STORM
COMMAND

STORM COMMAND

A Personal Account of the Gulf War

General Sir Peter de la Billière

MOTIVATE
PUBLISHING

Middle East edition published by:
Motivate Publishing

PO Box 2331
Dubai, UAE

PO Box 43072
Abu Dhabi, UAE

London House
26/40 Kensington High Street
London W8 4PF

A catalogue record for this book is available
from the British Library

ISBN 1 873544 46 4

Set in Meridien by Rowland Phototypesetting Ltd
Bury St Edmunds, Suffolk, United Kingdom

Printed and bound in the UAE by
Rashid Printers, Ajman

CONTENTS

ACKNOWLEDGEMENTS

I am much indebted to the following for contributing information and advice:

Margaret Aldred, Captain Mark Chapman, Brigadier Patrick Cordingley, Commodore Christopher Craig, Brigadier Arthur Denaro, Nigel Gillies, Brigadier Tim Glass, Brigadier Christopher Hammerbeck, Air Chief Marshal Sir Patrick Hine, Lieutenant Colonel David McDine, Air Vice Marshal Ian Macfadyen, Sir Alan Munro, Major General Rupert Smith, Brigadier Tim Sulivan, Colonel Ian Talbot, Brigadier Martin White, Lieutenant General Sir Michael Wilkes, Air Marshal Sir William Wratten.

There are two other people to whom I am particularly grateful: my wife Bridget, who urged me to use my letters home as the basis of this book; and Duff Hart-Davis, without whose editorial and moral support I could never have taken on this endeavour.

Peter de la Billière
July 1992

Author's Note

I should like to emphasize that this book is in no sense an official history of the Gulf campaign.

Although the Ministry of Defence was exceptionally helpful in correcting errors of fact, this is essentially a personal account, and the opinions expressed in it are my own.

LIST OF ABBREVIATIONS

ARCENT	(US) Army Central Command	FMA	force maintenance area
ASMA	air staff management aid	G-Day	start of ground war
AWACS	airborne warning and control system (aircraft)	GPS	global positioning system
		HAS	hardened aircraft shelter
BDA	battle damage assessment	H-Hour	start of air war
BERM	sand barrier	KTO	Kuwait Theatre of Operations
Blue on blue	incident in which own troops are hit by friendly fire	MARCENT	(US) Marines Central Command
Bluey	forces' airmail letter	MCMV	mine counter-measure vessel
CAP	combat air patrol		
CBFME	Commander, British Forces Middle East	MRLS	multiple rocket launch system
CENTCOM	(US) Central Command	MSR	main supply route
CNN	Cable News Network	NBC	nuclear, biological and chemical
Compo	Composite rations		
EOD	explosive ordnance disposal	ROE	Rules of Engagement
		SAM	surface-to-air missile
FBS	Forces' Broadcasting Service	SNOME	Senior Naval Officer, Middle East
FFMA	forward force maintenance area	Triple A	anti-aircraft fire
		Zulu	Greenwich Mean Time

PICTURE CREDITS

Section 1

Lieutenant General Prince Khalid bin Sultan © General Khalid bin Sultan
Air Chief Marshal Sir Patrick Hine © Air Chief Marshal Sir Patrick Hine
Air Vice-Marshal Sir William Wratten © UPPA
Brigadier Patrick Cordingley © Richard Maw/Sportsphoto
Brigadier Martin White © Brigadier Martin White
Commodore Christopher Craig © Crown copyright. Reproduced with permission of
   the Controller of HMSO 1991
Major General Rupert Smith © Major General Rupert Smith
A hands-on man: Tom King © Rex Features
Mr Major with servicemen © Sportsphoto
Mr Major with King Fahd © Richard Maw/Sportsphoto
Desert Parade © Rex Features
Prince of Wales, Norman Schwarzkopf and author © Capt. Mark Chapman
Harry Secombe © Frank Spooner Pictures
HMS London © Capt. Mark Chapman
Author giving briefing © Capt. Mark Chapman
An ear to the ground © Air Vice-Marshal Ian Macfadyen
Patrick the Jerboa © 7th Armoured Brigade/Terry Mayles
Author serving Christmas lunch © Queen's Royal Irish Hussars
Christmas cake parcels © Capt. Mark Chapman

Section 2

Legion of Merit. Courtesy of Prime Minister's Office, London
Order of Abdul Aziz © Image Studio
Sheikh Zayed Al Nahyan. Courtesy of Presidential Palace, Abu Dhabi
Sheikh Mohammed Al Maktoum. Courtesy of Ruler's Office, Dubai
Sultan Qaboos Al Said © Mohammed Mustapha
Sheikh Hamad Al Khalifa. Courtesy of Ministry of Information, Bahrein

Section 3

Bomb crater © Capt. Mark Chapman
JP233 bomber © Air Vice-Marshal Ian Macfadyen
Tornado pilot © Rex Features
Air Commodore Ian Macfadyen © Air Vice-Marshal Ian Macfadyen
Lieutenant Colonel Arthur Denaro © Queen's Royal Irish Hussars
Safwan peace talks © Major Alan Cardey
Islamic troops in Kuwait City © Rex Features
Postwar reunion at Heathrow © Rex Features

THE GULF WAR THEATRE

Turkey

Cyprus
Mediterranean
Sea

Syria

Lebanon

Damascus

Amman–
Baghdad road

■ Tehran

Baghdad

Iran

Israel
Tel Aviv ■

Amman

Iraq

Wadi al Batin

Jerusalem ▲

Jordan

Cairo ■

Qaysumah

Basra
Raudhatin Oilfield
Bubiyan Island
Kuwait
Faylaka Island

The Gulf

Egypt

King Khalid
Military City

Khafji

Jubail
Dhahran

Bahrein

Qatar

Straits of Hormuz

Riyadh ■

Saudi Arabia

UAE

Muscat ▲

Oman

Jeddah
Mecca

Red Sea

Sudan

Khamish
Mushayt

Straits of Bab el Mandeb

Khartoum ■

Yemen

Ethiopia

Aden

Key

○ Allied Airbases

□ Iraqi Airbases

⋀ Missile Plants

✳ Chemical/Biological Weapons Plants

Kilometres
0   360

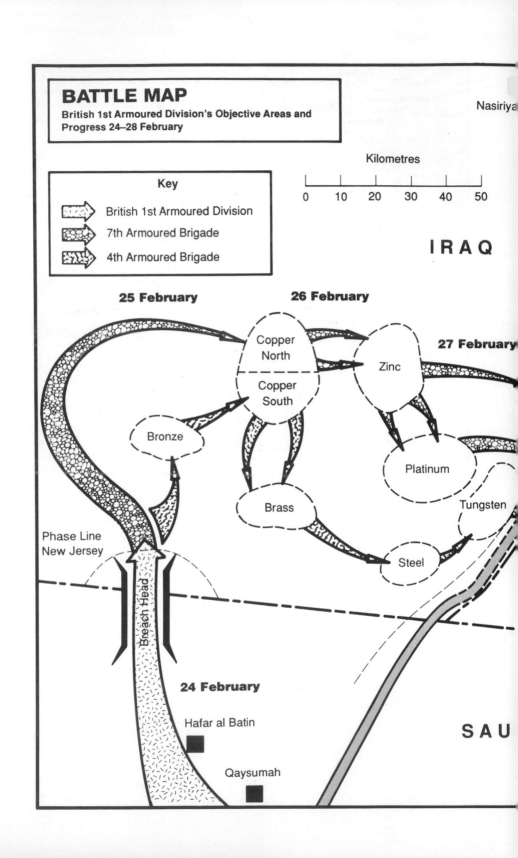

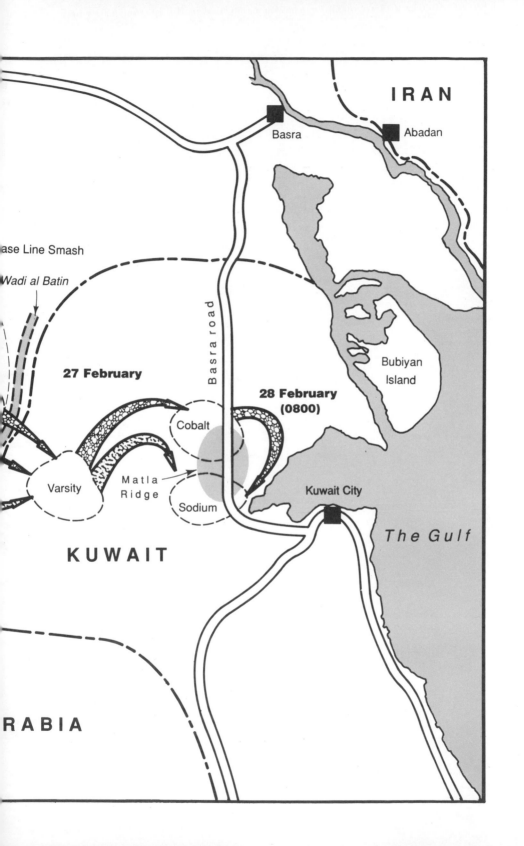

When I made a brief visit to our forces in the Gulf just before
Christmas 1990, I was struck by three things above all. The
first was the sheer size of Operation Granby - the biggest
operational deployment of British forces since the Second World
War. The second was the very great professional skill of our
servicemen and women. The third was the irrepressible sense of
humour they displayed despite the fact that many were living in
conditions of extreme discomfort in the desert during one of the
worst winters seen in that part of the world. I may be wrong,
but I have come to the conclusion that humour, constant and
imaginative training and good leadership are vital ingredients
for any successful military operation - and Peter de la Billière
certainly helped to provide the latter.

Everyone knows that, when the battle to free Kuwait eventually
began, it was short and sharp. Far less well documented are the
months of careful preparation which made such an outcome
possible. "Storm Command" shows the tenacity with which General
de la Billière fought to obtain everything his forces needed -
from more armour and men to a broadcasting station, a force
newspaper and telephones.

This fascinating and immensely readable account also brings out,
with warmth and humour, the quality of the 45,000 men and women
under his command. It was no surprise to me that, when the time
came, those men and women responded to their Commander's call so
positively and so professionally, fulfilling the task of
liberating Kuwait with their coalition colleagues more
efficiently and with fewer casualties than any of us had dared
hope.

PREFACE

My primary aim in writing this book is to demonstrate the importance of individual human beings in modern warfare. In the battle to drive the Iraqi army out of Kuwait, Coalition forces used every form of high-technology weapon available; yet in the end success depended on the performance of individuals, whether they were pilots, divers, tank drivers, mechanics, engineers, cooks, radio operators, infantrymen, nurses or officers of all ranks. It was these ordinary people who, at the end of the day, were going to put their lives on the line and risk their necks when their Government decided to go to war.

My account of the campaign is designed mainly for readers without a military background, who may be interested in the way that a large-scale international operation is managed. I hope the book will illustrate the human problems involved in holding high command during a major conflict, and show what pressures – military, diplomatic and political – a senior commander comes under. I hope, also, that it will demonstrate the importance of establishing and maintaining good personal relationships with other national commanders, thus ensuring that international relations prosper along the lines desired by the various governments involved.

The British contingent of forty-five thousand men and women, though less than a tenth the size of the American force, was nevertheless the third-largest element in the Coalition after America and Saudi Arabia. This lent us considerable influence on the international scene and meant that, together with the United States, we were able to give a lead to our other partners in the Coalition.

Inevitably, our preparations for war took a long time. For one thing, we were a very great distance from home – the Americans twelve thousand kilometres, the British six thousand kilometres – so that logistic problems were formidable. For a second, the operation was immensely complex, with more than thirty nations involved in the Coalition. For a third, our objectives kept changing. Having gone to the Middle East to protect Saudi Arabia from further aggression by the forces of Saddam Hussein, we came round in various stages to the conclusion that we would have to evict his army from Kuwait by force, and this demanded constant revision of our plans.

The build-up, both political and military, had to be conducted with care and patience. When war came at last, it was short, sharp, and (for us) extraordinarily successful, with minimal Coalition casualties. But if our preparations had been skimped, or if our force levels had been inadequate, the result would have been very different: the land battle would have lasted much longer, with far higher casualties, particularly among the Iraqis, who would have lost very large numbers of men if the fighting had been protracted.

This, then, is a personal account of a campaign which proved a triumphant success. I hope it will be seen as a tribute to the resolution and common sense displayed by the British people, and by British servicemen and women, when faced with a major challenge.

STORM
COMMAND

CHAPTER 1

BACK TO ARABIA

At the beginning of August 1990, after thirty-nine years in the army, I was stationed at Aldershot as General Officer Commanding South-East District. I had four more months to go before retiring, and my thoughts were turning increasingly to civilian pursuits, with sailing, farming and the traditional rearing of livestock high on my list of priorities. I had long cherished an ambition to take a yacht to New Zealand, and now planned that in September my wife Bridget and I should spend a week sailing in the Solent as a kind of training exercise, to see whether or not we could manage a small boat on our own. I had also been on a week's butchery course with the Army Catering Corps, honing my skills for the management of a retail meat outlet for the farm partnership which I planned to develop as a second career.

Then, on 2 August, Saddam Hussein's troops invaded Kuwait. We heard the news on the car radio as we drove towards Winchester County Hospital, where Bridget's father, Colonel Basil Goode, lay mortally ill after a stroke. Although he never knew it, he made a substantial contribution to the war in the Gulf for, as an officer in the Loyals, he had spent much time developing the 105mm gun, predecessor of the 120mm gun fitted to our Challenger tanks. Now at the end of his life, though barely conscious, he registered the fact that Kuwait had been invaded. He died two days later, much mourned by all of us in his family.

Instinct told me that the crisis in the Middle East would grow worse before it grew better, especially when, a week later, in response to American and Saudi requests for help, the Ministry of Defence launched Operation Granby* and hastily deployed Tornado and Jaguar squadrons of the RAF to help deter Saddam from further aggression. In a lifetime's soldiering I had never known a dispute on that scale resolve itself peacefully, and I suspected that other nations would soon be drawn into Kuwait's confrontation with Iraq. Even so, there seemed no reason why Bridget and I should not take our sailing leave as planned, and early in September we set out from Whale Island, near Portsmouth, in *Craftsman*, a twenty-eight-foot boat with an engine which turned out to be thoroughly unreliable, despite the fact that its august owners were the Royal Electrical and Mechanical Engineers.

The trip was a disaster. We did have one enjoyable night moored up an estuary near Wareham, but the week as a whole confirmed emphatically that Bridget is no natural sailor. The trouble is not that she is frightened of the sea; rather, she is bored by it. Having poor natural balance, she is easily sea-sick and has no aptitude for sailing. On this voyage she hoped that at least she might prove efficient at handling the boat in harbour; but with the engine constantly liable to cut out, accurate manoeuvring was impossible, and all she could do, whenever we came into port, was to put in a high-speed run at the jetty, which made us look foolish to anyone on shore and did nothing to improve her temper or mine, let alone our nautical reputation. Our final humiliation came after a pleasant day's sail out from Poole towards the Solent: the wind and our engine both died on us and, when the tide turned as we reached the Needles, to avoid drifting out into the Channel we were obliged to hail a passing yacht for a tow into Yarmouth. The fiasco left me worrying about how I could adapt my long-distance sailing plans to suit Bridget: in the twenty-five years of our marriage I had been separated from

---

* The name baffled our American allies, who had never heard of the Marquess of Granby, the distinguished eighteenth-century commander who fought in the battle of Minden during the Seven Years War. The name was chosen from a list in the Ministry of Defence computer, awaiting the next major operation. To the Americans, the deployment was initially known as Operation Desert Shield. The name of the Naval Task Group, 321:1, was chosen in the same way.

her far too often by overseas postings and I was determined
not to leave her behind again.

My ruminations were cut short by the six o'clock news,
which we heard as we drove home towards Aldershot on the
evening of 15 September. Tom King, Secretary of State for
Defence, had announced that 7th Armoured Brigade was to
be deployed in Saudi Arabia, and that a Joint Force Headquarters was to be set up.

The news set my adrenalin racing. Until then, the naval
and air units in the Gulf had operated under their own independent commands; but now that a large army force had
been designated for the theatre, all British forces would come
under a single tri-service commander, and I simply felt that I
was the man for the job. I turned and looked at Bridget and,
even though I had not spoken, she knew what I was thinking.
The moment she heard the news, her heart sank, for she
knew that a love of challenge, and of campaigns, had shaped
the course of my life.

Here was an immense challenge. The job of commanding
British forces in the Gulf would test me to the full; things
could go badly wrong and, if they did, failure would destroy
such reputation as I had and wreck what until then had been
a relatively successful career. Nevertheless, this seemed to be
a task for which the whole of my life had prepared me.

The only reason I joined the Army in the first place was to
go on operations, and I had spent most of my life looking for
trouble-spots. Fortunately for me, I had always managed to
find unrest somewhere in the world, and now, when I saw
an opportunity of becoming involved in operations at the age
of fifty-six and the rank of Lieutenant General, I grasped it
eagerly. Few officers of that age and seniority ever get the
chance to go on active service, and it never entered my head
to do anything but apply for the post of commander: to have
passed up the chance would have been contrary to the whole
thrust of my soldiering life. Somebody had to take the job, I
reasoned: if I did not get it, someone else would. It was not
as if I was creating a war to keep myself busy. War was
coming, and I felt I could make a contribution by going to it.
I saw retirement as something for which I had conditioned

myself to prepare, not an excuse to stop doing all those things for which I had trained so long. Altogether, it would have seemed very strange to me *not* to volunteer.

Waiting for me at home I found an official letter from Lieutenant General Sir John Learmont, Military Secretary at the Ministry of Defence, who informed me that I was to retire on 20 January 1991. Ignoring that instruction for the moment, I telephoned the Commander-in-Chief of UK Land Forces, my long-term friend General Sir Charles Huxtable, with whom I had fought in Korea in 1953, and asked him to put my name forward. He said that he had already done so, and that the Chief of the General Staff, General Sir John Chapple, had accepted the nomination. When I added that if I got the job I would postpone my retirement and serve on as long as necessary, Charles said, 'Don't worry. We haven't forgotten you. Your name's already in the hat.'

That evening I made myself some notes and, under the heading THE GULF (WAR?) 1990 – OPERATION GRANBY, I wrote, 'This is for me.' I then listed the reasons which, in my view, made me a contender for the post:

1 I had seen a great deal of active service in the Middle East. I spoke some colloquial Arabic, liked and respected Arabs, and understood their way of life.

2 I had served with the Americans in the Korean War, albeit a long time ago, and since then had often worked with them on counter-terrorist operations.

3 As Commander of British Forces and Military Commissioner in the Falkland Islands from 1984 to 1985 I had gained valuable experience of tri-service command – the difficult art of inducing all three Services to adapt their single-service habits and procedures so that they can work smoothly together (tri-service personnel are known as 'purple', a combination of the red, blue and sand colours worn by the individual services).

4 My tour in the Falklands had also given me valuable political experience: I knew that if war broke out in the Gulf, it would be a highly political conflict.

5 One of my roles in South-East District for the past
   three years had been that of Permanent Peacetime
   Commander (PPC) of the standing organization
   known as the Joint Forces Operational Staff. This is
   the skeleton command group which forms the basis
   of any tri-service headquarters which may be needed
   suddenly, and which rapidly sets about the task of
   calling in officers to create such a headquarters when
   a major operation breaks.

Of these qualifications, the first struck me as the most important. My involvement with Arabs began when I was at
Harrow, where my fellow pupils included two future kings:
Feisal of Iraq and Hussein of Jordan. Although I did not know
either well, the mere fact that I had been at school with them
gave me an advantage later on, particularly in Jordan.

My introduction to the Middle East came in October 1953
when, as a nineteen-year-old platoon commander in the
Durham Light Infantry, I sailed in a troopship from Korea to
Egypt and served in the Canal Zone as part of what was, in
effect, an army of occupation. I was also sent on a detachment
to Jordan, where I spent four enjoyable months at Aqaba –
then little more than a few mud huts – and made my first,
unforgettable visit to Petra, John William Burgon's 'rose-red
city – "half as old as time"!'

In 1956 I transferred to the Special Air Service and it was
with them, over the next twenty years, that I repeatedly
became involved in Arabian operations, most of them covert.
The first was a short but interesting campaign in the Jebel
Akhdar, the mountainous interior of Oman. Although we
never achieved our ultimate objective of eliminating or capturing Ghalib, Talib and Suleiman, the three dissident leaders
at large in the mountains, we did manage to secure the mountain top and drive them into exile, from which they never
returned. We could also claim to have been the first foreigners
to reach the top of the Jebel since the Persians in the tenth
century.

Next I found myself in Aden, where I was posted on loan
service as an Intelligence Officer in the Federal Regular Army

(FRA). It was there that I came to know the Arabs well, to appreciate their fine culture and to respect their way of life. For almost two years I served with the FRA, an Arab army then commanded by the distinguished military historian Brigadier (now Major General) James Lunt and during that time, in 1962, I gained a colloquial grasp of the language (I would have learnt it more thoroughly if the Arab officers had not all spoken English). I found that the Arabs like and respect a foreigner who has taken the trouble to learn their language, since he has made an effort not only to master their speech, but also to understand their religion, culture and history.

Later came another vicious campaign in Aden, during which two of my squadron were killed and decapitated by dissident tribesmen, who, in accordance with their custom, took the heads of their victims back to their ruler in Taiz, to prove that they were dead. Later still, in the early 1970s, came a lengthy operation in Oman, where the SAS conducted a secret campaign against a communist-led insurrection which rumbled on for four years. In the end it was the Omanis who, by their own efforts, turned the tide in their favour, albeit with some assistance from the SAS.

Next came another difficult campaign, when a guerrilla force established itself in the Musandam peninsula, an exceedingly wild promontory which sticks out from the north-east tip of Oman into the Straits of Hormuz, the very throat of the Gulf. The rebels' aim was to disrupt the with-drawal of conventional British troops from the region, in which we had maintained a presence for half a century; but a night parachute drop by the SAS into Wadi Rawdah, a huge, circular bowl high in the mountains surrounded by peaks rising four thousand feet above its floor, and then seaborne attacks on the two guerrilla coastal strongholds, effectively put them out of business.

Later in the 1970s I was posted to the Sudan. Taking Bridget and our three children, I travelled out from England to Egypt, crossed Lake Nasser and then, in the full heat of summer, we all made a four-day transit of the Nubian desert by Land Rover – a testing experience which appealed to me more than to other members of the family. Arriving in Khartoum, I took command of the British Army Training Team attached to the Sudanese army and remained there for twenty months.

Thus in all I spent nearly eight years in Arab-speaking countries, and I developed a strong affection for the desert, which, when I first knew it, had not changed for thousands of years. I loved the vast open spaces, the brilliant freshness as dawn breaks, the wonderful feeling of freedom and independence and solitude with which the sands inspire the human soul. Had I never married, I might well have stayed on indefinitely and joined that small band of eccentric Englishmen who have devoted their lives to Arabia.

How much all this would count for in the autumn of 1990, I could not tell. But there followed an aggravating delay, twelve days long, tense for me and damaging to the prospects of the man – whoever he might be – who was eventually appointed Commander of British forces in the Middle East. Under what is known as the shopping-basket system, officers were already being called in and appointed to positions in the tri-service headquarters without the so-far-unchosen commander being able to have any say in their selection. *Any* commander, given the opportunity, would prefer to select the key people for his own headquarters, especially if it is being tailor-made for the task in hand, as was happening here. Advice on the shape of the headquarters was coming in from Air Vice-Marshal Sandy Wilson, commander of the RAF detachment hastily flown into the theatre as a deterrent. On the whole his ideas were very much in line with my own; nevertheless, as the one who had to make things work, the commander should have had a say in the structure of the headquarters, and in the choice of people to fill key roles.

Having sent in my nomination and *curriculum vitae*, I could do little but keep my ear to the ground. Against me, I thought, might be the fact that I was so close to retirement: if the Service Chiefs decided to nominate somebody whose career had longer to run, and who might therefore benefit more from the experience, it would be perfectly understandable. Soon I heard that the RAF were pressing the merits of Sandy Wilson as their contender for the post. A highly intelligent and able former fighter pilot, he had the advantage of being already on the ground and fully in touch with the situation; yet there were, in my view at least, two flaws in his candidacy. First, he held only two-star rank, whereas this was a three-star appointment; and second, since the Army contingent in the Gulf was going to outnumber those of the RAF and Navy several times over, there really was a need for a man who had Army and tri-service command experience.

Without waiting to see what the outcome of the leadership race would be, I commissioned a pamphlet of information and advice for anyone who might become involved in Operation Granby. This *aide memoire* contained basic facts about travel arrangements, vaccinations, passports, pay, the strength of the Iraqi forces and so on; but it also included an introduction to the Arabs, their way of life, and the Middle East as a whole. This emphasized the importance of religion in Arab culture, sketched outstanding features of the Arab character, and gave hints on how to behave in Arab society ('If invited to a meal in the countryside, you may be eating with your hands. You may have to take off your shoes. If so, you should not point the soles of your feet at anyone . . .') The pamphlet concluded with a basic vocabulary and some medical advice on dealing with chemical poisoning and battle shock. Altogether, I believe it was a useful publication.

On 25 September I heard that my name had been accepted by all three Services, and that the Chief of the Defence Staff, Marshal of the Royal Air Force Sir David Craig (now Lord Craig), was putting it to the Secretary of State for Defence, Tom King. It appeared that the Navy had been won over partly by General Sir John Chapple, the CGS, and partly by the fact that I had got on well with them in the Falklands. 'I shall have to become truly purple if I am to keep the other Services alongside,' I noted that evening. 'I must also see I get the best people available for the jobs in my headquarters – no kind-hearted jollying along of those less than competent.'

That same day I received a visit from Lieutenant General Michael Wilkes, a powerfully built and snappily dressed Gunner of rather youthful appearance and an old friend. By then the Army Commander – the man in charge of all the Army's fighting units based in the United Kingdom – he had just returned from the Gulf and told me that political wrangling had already started over the number of troops to be sent out. In a phrase which was attributed to the Prime Minister, Margaret Thatcher (now Baroness Thatcher of Kesteven), and which later became a kind of watchword, the Government was anxious 'not to get its arm caught in the mangle' – not to be dragged into a conflict which would demand ever-increasing commitment of men and resources. At first White-hall wanted to keep numbers down to about six thousand. The Army had bid for ten thousand, but was prepared to settle for seven thousand five hundred. And yet the total requirement identified after an in-theatre reconnaissance soon reached eleven thousand five hundred, a fact which had yet to be communicated to the Prime Minister.

And so, before my appointment had even been confirmed, I found myself being drawn into the numbers game. Soon it became clear that the Cabinet wished to retain close control over the personnel and equipment being deployed, so that they could keep a check on final costs and measure the extent of the United Kingdom's commitment. Thereafter, control of numbers was always high on the agenda, and the 'arm in the mangle' outlook prevailed. At first they had some justification for their cautious attitude, since Operation Granby was launched as a deterrent, to prevent a war rather than to pro-voke one, and it was natural that Whitehall should not want to commit forces larger than were necessary to make a worth-while political gesture. The trouble was that later, when our aim changed from defence to offence, from my viewpoint in the field there appeared to be continual hold-ups caused by questioning of the reinforcements which I considered neces-sary for the job. The delays undoubtedly reflected the debate which every request set off, but they caused us boundless chagrin.

In September, at the outset, the Army was of course keen not to miss out on an operation which looked as if it might develop into a major campaign: we were anxious not to make the bill, in terms of either cash or political commitment, so great that the whole idea of a large-scale military deployment might be discarded. We therefore tended to be cautious in our early estimates of manpower needs. Yet all of us knew that initial estimates invariably prove too small: when a detailed reconnaissance is made, unforeseeable extra tasks become apparent and numbers rise inexorably.

Mike also told me that Mrs Thatcher herself was pressing for my appointment and indeed had threatened that, if I was passed over, she would make me her special adviser on the Middle East – a fact which she has since confirmed to me personally. (Cynics later remarked that this was the factor which clinched my nomination: the need to remove me from Whitehall as far and as fast as possible.) Yet still there was no definite news.

By the evening of 26 September I knew that my name had reached the Secretary of State's office. All the same, pressure was building inexorably, for the Joint Force Headquarters had been told to form up immediately and, while it remained headless, the Services were posting to it shopping-list nominees who were not necessarily of the right quality or equipped with the right qualifications. 'Thank God for Mike Wilkes,' I noted. 'He and I are of one mind and work hand in glove. He is trying to slow down the form-up of the Joint HQ until I am around officially.' By then it had been widely blazoned in the Press that I would be appointed and Sandy Wilson telephoned from Riyadh to make me welcome. 'A most generous gesture', I noted, considering that no announcement had been made.

Then at last, on 28 September, things began to move. That morning in my office at Aldershot I held a meeting with John Hoddinott, the Chief Constable of Hampshire, in one of a regular series of conferences at which we discussed counter-terrorist measures. Because this was my field, I held very firm views about how we should conduct the counter-terrorist battle, with Army and police working closely together. John represented the five Chief Constables whose territory lay within the area of the South-East Command and we would meet with our intelligence staffs every two or three months to exchange information, assess how the campaign against terrorism was going and decide on adjustments in policy.

That morning there were eight or nine people round my

office table, including my Chief of Staff, Brigadier Robert Ackworth. The meeting began at 0930 and was scheduled to last until lunchtime, but after no more than forty minutes my personal assistant, Julie Morris, hurried in: Tom King had invited me to a sandwich lunch at the Ministry of Defence in Whitehall. Such a summons could only mean that, my nomination approved by the Army Board and the Cabinet, he wanted to make a final, formal assessment of my qualifications for command in the Gulf.

I made my apologies and left the meeting at once. The only way to reach London in time was by helicopter, so Mark Chapman, my Military Aide, immediately arranged for a Lynx to lift us into the capital; but before we took off from the playing field in front of my headquarters I changed into civilian clothes and told Mark to call the outer offices of both the Chief of the Defence Staff and the Chief of the General Staff to make sure that they, my military superiors, knew that I was on my way to the Secretary of State, for I did not want them to think that I had gone to see him over their heads. To my consternation, I found that neither had heard about my impending visit. Here immediately was an instance of TK (as he was affectionately known to the Services) by-passing the normal chain of command — something which I was determined not to do myself.

The flight from Aldershot to Chelsea Barracks took only fifteen minutes. As we skimmed freely over the traffic jams and roadworks with which other mortals were struggling, my mind seemed to be whirling as fast as our rotor blades with ideas and plans. In Chelsea a car was waiting and I reached the Ministry of Defence's huge main building in good time. At the reception desk I went through the usual procedure of establishing my identity and the purpose of my visit; then I was shown to the special lift programmed to travel only to the sixth floor, which houses Service chiefs, officials and ministers.

Tom King's spacious panelled office had a handsome appearance, slightly impaired by the blast-proof net curtains over the windows. Oil paintings of sea battles adorned the walls and behind his desk hung an impressively large map of the world.

At that stage we did not know each other well. Although we had met several times, we had never had much conversation, but I had always found him pleasant and easy to get on with, and now he was no different. We sat down to talk at an octagonal mahogany table at one side of the room and his Private Secretary Simon Webb arranged for some excellent sandwiches and a glass of beer to be brought in.

At first the Secretary of State took a challenging, almost aggressive attitude about the way in which the newspapers had repeatedly touted my name as the most likely man to command British forces in the Gulf. He seemed acutely sensitive about the Press: he was convinced that there had been a leak and, although I emphatically assured him that I had not spoken to any media man, it was hard to persuade him that some bright journalist had simply put two and two together and come up with a reasonably intelligent answer.

His next question was easier to knock on the head. How, he wanted to know, had word of our private lunch meeting reached the Service chiefs in the Ministry so quickly? 'Because I warned them about it,' I replied, and I went on to explain with some emphasis that I had never been in favour of trying to by-pass a chain of command. To do so might confer a temporary advantage, but in the long term it always proved a certain way of creating problems in the relationships between Services and politicians, and could only breed distrust.

The Secretary of State took my point, but immediately went on to describe himself as 'very much a hands-on man' and to say that, if I became commander in the Gulf, he would require direct access to me, so that he could always be fully briefed with the latest plans and intelligence and thus able to hold his own in front of the media or the House of Commons. This seemed to me reasonable enough and I said so. Several times during the Falklands campaign ministers had been put at a disadvantage by information reaching the media before it came to them. With back-pack satellite communications available to every reporter, I foresaw that the media would run riot if the Services did not make sure that they kept ministers ahead of the game. Yet I also made it quite clear that, when it came to decision making, I should have to deal through the

chain of command and not direct to him: it would be dangerous for me to have my decisions approved by the Secretary
of State and for my superiors to hear about them afterwards.

This, too, he seemed to accept and he went on to cross-
question me on my qualifications. I recapitulated my combat
experience with the Americans in Korea, my eight years'
service in Arab countries, my understanding of Arabs and
their way of life, my experience of tri-service command in
the Falklands . . . Without, I hope, sounding conceited, I
said that for this appointment I thought I was unique, in
terms of experience, among three-star officers in any of the
Services.

Satisfied at last, he told me that the job was mine, but then
immediately alarmed me by insisting that the matter be kept
between the two of us until it had been cleared with the
Cabinet, the Prime Minister and the Queen. Had he not taken
in my remarks about the chain of command made a few
minutes earlier? I said that I must at once let Sir David Craig
and Sir John Chapple know the outcome of the meeting,
otherwise I would be failing to inform my superiors of something which they should know.

He saw my point, accepted my argument and immediately
left the room to walk down the corridor and tell the Service
chiefs himself. This cleared the way for me to talk to both of
them before I left the building.

I had long liked and admired Chapple as a man of enormous
ability and I respected his many qualities, not least his readiness to stand back from the minutiae of day-to-day decision-
making and let his generals get on with it. Now he told me
that he had just returned from Germany, where he had visited
7th Armoured Brigade. He had been most impressed by the
vigour and enthusiasm with which the unit was preparing for
its departure to Saudi Arabia and he lent me the excellent
notes which he had used to brief the troops on the situation
in the Middle East.

The question of how we were to keep the Secretary of State
adequately informed seemed to me so important that I raised
it there and then. Quickly we decided that we must meet his
requirement, rather than fight it; but to do so would mean

acquiring special communications equipment and setting up special briefing arrangements. Much of the information would be classified; moreover, it would have to be sent back without any delay. This meant that we would need highly efficient briefing arrangements, and a secure telephone system, so that messages could travel by voice or facsimile without fear of interception.

During our earlier discussion the Secretary of State had talked about being able to speak directly to the Brigade Commander. This I was most anxious to avoid, as it would have cut across my own command chain. Instead, we arranged that Tom King would communicate with me by means of routine weekly calls and that he would be able to telephone me at any other time, should he consider it necessary. I felt sure that the way to ease his concern was to build up confidence on both sides. Once he was receiving all the information he needed – and moreover was confident that he was getting it – he would have no need to interfere, because he would feel fully briefed and in control. Only if he were denied legitimate information, or caught short by the lack of it, would he worry that he had been kept in the dark.

Farming and butchery took a back seat. To Bridget's unbounded relief, thoughts of long-distance sailing trips disappeared over the horizon. Having been forced to mark time for the past two weeks, I was suddenly at full stretch in a whirl of briefings. Mark Chapman found it difficult to obtain up-to-date, reliable information about the situation in Riyadh. It seemed to him that the various levels of command were having trouble in switching from the inertia of peacetime to the high rate of activity needed in the run-up to major operations. Yet once he and I were launched on our new trajectory, we never stopped.

Next morning, together with Mike Wilkes, I flew by helicopter through fog, wind and rain to the Headquarters of RAF Strike Command in a leafy encampment on a hill outside High Wycombe. Since I was still sworn to secrecy about my new role, I wore civilian clothes in the hope that I would thus prevent staff officers drawing otherwise-inevitable con-

clusions. Our meeting was with Air Chief Marshal Sir Patrick
Hine, who had already been appointed Joint Commander of
Operation Granby, and so would be my immediate superior
as long as the campaign lasted.*

I had known and respected Paddy Hine for many years: an
extremely intelligent man, always very well turned out (and
often reminding people of President Bush), he has the cardinal virtue of being prepared to listen to the views of others.
He is thus an easy colleague to work with and I much looked
forward to the prospect of coming under his command. He
told me that Sandy Wilson, the air commander already in
theatre, would be my deputy and asked me to say when I
wanted to go out to Riyadh. As soon as possible, was my
reply, once essential briefings had been completed, perhaps
in five or six days' time.

There followed a briefing on the situation. Thanks to the
prompt and generous support of Sultan Qaboos, the Ruler of
Oman, we had been able to deploy RAF aircraft to Thumrait
and other bases at zero notice. Sultan Qaboos's immediate
cooperation proved a major factor in enabling us to react so
swiftly in the early stages of the campaign. At that stage, as I
say, our reaction to Saddam Hussein's occupation of Kuwait
was purely defensive: we had deployed Tornado and Jaguar
squadrons, together with Nimrod maritime surveillance aircraft, to support the international Coalition in deterring him
from further aggression, and in particular to stifle any ideas he
might have of making a pre-emptive strike on Saudi Arabia.

At 2230 that evening, 29 September, I learnt that both the
Queen and the Prime Minister had approved my appointment, so that at last it could be made public and I could openly
start to make plans. Next morning I moved Mark Chapman
to a desk in the Joint Headquarters at High Wycombe. A very
keen but relaxed young officer from the Light Infantry (my
own parent regiment was the Durham Light Infantry), Mark
had worked for me for fifteen months and we had a good

* Whenever a major, tri-service operation breaks overseas, one of the four-star
Commanders-in-Chief of the Army, Navy and Air Force, based in the United
Kingdom, is appointed its Joint Commander. In this case Hine was chosen and a Joint
Headquarters was set up at RAF Strike Command.

understanding of each other's strengths and weaknesses. His tour was due to end, but I was determined that he should accompany me to the Middle East, partly because he was such a crucial member of my staff, and partly because I knew that Operation Granby would give him invaluable experience. This change of plan came as no small shock to him, especially as he had recently married Ruth, a specialist teacher. It was typical of the Army that the comfortable way of life which he had just established should be suddenly disrupted and that Ruth, like thousands of other Service wives, should find herself abandoned at short notice for an indefinite period.

The next couple of days were packed with further briefings: at the Ministry of Defence in London, Fleet Headquarters at Northwood, UK Land Forces' Headquarters at Wilton, near Salisbury, and at several locations in the British Army of the Rhine, in northern Germany. Among the subjects covered were the Iraqis' ability to wage chemical and biological warfare: we suspected that they had substantial stocks of chemical weapons and possibly some biological capability as well. Saddam Hussein had used poison gas extensively during his war against Iran and against his own Kurdish minority: it seemed likely that, if a suitable opportunity presented itself, he would use it against the Coalition forces, or against the civilian population of Saudi Arabia.

On the basis that a new commander needs to know as much as possible about his principal enemy, I sought information about Saddam, only to discover that at that stage we seemed to possess very little. It appeared that during the eight years of his war against Iran, we had concluded that he was not in a position to make trouble elsewhere: so long as he remained locked in a battle of attrition with his expansionist neighbour, he had no chance to pursue wider ambitions. Now, however, he demanded our closest attention. A detailed analysis of the Iran–Iraq conflict now yielded useful lessons and after consulting the British Embassy in Riyadh we put together a character sketch which brought out some of Saddam's weaknesses. Clearly a robust individual, he was also completely ruthless – a brutal dictator who ruled through fear and treated human beings as expendable pawns in pursuit of

his own ambition. Stories of how he invited people to meetings and then shot them with his own pistol as they drank
tea at his table were doubtless exaggerated but hardly reassur-
ing. If not clinically insane, he was at least irrational and
therefore dangerously unpredictable. His military record
made it obvious that, however much he might posture and
dress up as a soldier, he was useless as strategist and tactician.
His mistakes in the war with Iran were legion and now it
seemed that he had made a major strategic error in invading
the whole of Kuwait. Had he merely seized the oil field of
Raudhatin and the island of Bubiyan to the north of the city,
he might well have kept them: even if the world had made
a great fuss, it would hardly have gone to war. But no, greed
and bravado had caused him to seize the entire country, and
there was no telling how wild his ambitions might become.

We already knew from aerial surveillance that his military
airfields were extremely large and spread the length and
breadth of Iraq, giving him the capacity to threaten all his
neighbours – not only Saudi Arabia, but also Jordan, Syria and
Turkey as well. We knew, for instance, that the airbase at
Balad, north-east of Baghdad, was four times the size of Heathrow and in military terms incorporated massive redundancy;
that is, it was infinitely larger and more expensive to maintain
than its present level of use warranted, and aircraft would be
able to go on using it even if it were extensively damaged.

One of my most fascinating briefings was at the Foreign
Office, which had established a centre for the exchange of
information about the hostages whom Saddam had seized
and deployed around his air bases as human shields. The
Foreign Office was widely accused of having done little or
nothing to secure the release of these political prisoners; in
fact, as I now discovered, strenuous efforts were being made
on their behalf and an information service had been established so that families and relatives could telephone in for the
latest news. It immediately occurred to me that Special Forces
might be tasked to explore ways of rescuing the hostages and
I passed the idea on to Paddy Hine's staff.

On the evening of 3 October we had what I described in
my diary as a 'rather tense family supper' at my daughter

Phillida's flat in London. Our three children were all there and I hoped that we would have a relaxed family evening. It did not turn out like that, partly because everyone was naturally anxious about the future, and partly because I was going down with what, in Saddam Hussein's terminology, could only have been called the 'mother of all colds'.

Since my earliest days in the Army I had maintained the practice of taking a run and a cold bath before breakfast, in the belief that physical fitness keeps one mentally alert; but now not even this Spartan regime could ward off the invasion of germs, and in the morning I felt so ill that I seriously considered postponing my departure for the Gulf. Yet the need to reach the theatre was so urgent that I forced myself to carry on with the next item on my schedule, a flying visit to the British Army of the Rhine.

My first appointment in Germany was with a doctor, for whose services I had radioed ahead. General Sir Peter Inge, Commander-in-Chief, BAOR, summoned one to his office and he gave me an examination there and then. Fortified by the antibiotics which he prescribed, I plunged into talks with the Commander-in-Chief and with Lieutenant General Sir Charles Guthrie, Commander of 1st (British) Corps. Both were old friends with whom I had worked at different stages of my career, and Guthrie and I had once served together.

Our meetings soon confirmed my suspicion that the effort of producing one fully operational armoured brigade had turned the whole system inside-out. Some of our armoured vehicles were old and plain worn out; others were run down and not properly maintained or else not used, due to the lack of spares, money and training. To bring 7th Armoured Brigade up to the strength which was needed to fight a desert campaign, we decided to take people and equipment away from other units in Germany; when 4th Armoured Brigade also moved out, those units remaining were left with barely enough men to guard their own installations, let alone to carry out any training. In effect, the whole of BAOR became seriously degraded in operational terms, for as long as the campaign in the Gulf lasted.

Nor was this all. Like any other commander landed with a

major commitment, I was already looking round for ways of increasing the number of troops at my disposal. If we went to war in the desert with one armoured brigade, it would have to be attached to an American division and fight under an American divisional commander, which would severely limit its freedom of action. If, on the other hand, we had a British division, it would have far more scope to do itself justice. And yet, to raise a complete division from BAOR would leave defences in the British zone of Germany substantially depleted.

Every possible permutation had to be discussed in detail and the senior officers in Germany behaved superbly. It can never be much fun for a commander to emasculate his command for the benefit of someone else, yet to my undying admiration Peter Inge did just that without so much as a hint of complaint or a single unpleasant aside. I flew home much impressed with the spirit being shown by all ranks and with the character of Brigadier Patrick Cordingley, commander of 7th Armoured Brigade, who was about to depart for the Middle East, and whom I had met for the first time. A friendly and direct man, with a long, narrow face which twisted engagingly to one side when he smiled, Patrick immediately struck me as just the sort of leader we would need in the desert.

On 5 October, back in England, I was briefed by Joint Headquarters on our outline plan, which at that stage was extremely vague: defend Saudi Arabia against aggression. As further troops arrived in the theatre, more ambitious plans were put together; but at the outset we were deploying simply to protect Saudi Arabia, not to free Kuwait.

That evening I said goodbye to my staff at Aldershot. After working with them for two-and-a-half years, I would have liked to go round and thank each of them individually for all the help they had given me; but events had moved so fast that there was no time for such niceties, and the best I could do was to bid them a mass farewell outside the historic Victorian headquarters building. I addressed them from the steps beneath the pillared portico of the main entrance, flanked by two ancient cannons, scene of innumerable highly charged departures, among them that of Earl Haig, who went from there in 1916 to command the armies of the British Expeditionary Force at the start of the First World War.

About a hundred people gathered round in a semicircle and, because dusk was already falling, I failed to notice that the throng included Larry Signy, Defence Correspondent of the *Aldershot News* and a staunch friend of the Army. He had every right to be there and report the event as he had been officially invited; but my staff had failed to tell me that the Press would be present and I was less than cautious in my remarks. I confirmed that the cause of my premature departure was the tension in the Gulf and I suggested that people should watch their newspapers closely in the period leading up to Christmas. The message I intended to put across was that developments would be taking place by then, *not* that a war would have started. But that was how Larry's report was interpreted by Reuter's. Later that evening, as Bridget and I were casually watching the nine o'clock news, I was appalled to hear the announcer say, 'NEW GULF COMMANDER PREDICTS WAR BY CHRISTMAS.'

I felt badly let down. If I had known that a reporter was present, I would never have mentioned the Gulf at all. 'This is going to cause embarrassment for days to come and could affect my overall position,' I noted. Since I was brand new in my job, the last thing I wanted was to be seen posing as a great military adventurer on his way out to the Middle East to start a war, and at the first possible moment I wrote to the Joint Commander explaining what had happened. Later, however, I found that even if I had damaged my standing in the United Kingdom, I had positively enhanced it in the Gulf, where rulers such as Sheikh Isa of Bahrein were to congratulate me heartily on taking such a vigorous approach.

My last two days in England flew past in a flurry of final briefings and personal preparations. Our home in the west of England, let for the past few years, was back in our hands, but we were still living in the General's house at Aldershot, so it was there that I did my packing. Limiting myself to bare essentials of clothing and personal equipment, I eschewed extras such as books, which I knew there would be no time to read, and took only a small radio which could receive the vital BBC World Service on short wave. I allowed myself only two small luxuries: a photograph of Bridget and the family, and a dagger-shaped paper knife given me by the Australian SAS.

I drew up tropical uniform and had it fitted by the military tailor in Aldershot. I also drew my own NBC kit and practised putting it on under operational timings. Out came old desert boots and medal ribbons and badges of rank for tropical kit which I had thought I would never need again. On two beds we laid out everything that I might need for an indefinite stay abroad. During one of his final telephone calls to Riyadh, Mark had been astonished to hear Sandy Wilson's Personal Staff Officer say casually, 'Oh, and don't forget to bring a dinner jacket.' I was equally amazed by this advice. What were we going to Saudi Arabia *for*, to live it up or to fight a war? Nevertheless, because there seemed to be plenty of space, I put my dinner jacket in (and never during my six months in Riyadh did I wear it). During all these preparations Sergeant Larry Jones, my House Sergeant for the past three years and a pillar of unobtrusive efficiency, kept me firmly on the rails.

Then, on the evening of 6 October, my driver, Sergeant Alan Cain, took me to RAF Brize Norton in Oxfordshire. Alan had driven me around the south of England for nearly two years; he was trained in close-protection work and had become an indispensable member of my staff. A small, taciturn man, not given to unnecessary chatter, he not only knew my personal habits but also, on a professional level, was able to identify those moments when it became most necessary to maintain a high state of alert against possible terrorist attack or ambush. I had arranged that he would join me as my personal driver in Riyadh, but for the moment I said goodbye to him and he left to go on a week's refresher course in close protection, run by the Royal Military Police.

The RAF TriStar was loaded with freight; at the front, however, were some comfortable seats. Ensconced in one of these, clearing papers and writing confidential reports, I found that the six-hour flight passed extraordinarily fast. After what seemed a very short time we started our descent and a few minutes later, at 0200 local time, I stepped out into the hot darkness of Riyadh. As I felt the dry, desert air on my face and smelt its familiar scents, a surge of memories came at me, and I rejoiced in the knowledge that another Arabian adventure had begun.

CHAPTER 2

'WAR BEFORE CHRISTMAS'

At the foot of the aircraft steps a small Saudi honour guard stood waiting, and there to greet me was Sandy Wilson. Considering that he had been working under great stress, I thought it extremely good of him to turn out in the early hours of the morning. We bundled into a Mercedes and drove off along a huge motorway which carried us over the desert as smoothly as a magic carpet, with never a pothole in its immaculate surface. My first glimpses of Riyadh at night showed me that Arabia had changed beyond belief, even since my last visit. As it happened, I had never been to the Saudi capital; but equally, in all my travels I had never seen an Arab city to rival this, with its immense dual carriageways and spectacular, futuristic buildings, their modern lines given an exotic, oriental look by arched doorways and windows and fretted screens.

Mark, following with the luggage in another car, was equally amazed. Our departure from England had been so rushed that he had had no time to bone up on the situation in Riyadh and he arrived in the dark in more senses than one. He expected that we would proceed to some fortified compound on the outskirts of the city and when his driver, in answer to a question, said that we were going to 'the Hyatt', he assumed that this was the Arab word for a fort. In fact we were heading not for the Hyatt Hotel but for the Sheraton, where a suite had been reserved for me.

The manager had stayed up half the night to welcome me. The suite was the last word in luxury, right down to a huge bowl of fruit set out on a table. Yet the place filled me with misgiving: for one thing, I had come out to fight a war, not to live in five-star comfort; for another, the building was hopelessly insecure, its corridors alive with strangers, any of whom could be a potential threat. As soon as the manager was out of earshot, I said to Mark, 'For Christ's sake, let's get out of here as soon as we can. Start looking for somewhere else tomorrow.' Late as it was, before going to bed I wrote a note to Bridget – the first of a series of letters which I sent her every day, as I always have while on operations.

Morning confirmed my distaste for hotel living, which has always struck me as a completely artificial form of existence. The Sheraton had the added disadvantage of harbouring a large number of exiled Kuwaitis, including members of the ruling family, to whom the Saudis had generously given refuge when they escaped from their homeland. Dozens of children, bored to distraction, raced round the hotel corridors screaming at all hours of the day and night and constantly dialled random numbers on the room telephones. I was to some extent protected by a tri-service team of bodyguards, one of whom was stationed permanently outside my door and could turn people away, but even so the noise was infuriating.

For me, the redeeming feature of the hotel was its small gym, in which I was able to clock up four or five kilometres on a running machine every morning. Running in the open was inadvisable, both because of the heat and because it would have made one very exposed. The gym was an excellent alternative and enabled me to work up the good daily sweat which I find indispensable to well-being. In an environment of that kind, when one is working at high pressure, it is tempting to give up physical exercise altogether; but I knew that to do so would diminish my mental alertness and so impair my efficiency.

Mark was much concerned about my safety – as indeed he was paid to be. Having known two Iraqi soldiers at Sandhurst and seen how competent they were, he felt certain that Saddam Hussein must have some special forces operating in Riyadh and that the British Commander would be a prime target for an assassination squad. He therefore made sure that I was well protected, both in the hotel and while on the move around the city. Inside, one of the bodyguards came with us when we visited the gym; then, before we went down to breakfast, one man preceded me along the corridor while another checked the dining room and had a table cleared. Outside, we tried to avoid establishing any pattern: by varying time and routes, we sought to present the most elusive target possible. I also took the precaution of removing my beret and draping a civilian jacket over the top of my uniform whenever I travelled by car. I always moved with two, sometimes three, unmarked, identical blue Mercedes so that if ever any other car tried to cut in on mine, we would have the means of heading it off, and I was always accompanied by at least two members of the bodyguard team, armed with sub-machine guns.

Whether or not these precautions were essential, I could never decide, for in spite of Mark's apprehension the terrorist threat seemed slight. But my personal bodyguard Sergeant David Green and the rest of the close-protection team under Staff Sergeant Worzel Young of the Royal Military Police knew their business, and they had an extensive communications system which linked all the teams in the city, so that their headquarters in my compound always knew exactly where I was and what I was doing, and a reserve force could have been deployed at very short notice if trouble had developed. Much as I disliked always being hemmed in by security men, I knew that to have dispensed with guards altogether would have been excessively foolish – rather like going over the top in an infantry attack without a rifle. Furthermore, without such trappings of power, the British Forces' Commander would have lost face in the eyes of the Arabs and other members of the Coalition. I knew from previous visits how much image and presence count for in Arabia: it was essential that I should exercise privileges which might seem superficial elsewhere, purely to demonstrate the importance which Britain placed on Operation Granby.

My abrupt arrival in Riyadh demanded an energetic effort of readjustment – to a climate which, in autumn, was still producing daytime temperatures of 40°C; to a society in which the Matawa, or religious police, would confront in public anyone whom they considered to be transgressing the strict laws of Islam; and to a country from which alcohol was banned. 'The whole theatre is dry and I don't miss my booze at all,' I reported home after a few days. Slightly to my own surprise, the second half of that statement was as true as the first and a week later I wrote, 'When nobody can drink and booze isn't available, it's not difficult to live without it.' Because the British servicemen in Saudi Arabia were allowed no alcohol, I decided that I too would not drink while I was in theatre. I have always made a habit of not drinking while on operations and now I had the added incentive of not wanting to enjoy a privilege which my men could not share. I therefore drank no alcohol during my six months in the Middle East – with considerable benefit to my health. (The Americans were even stricter than us in exercising prohibition: if any US serviceman was found with a bottle sent in from the States, he was fined $1000 on the spot).

As for work, it was hard to know how to start. I was in the extraordinary position of suddenly becoming the managing director of a business with several thousand employees but absolutely no structure or facilities. Troops were pouring into the airport at Jubail, on the coast, and their heavy equipment was beginning to arrive by sea at the port nearby, but the men had no accommodation or communications beyond what they brought with them. Everything had to be created from scratch.

Daylight on my first morning showed how fast the city of Riyadh had expanded outwards into the desert. Between many of the new buildings stretches of level sand still lay undeveloped, and vast dual carriageways carried streams of traffic in every direction.

The headquarters which Sandy had established was on one floor of a modern office block, the rest of which was occupied by the US Marine Corps as their rear base. The building was guarded by Americans and could be approached by car only through a sequence of very tight road blocks. On our floor major adjustments were being made to accommodate staff and communications equipment – some walls were being knocked down, others built, all the cable ducting renewed – and the place was full of packing cases. My own office proved bigger and better than I had expected, with a good desk, a comfortable chair and a table large enough for conferences. The room's main deficiency was that it had no map boards, but I put that right by commissioning carpenters to make some immediately. Soon it became clear that this first building could only be a temporary home. Within weeks – within days, almost – we were bursting out of it and had to look for more spacious accommodation.

Already, with Operation Granby still in its early stages, information was flowing strongly to us from two directions: out from the United Kingdom and in from our forward units in the east of Saudi Arabia. My headquarters was the interface where all this information had to be processed, acted upon or passed on as necessary, and somehow we had to create a structure which could handle it.

'It's all incredibly artificial, complicated, political and a bit disconcerting,' I wrote to Bridget on 7 October, my first full day in Riyadh:

> I've never seen a country so outwardly wealthy, with never a tatty car in sight, vast great motorways scything through everything, buildings constructed without regard to expense, marble floors and deep pile carpets even in the Ministry of Defence. The war which hangs around seems quite unreal, and it's difficult to come to terms with it.

My own paramount need was to make personal contact with the senior commanders of the main Coalition forces – the Americans and the Saudis – and with the rulers of those states such as Bahrein, Dubai and Abu Dhabi who felt directly threatened by Saddam Hussein's aggression. The essence of an international operation such as we were mounting is that the people in charge should know and trust each other, and in my first few weeks I devoted much time and effort to visiting leaders both military and civilian.

Sandy Wilson had already established an excellent working relationship with the British Ambassador to Saudi Arabia, Sir

Alan Munro, who had lent him some rooms in the Embassy for use as offices. The two had been meeting several times a week: because Alan had worked in defence sales, he understood the Services very well and did everything in his power to help them. 'Ambassador is a super man and right on side,' I told Bridget. 'I've never had such cooperation as I receive. He is bright, cheerful and intelligent, and gives me all the information he possesses.' I could also have said that he was short, dark, balding and incredibly energetic, with the stamina to work right through the night if need be and a cheerful, boyish enthusiasm for every task he undertook. Visits to the Embassy quickly became a pleasure, not least because Alan had a most efficient personal assistant called Lisa Jacobs whose attractions were such that my military aides were always very keen to accompany me when I went to see him.*

Another vital recruit found for me by Sandy was Commander Colin Ferbrache (cordially known among his colleagues as 'Hairbrush'), who had come out to Riyadh as the Senior Naval Officer in the headquarters. To the Navy's horror, Sandy had hijacked him as his Military Assistant and I lost no time in doing the same. A Channel Islander in his late thirties, with a strange slow accent – almost a drawl – and a laid-back manner which belied his great competence, Colin had the priceless gift of being able to get on with anybody: whether he was speaking to Prince Charles or to a REME mechanic, he was always exactly the same. The experience of commanding a ship made him a good man off whom to bounce ideas and I found it valuable to talk things through with him, as I always got a sensible and mature response. (Also, if I was talking nonsense, he did not hesitate to say so – but in a way that never gave offence.) Altogether he was extremely useful to have around and he became my personal right-hand man, running my outer office, managing meetings, making arrangements and liaising with the Embassy. He also travelled extensively with me, which suited me well, as

---

* Alan had been awarded the KCMG in the New Year Honours of January 1990, but had been too busy to return to the United Kingdom to receive the award – a trip which he eventually managed in November.

I liked to be seen with a member of a Service other than the Army. Mark Chapman became my AMA, or Assistant Military Assistant, and also did admirable work, maturing noticeably during the six months of the campaign. Dispensing with a brief case, he always carried what he needed in a small ruck-sack, which he thought looked much more operational.

Among the Saudis, no one was more important to me than His Royal Highness Prince Khalid bin Sultan bin Abdulaziz, whom I met for the first time on the night of 7 October. A solid, well-built man of about forty, clean-shaven except for a moustache and smartly dressed in light-blue uniform, Khalid is a nephew of King Fahd and was then Chief of the Saudi Air Defence Force. In October 1990 he had also become, *de facto*, the leading Saudi representative – a position which he had established in his early meetings with the United States Air Force chief, Lieutenant General Charles (Chuck) Horner. During the build-up to war he played a vital role in recon-ciling his country's political and military necessities and in liaising between the Saudi ruling family and the foreign forces which had come to their aid.

At our first meeting he had a filthy cold, but made a point of emerging from his office at the Ministry of Defence to greet our party with elaborate courtesy in the doorway. When I greeted him in Arabic he was delighted and ushered me to the leather-covered armchair on the right of his own. Our delegation consisted of myself, Alan Munro and Sandy Wil-son, together with a couple of note-takers, and we filled the modest office to bursting point. As it was already 2200, and I had been working flat-out all day, I felt so tired that I feared I might fall asleep during the conversation; but our host revived me with his fluent English and ease of manner – evidently the result of his Sandhurst training. As we exchanged compliments and swapped information about our backgrounds, I soon found that he had an engaging sense of humour and also that he had taken a major technological step forward in the matter of providing his guests with refreshments: instead of the small cups of tea which are ubiquitous in Arabia, he offered chocolate biscuits and first-class coffee from a cappuccino machine.

When at last our conversation turned to business, I began
to see that King Fahd's decision to invite British and American
forces into his country had been an act of very great courage.
In Arab eyes, the only way to make the mass arrival of
foreigners tolerable was to place the armies, at least nom-
inally, under the command of a Saudi officer; and since in
Saudi Arabia all political leaders tend to be members of the
ruling family, it was essential that the Commander-in-Chief
should both be a serviceman and have direct access to the
King and his closest advisers. For this crucial position Prince
Khalid was the natural choice. Not only was he already Chief
of Air Defence, he was also a son of the King's brother Prince
Sultan, the Minister of Defence. Besides, his time at Sandhurst
had given him valuable military training, and some experience of the West. Although his appointment as Commander-
in-Chief had not yet been officially confirmed, he was in effect
the Saudi leader with whom the Coalition did business.

A man of ability and ambition, he was broad-minded
enough to listen to other people's views and, whenever persuaded by the strength of an argument, to change his own
plans accordingly. The pressures on him from the Saudi side
were immense: he had with one hand to prepare for war,
with the other to keep the behaviour of all the foreigners
within bounds which the radical elements of the Saudi population would tolerate. In the eyes of devout Muslims, the
provocations inflicted by the military build-up were intense.
Not only were the infidels tearing up roads with tracked
vehicles, taking over buildings and trying to fire live ammunition on some of the best camel-grazing areas in the desert,
they had also brought with them potentially disruptive inno-
vations in the form of women drivers, alien religious beliefs
and a horde of uncontrollable Press reporters.

My first meeting with Khalid went well and before it ended
I asked him to call me Peter – which he did from then on. He
said he wanted to see me at least once a week, and this I
welcomed: I made a mental note that I would hold him to
the agreement, even if I had no pressing matter to discuss, as I
felt that regular communication was going to be of the utmost
importance. Thereafter I addressed him as 'Your Royal High-

ness', and whenever I wrote to him (as I had frequent occasion to) I would begin with the formal Arab salutation 'After greetings' before proceeding to business.

Still more vital to the coalition than Prince Khalid or the Ambassador – and certainly a good deal larger than either – was the Commander-in-Chief of the American Forces, General Norman Schwarzkopf, generally known in his headquarters as 'the CinC' (pronounced 'Sink'). A big, imposing man – six foot three and seventeen stone – he gave off a feeling of confidence which I found immediately inspiring. As I shook his great paw of a hand for the first time, I felt straight away that here was a man I could like and respect, a man with whom I could do business. Press reports later claimed that our initial relationship was cool. That was nonsense. From the moment I walked into his office, everything came right between us. Of course a degree of formality persisted for a while, as it must between strangers, even if they share the same profession, and we spent some time sizing each other up; but because we were both under heavy pressure, the normal process of getting to know each other was greatly accelerated.

Sandy Wilson had established an arrangement whereby he, the senior British officer in theatre, attended Schwarzkopf's evening briefing at 1930 every night (known as 'Evening Prayers'), along with the American component commanders (the heads of the various forces). This was an important privilege, granted to us because of our commitment to place British forces under American command. As soon as I took over Sandy's chair at the meetings, I saw that my position was extremely valuable, although at the same time very fragile. The company would be briefed on what had happened that day, on plans for the next day and on how things were going in the American forces as a whole. To hear all this inside information put me in a position of trust: it was taken for granted that I would maintain strict confidentiality, which of course I took good care to do.

I quickly decided that the only thing to do was to establish a frank and open relationship with Schwarzkopf. He and I were going to have to trust each other completely and tell each other what was going on, even if it meant, on occasion, sharing information which our own governments might have preferred to keep to themselves. Without such an understanding, we would never have known whether we were telling each other the truth or only the half-truth, and we would never have built up the trust necessary for taking major decisions.

The best way to establish the right kind of understanding, it seemed to me, was to tackle the problem head-on. One evening I therefore asked Schwarzkopf if he could spare me five minutes after the main briefing and when we were alone together I went straight to the point. 'Look,' I said, 'if things are going to work, we've got to understand and trust each other. I hope we can both be totally frank in exchanging information and establish such a good relationship that if we get some bad news, which one of our governments isn't going to like or which we don't want passed on, we can share it in the confidence that it won't be abused.'

'No problem!' he said at once. He agreed, giving me his categorical assurance that he would share everything – which he did. This was a generous acceptance, for we were both well aware that America was running the show, that Schwarzkopf himself would always be the main source of information, and that I stood to gain most from our deal: it was I who wanted to be sure that every significant detail was at my disposal so that I would be able to make my own judgments as to whether a particular course of action would be acceptable to the British and fit the political directives which I was being given. I wrote to Bridget that night:

> Had an excellent one-to-one meeting with Schwarzkopf. We spoke as one soldier to another, and he agreed we would be frank and honest and not hide problems on national constraints. As a result, we are at one and I have cleared down all my requirements to his satisfaction. Thanks to the arrangements made by Sandy, I already see him daily and I have a seat at his table if war starts.

Our private arrangement, quickly made though it was, proved by no means easy to develop and sustain. On the contrary, it often demanded judgment and personal willpower. Of course I warned my immediate superior, Paddy Hine, that I might sometimes be unable to tell him what was going on in theatre because Schwarzkopf had asked me not to. Paddy accepted this, and allowed me to use my discretion – for which I was grateful. Even so, there were occasions on which I found myself in difficulty, when Schwarzkopf told me something which I knew was of immediate concern to the British Government, but which I could not pass on. Was I, in that case, being disloyal and unpatriotic?

Experience has taught me that very few people are able to keep a secret: almost everybody feels the need to impress some friend or colleague by revealing new information. One person tells another, that person tells two more and the secret is a secret no longer. Riyadh, London and Washington proved no exception to the rule: within hours, within minutes even, leaked information would be back in one of the Western capitals and somebody would be on the telephone demanding to know where it had come from. For this reason, I kept my agreement with Schwarzkopf to the letter, and he did the same. Once it became clear that we could both hold our tongues, information flowed much more freely.

The longer I worked with Schwarzkopf, the more I came to admire him, for I saw that he was far more than the rough, tough soldier which he at first appeared to be, and that if tact was not one of his virtues, he had many others. First, because as a boy he had spent holidays in Iran, where his father was attached to the police as an adviser, he understood the Middle Eastern mentality and ways of operating, which gave him a flying start. Second, he was a true professional soldier, a brilliant strategist and tactician. Having studied history and learned many lessons from it, he would often draw an analogy between events in the past and those of the present. No matter that he looked a bull of a man: he was highly sensitive and his quick mind could cut through to the core of a problem and come up with the right solution.

His third great strength was his political awareness. Because he had travelled widely, lived in the Middle East and seen active service in many countries, he understood that if a military solution of the Gulf crisis was to have any chance of success, it must take account of the political situation – in other words, he saw that there was no point in trying to force through military plans if these were going to upset the Saudis, the British or the French, because in the end the Coalition would break up. Thus he was always prepared to compromise on the military front if faced by a political imperative – and perhaps it was this above all which made him so successful in the Gulf, a truly great leader.

Like everyone else, he had failings, among them the quick temper which gave him his nickname, Stormin' Norman. He could certainly flare up – or, as his staff described it, 'go ballistic' – and when he did so, he became very frightening. Yet in my experience, this did not involve losing his temper with any one man; rather, he lost it with events, with things which had gone wrong. Of course, if you happened to be the man controlling those events, the abuse could become rather personal, but he would never turn on you because you had irritated him, only because you had taken unnecessary risks or caused some disaster. Another characteristic of his rages was that they blew over very quickly. A Norman storm was like a squall in the Pacific: huge and thunderous while it lasted, but soon over; and usually, by means of a softer word or two, he would go some way towards restoring the man he had just chewed up. I sometimes felt that the storms were controlled and deliberate, laid on to keep people sharpened up, but I also reckoned that his short fuse tended to stilt his staff officers. His immediate staff respected him – as everyone did – but they were also frightened of him, and reluctant to take decisions unless he backed them, with the result that he lost some input from them.

When not stormin', he had a strong sense of humour and a lightning wit. One evening, during the domestic part of the briefing, his Home Affairs Officer said, 'You'll wish to know, General, that yesterday, back home, Mrs Brenda Schwarzkopf addressed a group of wives whose husbands are over here – and got a standing ovation.'

'I should very much hope so,' growled Schwarzkopf

instantly. 'Anyone who's been married to me for twenty-two years *deserves* a standing ovation.'

All the senior American commanders had earthy turns of phrase, and none more so than Schwarzkopf's deputy, Lieutenant General Calvin Waller, who was ebullient, swanky and nearly as big as the CinC himself. Whenever Waller was about to go and answer a call of nature, he would announce, 'Well, I'm gonna choke my chicken,' and once during the air war, when somebody said that it was taking a long time to knock out the Iraqi army's fighting capability, he came up with a classic explanation of the difficulties involved. 'Well,' he said, 'it's like trying to stuff spaghetti up a wild cat's ass. You don't achieve much and you just get your hand covered in scratches.'

After Schwarzkopf, the American whose ability I admired most was Chuck Horner, the Air Force general. With his slouching posture, his crumpled bloodhound face and his habit of cussing and swearing, he neither looked nor sounded much like a top-class officer; but his professional ability was phenomenal. He knew his aircraft and his pilots inside out, and the plan for the air war which he worked out with his assistant Brigadier General Buster Glosson (another Vietnam veteran) was nothing short of a masterpiece.

Vital as it was for me to meet the leaders of the Coalition in Riyadh, I felt it was no less urgent that I should visit its other elements: 7th Armoured Brigade, whose equipment was already coming ashore at Jubail; the United States Marines, with whom the brigade would be training; the Royal Navy, which was building up its strength; the United States Navy, whose local commander had his flagship alongside in Bahrein; and last, but by no means least, I wanted to make contact with the Rulers of the Gulf states who felt threatened by Saddam Hussein's aggression.

The result was that for my first few weeks in the theatre I was constantly travelling. Fortunately I had at my disposal an HS125 seven-seat executive jet, white, with a smart blue stripe along each side. This little aircraft, complete with pilot and steward, proved an indispensable tool of command, without which I should not have been able to cover the immense area under my control, which included almost the whole of Arabia. The distance from Riyadh to Jubail, for instance, is nearly six hundred kilometres, but the 125 could cover it in under an hour. Abu Dhabi lies more than eight hundred kilometres east of the Saudi capital, but I could be there in an hour and a bit. It was possible for me to fly down to Oman and return to Riyadh on the same day; and Tabuk, the airfield in the west, was only ninety minutes away. The 125 was in effect my private jet: I could take staff along with me, hold conferences and briefings on board, catch up with paperwork. I could also sleep, carry secret documents and escape from the telephone for a while. Far from being a waste of time, air journeys were extremely valuable.*

One of my first, on 8 October, was to Jubail, an immense, modern port built for show on Saudi Arabia's east coast with oil revenues, and now being used to capacity for the first time as Allied equipment poured in. Most of the ships came from Cyprus, Panama, Liberia and many European ports. The Ministry of Defence had bid on the commerical market for ships to carry our armour and logistic supplies to the Gulf, and it was a commentary on the state of our merchant navy that of 146 ships sailing from England, only four or five were British. This fact seemed to reflect the high costs of chartering British, the small size of our merchant fleet and the fact that most British ships were already employed.

Fortunately I had in Jubail an exceptionally able Commander of the Force Maintenance Area (FMA), or depot, in the form of an officer from the Royal Corps of Transport, Colonel Martin White. Already a logistics expert with wide experience in Europe, Martin now proved himself a genius at setting up an operation which began on a big scale, which grew ever larger, and for which there was no precedent. Starting from the basis that he was going to provide ammunition, fuel, food and other essentials for one armoured brigade to

---

* Our crew, genially exasperated by my constant mid-air demands for coffee, which they were bringing me from the galley in inadequate, RAF-issue cups, went off to the souk and bought me a vast cup and saucer holding at least a pint.

occupy a defensive position not far north of the FMA, he progressed rapidly to a position in which he was called upon to supply an entire division which would fight a fast-moving offensive campaign with a start-line some four hundred kilometres from base. No praise can be too high for his efficiency or for the cheerful way in which he rose to meet one new problem after another. Such was his responsibility that, as soon as it could be arranged, I had him promoted Brigadier.

On a reconnaissance visit in September he had discovered that Jubail had been built as a centre for oil and light industry, but that the industrial side of the port had never taken off, with the result that several hutted camps intended for workers were standing unoccupied. He promptly rented one of these (which became known as Camp Four) to house British servicemen in transit, but also built a tented camp capable of holding two thousand men in the port area. (This was soon christened Baldrick Lines, after the Blackadder television series.) Martin himself lived for several months in the bottom of the port fire station, alongside the US Marine Corps' chief logistician, Brigadier General Jim Brabham.

As 7th Armoured Brigade began to pour in, the men arriving by air were supposed to be met by their equipment coming in by sea, but often ships were delayed, with the result that large numbers of soldiers had to live in the port area for the time being, many in big sheds, which were exceedingly hot and uncomfortable. On my first visit to the port, the influx was just beginning and it was clear that Martin had an immense job on his hands.

From Jubail I flew northwards by helicopter into the desert to watch our Challenger tanks firing live ammunition. With me came Major General Jeremy Blacker, the officer in charge of equipment development in the United Kingdom, who had flown out for urgent discussions about the up-armouring of our tanks and armoured fighting vehicles – the fitting of extra armoured plates to protect their tracks – and about a wide range of other UORs, or urgent operational requirements.

Another early trip was to Bahrein, where the Emir, Sheikh Isa, had always been virulently opposed to Saddam Hussein.

Now his tiny state had been brought almost to a standstill: international airlines had diverted all their flights to safer staging points further south and Bahrein was in severe economic difficulties. Our party consisted of myself and the British Ambassador to Bahrein, John Shepherd. (Senior diplomats on station pay regular calls on rulers, to ensure that they know them well enough to maintain good relations; but they always take the chance of making an extra visit when an outsider arrives, both to offer advice during discussions and to gain an accurate view of what has been said.) After a brief wait in a magnificent, marbled anteroom, we were ushered into the presence of the Emir – a small, bright-eyed man, whose diminutive stature in no way detracts from the power of his presence.

As always, he was very positive, talking in a most straightforward way, with a twinkle in his eye that made conversation a pleasure. He seemed in especially good humour, for the remarks which I had made at Aldershot – recommending people to watch their newspapers before Christmas – had gone ahead of me and I found myself something of a hero for taking such a positive stance. 'War before Christmas!' was very much the Emir's cry.

I said what a privilege it was for the British to be back in Bahrein, renewing our long-standing friendship and helping contain the threat to Arabia. With a wry smile Isa replied that he wished we had never gone away, that we had never removed our garrison during the early 1970s. Soon he moved back to the present crisis and congratulated me on taking such an aggressive posture. When he mentioned the use of military force to remove the Iraqis from Kuwait, he spoke with some vehemence, several times repeating loudly in English, 'He must not be allowed to stay there! He must go!' As firmly as possible I pointed out that, much as we too wanted Saddam out, our primary objective was to establish a defensive position and deter the Iraqis from trying to make further inroads down the Gulf, either into Saudi Arabia or into the smaller states. There was no question of our being able to evict Saddam from Kuwait within the next few weeks: we had neither the political directives nor (as yet) the military muscle to do that job. War before Christmas was not a possibility.

If Sheikh Isa felt any disappointment, he did not let it cloud the friendly atmosphere of our meeting. Bahrein, being one of the least wealthy of the Gulf states, had not been able to make any significant financial contribution to the Coalition effort, but the Emir had already placed valuable facilities at our disposal, not least the airfield at Muharraq, where Tornados had been based since the first days of the crisis in August. When I asked if we could put still more aircraft in, he agreed at once that we could move our Jaguars up from Thumrait in Oman, thus putting them right in the centre of the operational area and dramatically increasing their effectiveness. Nor did he blench when I asked if he would contribute to the in-theatre costs of our forces – food and facilities. Altogether, our meeting was good-natured and constructive.

From Bahrein I went on to visit Sheikh Zayed of Abu Dhabi, another old and trusted friend of the British, who acceded to the throne during the 1960s and became a greatly respected ruler. Now in his seventies, he still looks very much the Bedu, with his long, sallow, hawk-like face and commanding presence, a man whom one instantly respects because of his manner and background. I knew of old his passion for hunting and his predilection for living out in the desert (where he still has houses) rather than in the bustling town of Abu Dhabi. I liked the wild element in his character and I was glad to see him again.

Speaking through an interpreter, Sheikh Zayed also expressed his anxiety for the United Arab Emirates and asked that action against Saddam should be initiated without delay. Only in Oman, a good distance further south, did I find a more relaxed atmosphere. I was to have called on Sultan Qaboos, but for various reasons had to cancel my appointment. Instead I saw Sayed Fahr Bin Taimur, the Defence Minister, together with General Khomeis, Chief of the Defence Staff, and I was fairly careful to remind them how much time I had spent in their country on operational deployments earlier in my life.

Another ruler on whom I should have liked to call was

Sheikh Maktoum of Dubai, and I was most disappointed that the rapidly increasing pace of events made such a visit impossible. I already knew, however, that he had pledged his enthusiastic support to the Coalition, and offered to make his country's facilities available to us. Such spontaneous support gave me a feeling of great confidence that the whole of the Gulf was behind us.

Because of the span of my command, I had a unique opportunity – denied even to ambassadors, whose responsibility ends at the borders of the country to which they are posted – of travelling right down the Gulf and checking the pulse of one state after another. The central impression which I gained was of how few people had any clear idea of the true situation in Iraq.

Returning from Oman to Jubail, I met Lieutenant General Walt Boomer, Commander of the US Marines' Expeditionary Force, with whom our own 7th Armoured Brigade were to operate along Saudi Arabia's eastern littoral. I found Walt – a tall, gangling man, quiet and likeable – doubled up in a tiny office which he had requisitioned in the port area and had a useful talk about his plans before he sent me off on a four-hour reconnaissance by helicopter, during which I called on American units to see how they were living and to gain a general idea of the country. The men were busy with a wide variety of activities – training, maintaining vehicles, moving up-country – but they all made me welcome and even that brief glimpse of the terrain gave me an important understanding of what our own troops might or might not be expected to do later. I gained the immediate impression that the desert there, which consisted of sand made rough by tussocks of grass, with many small undulations and soft patches, was not suited to the fast-moving, wide-ranging kind of manoeuvres for which our own armoured units had been trained: there were too many oil pipelines and other installations cluttering up the terrain. Nevertheless, the Marines needed our tanks and the eastern sector was the one to which our armoured brigade had been assigned.

Back in Riyadh, I encountered Norman Schwarzkopf, who had himself just been to see the Ruler of Bahrein. 'Hey!' he said. 'That guy Isa thinks you're a hell of a feller. He says you're going to crack Saddam by Christmas.'

'Well,' I said cautiously, 'we have a saying in England: "The higher the regard, the harder the fall . . ."'

'That's right,' Schwarzkopf snapped back. 'The higher up the flagpole the monkey goes, the more he exposes his ass.'

My strange new existence quickly settled into a pattern of non-stop activity. Mark Chapman was searching hard for better accommodation, but there was very little to be had, and until he found something we had to stay in the Sheraton. Every morning at 0615 I would go down to the gym and put in a couple of kilometres on the treadmill, imagining that our lurcher Kesty was running with me and that we were passing familiar way-points in the lanes at Aldershot or round our home in the borders of Wales. Then, after a shower and break-fast, I would be in my headquarters by 0730, in time to read through the night's signals before going into the morning briefing at 0800. If I had to spend the whole day in the office, I would send someone out for a sandwich at lunchtime – and soon I wished I might never again see a pitta filled with greasy lamb. If I was going visiting, I would set off on my round as early as possible.

With daily practice my colloquial Arabic was returning rapidly. I asked Bridget to send out a dictionary and made a point every day of having a word with the Saudi guards at the entrance to my headquarters. Soon I had established a rapport with a soldier called Ahmed Hussein, but I gave him a fearful shock one morning when I wound down my window and by mistake addressed him as 'Saddam Hussein'. He looked mortified, not sure whether or not I had meant it as some abstruse form of joke.

Another highly valuable ally was His Royal Highness, Prince Sultan, brother of King Fahd and for seventeen years his Defence Minister. Together with Alan Munro, I flew in the HS125 to meet him at his sumptuous offices in the southern city of Jeddah. To be granted an audience with such a busy man was no small privilege and we had done a good deal of homework before the meeting, putting together a list of points which we wished to raise. We took with us, for instance, a draft of the Memorandum of Understanding which would give our servicemen protection in their work – almost diplomatic immunity – from Islamic law. We also wanted Prince Sultan's views on the Iraqi presence in the Yemen and the Sudan, where Saddam's emissaries were said to be giving advice and training. I gained the firm impression that the Sudan was supporting Iraq, which put it in bad odour with the Saudis. Our concern was that Saddam might base aircraft or train guerrillas there, so that we might find ourselves under attack from the south-west as well as from the north-east. I also had the uncomfortable feeling that the Sudanese might try to hijack one of our supply ships which were pouring down the Red Sea: the idea of a consignment of tanks ending up in Port Sudan was not at all amusing.

Our audience proved a memorable occasion. Prince Sultan is easy to talk to: he has a relaxed manner, a ready sense of humour and a disarming smile, but at the same time regal bearing and presence. At the start of the meeting I felt it worthwhile making my own Arab credentials clear, so I reminded him how in the Yemen, many years ago, I had fought on the same side as he while running the campaign against the Republicans in support of the Royalists, whom the Saudis had been backing. Sultan had been in defence matters even then and when I explained my role in the war, I immediately hit on an area of common interest and created a bridge between past and present – a classic example of how my past activities gave me a degree of credibility which I would otherwise have had to earn anew.

After this good start, Sultan talked freely of politics both at home and abroad. He discussed the American mid-term elections looming in November, and the effect they were likely to have on United States' support of the Coalition. He expressed high admiration for Margaret Thatcher and said he would like to meet her – also Tom King. Again and again, however, our talk returned to Kuwait, Iraq and Saddam Hussein, who, we decided was 'one man against the world'. Prince Sultan, too, called for war before Christmas, to send the Iraqis packing. Once more I had to explain that a huge

modern army cannot go to war at a moment's notice, as the
Bedouin can, but that we needed time to build up our forces.
Prince Sultan accepted this and, to my slight surprise but
infinite relief, directed his staff to sign our Memorandum of
Understanding on the spot. Armed with this precious document, we now had the right to remove British offenders from
the country and try them under British law. When we also
secured Prince Sultan's agreement to bring a squadron of
Puma helicopters into the theatre, I felt we had done well.

We also made efforts to befriend the French, who were
contributing a sizeable contingent to the Coalition, but
through no fault of their officers or men were quickly pushed
off on to the sidelines and had no say in the central planning.
This was because the Defence Minister, Jean-Pierre Chevenement, insisted that all command decisions must go through
him in Paris – a requirement which made it impossible for
the French to work closely with the Americans and condemned them to isolation. Colin, Mark and I called on the
French General Michel Roquejeoffre, dined with him and
invited him back to dine with us, but no amount of social
effort could change the unsatisfactory position of his force.

At last, after a week or so, I found somewhere better to live.
This was a two-storeyed villa in a compound normally
reserved for employees of the Saudi British Bank. The cluster
of houses, within a high wall, was typical of the settlements
built by overseas firms in Arabian cities so that Westerners
can carry on a normal life: besides about thirty dwellings,
there was a tennis court, a squash court and a swimming
pool, in which women as well as men could swim – something forbidden by strict Muslims. Inside the compound it was
possible for expatriates to hold restrained parties, but even in
this foreign enclave the consumption of alcohol was illegal
and there was always a risk that the Matawa would make a
raid if they thought that people were drinking or creating an
offensive amount of noise.

The house allotted to me was plain and functional, with
white walls and sliding, aluminium-framed windows, but it
was perfectly adequate for me. Downstairs, it had a spacious

sitting room with a dining area off it, a kitchen and a lavatory (which we later turned into an air-raid shelter). Upstairs, there was a big landing, a master bedroom with bathroom attached, two guest rooms and another bathroom. I shared the house with a friend from the Foreign Office, but as he was often away, and self-effacingly occupied the smaller of the two guest rooms, that left a good-sized room free for occasional visitors.

To look after us, we hired a Filipino woman called Gloria, who was in her thirties and spoke reasonable English.

With the possibility of war looming, Gloria was nervous about staying on in Riyadh and talked increasingly of going home, but within her limits she worked hard for us, producing breakfast, cleaning the house, doing our laundry and cooking supper whenever we were going to be in. The house was in every way an improvement on the hotel. It was quiet, private and secure – the gate into the compound was guarded by Filipinos and my own bodyguards lived in another house a few yards away.

We had an attractive little garden, in which we ate breakfast while the weather was still hot and, still better, a swimming pool, which took the place of the hotel's tread-mill as my means of getting early-morning exercise: I would try to put in thirty or more lengths before breakfast every day.

So at least I had a comfortable base. But nobody could answer the key question of how long I was going to be in it. 'The future is no clearer than when I left,' I wrote home on 15 October, the day I moved in. 'It seems as if an alarm clock is ticking away to something – but what? When?' Everything depended on the actions of the madman sitting in Baghdad, and on Arab and Western reactions to him. My letter continued:

> Short-notice war is very much the most likely option. The Arabs are pushing for us to go in and get it over with before Christmas and Ramadan, and before a lack of purpose comes in at home. The Americans are currently playing it long – two years, said Colin Powell [Chairman of the US Chiefs of Staff], the other day. Thatcher has been playing it short, for results and action, so it is a most confused picture.

Christmas was of no strategic significance to the Coalition: we were merely citing it as a useful reference point. On the other hand, Ramadan, the holy month, was all important in our calculations. In Ramadan, daytime fasting is obligatory for Muslims, who may let no food or drink pass their lips between dawn and dusk; at sundown the end of each period of abstinence is signalled by loudspeakers or a shot from a gun. We knew that once the holy month began, on 15 March, the Arab forces in the Coalition would become less and less efficient through exhaustion and, although it was conceivable that the Saudi Government would exempt their troops from fasting – which it has the power to do in a national emergency – March would have been a most unsatisfactory month for the Arabs to go to war. Moreover, when Ramadan was over, the hot weather would have set in, making warfare in armoured vehicles and NBC suits an exceedingly unpleasant, if not physically impossible, proposition. Everything therefore pointed to the fact that, if we were going to have a war, we must finish it before 15 March, or at any rate have made such progress by then that hostilities could not be stopped. Summing up the possibilities to Bridget, I wrote:

> Saddam has four choices. One, he can play it long and wait for the allies to fall apart – attractive to him. Two, he can pull down the pillars and let the temple fall in – possible if he sees he's losing. Three, he can attack to win – unlikely, and he would fail. Four, he can withdraw unconditionally – out of Arab character and, in my view, unlikely. So, as you can see, it's anything goes. The whole thing is a fascinating political jungle. Add the Press to it and you have a jungle full of giant man-traps.

During those first two weeks I was uncomfortably aware of a growing problem: that I could not easily work with Sandy Wilson. He was very clever, with a brain that moved like lightning, and I greatly respected his ability. Besides, having been in the Middle East since the beginning of the deployment, he knew more about everything than I did, and understandably often took the lead. But his methods were not mine. When I give an order, I prefer to stand back and let the person instructed get on with carrying out the task – hands-off, as the Army has it. Sandy was exactly the opposite: like Tom King, he was very much a hands-on man. He liked to ask questions at every stage of an operation and always wanted to be closely involved.

I could see that my arrival had put him in a difficult position. Until my appointment, he had been running his own show, with the RAF the sole British representatives on shore while the Navy operated independently in the Gulf. Then, just as things were about to become interesting, and the possibilities of action were increasing, along had come a General to take over command, with a great mass of Army in tow. I know that I myself would have found such a development very difficult to live with.

It is to Sandy's eternal credit that he never allowed disappointment to interfere with his desire that I should have a really good hand-over. He had made first-class command and liaison arrangements before my arrival and he remained magnanimous to the end, giving me full support throughout his stay. No doubt it was a flaw in my character which made it impossible for me to adapt my methods to suit his, and before I had been in theatre a week my letters home were reporting a sense of strain in our relationship. Fortunately for both of us, Sandy had already been earmarked for service elsewhere: he was about to be promoted Air Marshal and had been assigned another appointment – Commander-in-Chief of the Royal Air Force in Germany.

CHAPTER 3

DIGGING IN

Flying repeatedly over Arabia brought home to me the immense size of my command. From the shore of the Red Sea in the far north-west, the desert stretched fifteen hundred kilometres across to Kuwait and the coast of the Gulf in the north-east, and a still greater distance southwards to the Arabian Sea beyond Oman and the straits of Bab-el-Mandeb in the south-west corner: in all, nearly three million square kilometres.* And yet, vast as the area was, I soon decided that it was not big enough and urgently asked London to extend my jurisdiction beyond the Arabian peninsula itself to a distance sixty kilometres out to sea and to include the Suez Canal. The reason for this was that at first I had no authority to deploy forces outside the Gulf and although I possessed the ships and aircraft to deal with any incident which might arise, I had no power to use them at sea.

This was clearly both absurd and dangerous. If Saddam had managed to hijack a consignment of our tanks, for instance, or if the Yemenis had fired a Silkworm missile at one of our ships as it passed through the Straits of Bab-el-Mandeb, the whole of our build-up would have been thrown into disarray: I should have had to arrange convoys, rather than letting

---

* Though predominantly yellowish-brown, the desert has become more and more thickly dotted with fields growing wheat and other crops, each a perfect circle produced by the rotating arm of an irrigation unit. Saudi Arabia now grows more wheat than any other country in the Middle East. From the air the fields show up as rings of darker colour in the sand, often set out in neat rows, with their circumferences touching.

ships sail singly, and divert aircraft from combat air patrols against Iraq to the task of protecting the merchantmen – all of which would have placed an enormous extra burden on our limited assets. Moreover, with command arrangements as they were, it would have been the responsibility of Joint Headquarters, in the UK, to respond to such threats. The unsatisfactory nature of the position was vividly illustrated by an incident which occurred late in October.

A merchant ship called the *Tadmur* was boarded by the Royal Navy south of the Straits of Hormuz, at the entrance to the Gulf, technically outside my area. When we found that she was carrying contraband flour destined for Iraq, we suspected that the cargo had been loaded deliberately, so as to test the effectiveness of our embargo patrols. Whether or not that was so, we had to decide what to do with it. The obvious answer was to off-load it in Oman. The Omanis did their best to help and agreed that the ship should put into a small port while matters were being sorted out. Eventually we agreed that she should go back out to sea and cross-deck the flour on to HMS *Brazen* – a difficult task, which was carried out successfully, but not before *Brazen* had sent out an agonized signal protesting that she was likely to be invaded by armies of weevils and cockroaches. In the end *Brazen* took the flour back into Muscat and dumped it, but the whole saga, which lasted over a week, showed how unsatisfactory our command structure was.

Since the *Tadmur* was intercepted outside the Straits of Hormuz, in the Arabian Sea, control of the incident was taken over by Joint Headquarters at High Wycombe, thus cutting me out of the chain of command which I had just set up. One minute I had been commanding the ships involved because they were in the Gulf, the next they were outside it and under Joint Headquarters, even though what they were doing was of direct concern to me. The operation was being run with my ships and resources, but outside my area of responsibility. We finished up with Joint Headquarters and the Foreign Office dealing with our ambassadors in Oman and Saudi Arabia, while *Brazen*'s captain kept me informed only out of common sense and courtesy. Meanwhile, I was having to brief Norman Schwarzkopf about events taking place outside my area of command.

The incident proved a valuable catalyst in support of my argument that my area of responsibility should be extended to include the seaboard surrounding the whole Arabian peninsula. Paddy Hine took up the matter with London, who readily agreed to the extension.

Less successful was our attempt to have Jordan included within my area of responsibility: the attitude of King Hussein remained a worry all through the crisis. At that time, throughout the Gulf and in Saudi Arabia especially, there smouldered a suspicion that the King had done a deal with Saddam Hussein whereby the two would share the spoils if the Iraqis managed to defeat Saudi Arabia.* Whether or not that was true, the Saudis felt that Jordan was exploiting the crisis for her own ends: certainly she was giving Iraq a lot of help and convoys of lorries continued to ferry essential supplies from the port of Aqaba up the desert highway to Baghdad.

The most complex early task which I faced in theatre was the creation of a new command structure for the British Forces. My time in the Falkland Islands had taught me that tri-service command is a peculiar art, difficult to manage until one is used to it. The Army, Navy and Air Force all have their own procedures and ways of doing things; it therefore needs a combination of tact and firmness to make them work together in harmony. Rather than issue sweeping orders and directives, one has to bring all three Services into line by gentle yet firm manipulation – and this was particularly so in the Gulf, where both Navy and Air Force had become well established before I arrived on the scene.

Most of the senior officers in the Gulf had never even met each other, let alone worked together, and most had never been members of a tri-service organization. There was thus

* During the 1920s King Hussein of the Hejaz (grandfather of the present King) claimed overlordship in Arabia and in 1924 the dispute between him and Ibn Saud, leader of the Wahabis, led to war. The Wahabis invaded the Hejaz and defeated Hussein. In 1926 Ibn Saud proclaimed himself King and in 1932 renamed his kingdom Saudi Arabia. Afterwards Jordan claimed parts of Saudi Arabia – although of course the Saudis reject the claims utterly.

an urgent need to pull them all together – and the only person who could do that was me. My aim was to set up a system which would bring all three Services round the table with me, so that we could together sort out a unified policy for the forces in theatre, with everybody making an input and everybody bearing responsibility. In my mind it was essential that Navy, Army and Air Force should be properly co-ordinated and have their efforts directed in such a way as to maximize the effect of the British contribution as a whole.

At the outset I found that the Navy were thoroughly well-intentioned, but that because for the past ten years they had been independently policing the approaches to the Gulf with the Armilla Patrol, they still favoured their old and established system of reporting straight back to Fleet Headquarters in the United Kingdom: a major change of the kind I was proposing held no apparent advantages for them. The RAF had set up a similarly independent single-service operation, with their own headquarters in Riyadh and communications back to the Headquarters of Strike Command at High Wycombe.

Somehow I had to convince the sailors and airmen, many of whom had powerful personalities and definite views on how things should be done, that they now needed to work as a corporate, tri-service group. I had to develop in them a sense of loyalty to me and my headquarters, and give them the feeling that the organization which I was setting up needed their active support. The way to do this – as I saw it – was to make each head of Service clearly responsible for his Service to me and to ensure he realized that at the end of the day I was the man who would be issuing the orders, and that he would not get the right answers by bypassing the system or going back up the single-service chain of command.

Much depended on the support which I received from my immediate superior, the Joint Commander, Air Chief Marshal Sir Patrick Hine. A former fighter pilot, he had flown all the RAF's latest combat aircraft, including Tornados and Jaguars, to keep his hand in, and for such an active airman it would have been natural to let the RAF go on working straight back to him at High Wycombe. In fact, to my unbounded gratitude, he backed me wholeheartedly in my determination to create a fully tri-service force. No field commander can ever have had a more sympathetic or flexible superior than Paddy Hine. Quick, practical, energetic, intelligent and perceptive, he won the respect of everybody concerned, both in the United Kingdom and in the Gulf, and he took an enormous weight off my shoulders by interposing himself as a barrier between me and the politicians and civil servants in London. No matter how uncomfortable the issue, he backed me up with unswerving loyalty. In my difficulties with Sandy Wilson, for instance, he was most sensitive and helpful, even though, as an airman, he must have felt inclined to side with the officer from his own Service.

On his visits to the Gulf – he would come for three or four days about every three weeks and stay in my house – he always made a point of calling on Prince Khalid and Norman Schwarzkopf, in that order, and maintained a close understanding with both of them, which again made my own task easier. His priority always was to produce the best possible deal for his officers and men in the Gulf – and, far from dreading his arrivals, as one does those of some commanders, I looked forward to his visits keenly.

With him, often, came Mike Wilkes, the Army Commander. I always found his presence an enormous help, as I knew him well enough to bounce ideas off him and discuss problems without ceremony. 'I'm so lucky to have Mike where he is,' I told Bridget after one visit. 'We can talk to each other without barriers, and I can accept comment and criticism from him which I would never take from anyone else.' The bigger the Army deployment became, the more I valued his help.

While Paddy was in England, he and I maintained frequent contact, talking on the telephone almost every evening, often for as long as two hours. By this means we were able to discuss and settle every problem which came up before it had time to develop into a major issue and after a while we understood each other so well that we were fully in each other's minds.

Our conversations at first took place through a form of scrambler called Brahms – a rather laborious device, which had to be specially set up every day by having a new crypto-graphic tape fed into it and was liable to go down in mid sentence. Also, since one had to press a switch while speaking and release it while listening, as with a radio, exchanges were rather slow. Yet Brahms had the advantage of being portable, so that I could use it at my house in the evenings. Later we graduated to more sophisticated systems which gave us secure speech up to top-secret level.

Those evening conversations, though essential, took up a great deal of time and lasted late into the Saudi night. People in the United Kingdom, three hours behind us, would feel that they had the evening ahead of them, but seven o'clock their time was ten o'clock ours, and by then, after a fifteen-hour day, I was often beginning to feel that some sleep would not come amiss.

I also talked frequently to Tom King, who, having himself been in the Somerset Light Infantry and then the King's African Rifles, took an extremely close interest in the build-up, especially of the Army. My calls to him were never off-the-cuff, but booked and carefully planned in advance. Before each of them my staff would make out a schedule of matters which they knew the Secretary of State wished to discuss and I myself would compile a list of points which I wanted to clear down. One of his early preoccupations was the issue of wriggly pattern desert combat uniform. When our deployment began, hardly any was available (allegedly because we had sold it all to the Iraqis), but Tom King was continually pressing for servicemen to have the new uniform as soon as possible and for them to be photographed by the Press wearing it. When the early consignments arrived in the second half of October, we equipped the front-line soldiers first and issued one suit per man initially, so that as many people as possible would have lighter, more comfortable gear. (I myself wore desert combat uniform as soon as it became available, together with an SAS beret and a tri-service belt.)

In my headquarters, we had never been able to check the security of the whole building and were concerned that Iraqi agents might have planted it with hidden microphones before we moved in. In the early days, we therefore restricted classified conversations to my office, one of only two rooms which had been electronically cleared. Whenever I wanted to discuss matters of strategic importance or political significance, I talked from there. To improve security still further, I had a portable compact-disc player turned on to make background noise whenever we held sensitive briefings or were planning conferences. Thus we discussed the latest ideas for breaking through the obstacle belt into Iraq with Kylie Minogue squeaking in the background and worked out how to clear mine fields for an amphibious landing at the head of the Gulf to crescendos from *Phantom of the Opera.**

In spite of my efforts, the three Services did not at first pull together and lacked the will to work in unison. No one was being obdurate: it was simply that at the back of their minds they were still individual operators and although they paid nominal deference to the new headquarters, they felt no loyalty to it. Part of my problem with the Navy was that communication between Riyadh and ships in the Gulf – using the Inmarsat satellite designed for merchant vessels worldwide – was very poor. But the main trouble at first was that the Navy maintained the essentially defensive strategy which it had evolved for the defence of civilian shipping and the operation of the embargo against Iraq.

I now wanted a fundamental change: I wished the Navy to make plans for war at the northern end of the Gulf – a far cry from their role in the area so far – and I instructed the senior naval officer, Commodore Paul Haddacks, to prepare a plan for offensive operations.† To back him up and provide him with specialized support, I had a team flown out from the Maritime Tactical School in the United Kingdom. Under its able and lively leader, Captain Steve Taylor, the team travelled about the area for three weeks, and made several

---

* Mark Chapman took upon himself the responsibility of seeing that I was up to date in my musical appreciation and advised on the purchase of suitable works for drowning out potential eavesdroppers.
† After some discussion, it had been decided that his official designation should be Senior Naval Officer, Middle East, rather than Senior Naval Officer, Gulf – partly because the acronym SNOME was more dignified than SNOG, but also because the first accurately reflected the fact that neither the conflict nor the command was confined to the Gulf alone.

follow-up visits, devising an admirable plan which became the basis of our maritime support for the Coalition effort.

Just as we had teething difficulties with the tri-service command, so at first my own headquarters did not pull together as I wanted. One problem was that we were having to create a structure for ourselves as we went along, and new people were constantly arriving. Beyond that, though, lay a more serious deficiency: my Chief of Staff had neither the rank nor the experience to do the job I required of him. This was not his fault, but one unfortunate result of the initial delay over my own appointment in September.

Had my nomination been announced more promptly, hence giving me a greater say in the selection of officers, I would have made sure that my Chief of Staff was of higher rank. In the event, he, an RAF man, was faced with an impossible task, as he was working *primus inter pares* with officers of the same rank from the other Services, all trying to play their own games. The task of setting up the headquarters and training everyone in it for war was a formidable one by any standards. I wanted everyone working and exercised together in the shortest possible time, with all communications fully tested, in case Saddam made the pre-emptive strike which was well within his capabilities; but somehow this never happened and, in due course, I decided to replace the Chief of Staff with an officer of higher rank and experience, particularly of tri-service operations.

In purely physical terms, many of our early problems were extremely basic – and none more so than that of water. As critical as food or fuel, water is a fundamental necessity for any army and, in a country where very little existed on the land surface, the provision of adequate supplies was a matter which demanded immediate attention. Even though in October I did not know how large our forces were going to be, it was clear that our requirements would run to hundreds of tons a day.

The most obvious source was the desalination plant at Jubail, which supplied Riyadh and in theory had the capacity to supply our forces as well. Yet as this was obviously a prime target for Iraqi attacks, we could not rely on it, especially as it was vulnerable to oil spillage in the Gulf. (Later, when the Iraqis deliberately released torrents of oil into the sea, I insisted that we should charter two ships loaded with water. Whitehall was reluctant to do this, as usual because of the expense; but the vessels came in extremely useful. Having taken on full cargoes at Jebel Ali, they were able to top up ships of the Royal Naval task force at sea and, at the end of the war, when the desalination plants in Kuwait had been sabotaged, they sold water to the Kuwaitis.)

The other main source was fossil water, which has accumulated over the centuries in enormous, prehistoric aquifers beneath the desert. Many of these were already being exploited for agricultural use, especially in areas where they lie not too deep beneath the surface; but I tasked the Royal Engineers to identify sources in the battle zone and find out what water might be available. Out went the Sappers to prospect the best sites for artesian wells, but that was only their first task. Once water had been found, they had to negotiate the purchase of it with local landowners and make arrangements for moving it to the areas where it would be needed, storing it in pillow tanks, chilling and purifying it. Fortunately the cool season was already setting in by the time our deployment began to build up, otherwise the water problem would have been even greater. As it was, it set the Sappers an enormous task, which they tackled with their usual efficiency. Although in the end they never drilled any new wells, they used many existing sources, especially one at Qaysumah, on which we drew heavily. They became expert at fitting reverse-osmosis plants to the wells and so converting the brackish artesian liquid which came up from beneath the desert to sweet water.

Another urgent preoccupation of mine was with the media. In the Falklands I had learned to appreciate the power of the media and the influence which they can exert, for good or ill. I had found, first, that if I could win reporters on to my side they would do a lot for the forces, and second, that if I put over a consistent message, that message would start to filter into the hearts and minds of people in the United

Kingdom. Further, that message would permeate through to every level of British society, because if one influenced the people of Britain, one began to influence politicians as well – and support across the whole political spectrum was essential for the kind of major overseas operation which we were mounting.

The media, in other words, were of crucial importance, especially with modern communications, which ensure that news is back in the United Kingdom almost before it has happened. It seemed to me vital that if war came, it should be reported properly and not from second-hand information; so in the Gulf I took a lot of trouble to bring the media alongside and gave them every possible facility. After that, if they reported something which was inaccurate, at least I would know that they were doing it deliberately. I was also concerned about their safety, for it was clear that many of them had little idea of what they were letting themselves in for.

The media corps which assembled to report the Gulf conflict was the largest in history and by the end of the year it numbered over fourteen hundred men and women. This, of course, horrified the Saudi authorities, who in the early days tried to keep the total of journalists down to a handful by restricting the issue of visas. In the end, however, the war gained such a high profile on the world stage that the Saudis eased up on their efforts to control the reporters and cameramen flooding in and out.

Western practices would not allow me to keep the media away from the war. Many Arabs could not see why it was necessary to have any media men present, but we reckoned it an essential part of our democratic way of life. Furthermore, my view was that, if we had bad news, we would be quite wrong to suppress it, other than for genuine reasons of security. If some revelation might give an advantage to the enemy or have an adverse impact on our own servicemen and their will to fight, there might be a case for withholding it. Otherwise, I felt that everything should be reported. At the same time, I was always disappointed when I read inaccurate reports written simply to attract attention and create a story where none existed.

I also found it difficult to accept that the Western media had any legitimate role in Baghdad. The principle of a free Press, as I understand it, is that the media report everything which happens. Reporters in the heart of enemy territory were completely muzzled and could send out only what Saddam Hussein allowed them to. They were, in effect, mouthpieces for the enemy, whose aim was to destroy and kill our own servicemen. I therefore thought that their reports should not have been broadcast or published, for they served no purpose as far as the Coalition was concerned and, in my view, offered no real extension of the information available to the public.

The media's stronghold in the Eastern Province of Saudi Arabia was Dhahran, and there, on 25 October, I threw a barbecue for the British contingent in the residence of the Consul. 'They're a very up-market lot when you meet them as normal citizens,' I reported to Bridget. 'I told them we both had a job to do and a responsibility to UK citizens.'

My own Press conferences convinced me that television had added an extra dimension to the conduct of modern warfare: commanders of the future will have to be trained not only to handle it, but also to allow enough time and resources for it to be used to fullest advantage. For someone like myself, who had deliberately kept a low profile throughout my career in Special Forces, it was a strange and unnerving experience to stand up in front of the cameras. Yet television is something that a modern commander cannot ignore. I found that if ever I left too long a gap between appearances, the media soon began to point out that although the American commander was constantly on the screen, there seemed to be something wrong with his British opposite number. Even the relatively few appearances which I did make produced an enormous fan mail. To people whom I knew, I replied by hand, but when I began to receive forty or more letters a day, I had to ask my private staff to answer them – and even they had a job to keep up.

Nobody was keener that our forces should have good Press coverage than Tom King and he followed the minutiae of individual reports with almost obsessive attention. When photographs of two soldiers clad only in shorts and vests but carrying their weapons and gasmasks appeared in *The Times* and the *Daily Express*, many people in the Ministry of Defence took temporary leave of their senses. Since the men were doing precisely what they had been ordered to do – keep their weapons and masks with them at all times, even when going to have a wash – there was absolutely no cause for uproar. The fact that *The Times* had frivolously captioned its picture 'Dressed for action' was in no way the fault of the men concerned. 'They're making a ridiculous fuss about two photographs which they say are "undignified", and I'm trying to quieten them down,' I told Bridget. 'It is absurd that this is all people in London can think about when they ought to be putting their minds to the very serious decisions they're going to have to make.'

As our ground forces began to spread out into the desert, I foresaw that there would be an urgent need to keep them all informed of what was going on, both in theatre and outside it. By the time the British contingent was fully deployed, we had more than 45,000 men stretched out over a distance greater than that from John O'Groats to Land's End – the largest force ever deployed in combat by the United Kingdom since the Second World War. What a soldier heard in a remote part of the desert, where he never moved far from his slit trench or armoured vehicle, might be totally different from the news which a sailor picked up inside the hull of a Type 42 destroyer plying the waters of the Gulf. It seemed to me essential that all these far-flung people should feel themselves part of a cohesive military force. They also had to know who their commander was and to feel that their gripes and grievances were being attended to.

The best means of creating a common bond, in my view, was a force newspaper and towards the end of October I gave a directive which led to the publication of that admirable organ, the *Sandy Times*. As a precursor, there appeared in early November two issues of a small, photocopied news-sheet called *Arabian Info*. The first came out with its eight pages numbered in the normal order, but the second contained a mock-apology for this oversight and a promise that Page 3 would never appear again. This neat reference to the *Sun* – which had produced two special editions for the Middle East, without its inflammatory naked girl on Page 3 – was maintained throughout the life of the Forces' newspaper, which appeared consistently with Page 2 followed by Page 4.

The first number of *Arabian Info* announced a competition to find a more memorable name for the new paper. Many of the seventy suggestions which came in were unprintable and to choose the best from a short list of six we held a boardroom-type vote after a Heads of Services meeting in my headquarters. *Omani Oracle* was a near miss, *Gulf Bits* not solid enough, *Hard Times* too gloomy. Eventually, in true democratic fashion, I allowed myself to be voted down and conceded to the majority that we should go for *Sandy Times* (I cannot remember what it was that I preferred.) From a small initial print run of two thousand copies in November, the paper rose to a peak circulation of ten thousand every fortnight (or sometimes every week) by the beginning of the New Year. Printed in large, handsome format on glossy paper, generally in two colours, and frequently carrying messages from VIPs such as the Prime Minister and the Secretary of State, it quickly established itself as essential reading among the servicemen, not least for the vigour of its correspondence column, which published numerous heart-felt complaints and so offered a useful safety valve for the frustrations of desert life.

Under the military guidance of Lieutenant Colonel Glyn Jones, the *Sandy Times* was edited by Squadron Leader Pat McKinlay and printed in Riyadh by a firm called Maramer. An article in the final issue revealed that the company had been engaged in error: the editors, lost while in search of another firm, found themselves in Maramer's print works, assumed it was the one they were looking for and went straight into business, not realizing until several weeks later that they had taken' on the wrong firm. Undeterred by this initial confusion (or by the fact that official permission for us to publish the newspaper had not yet come through from the Saudis), Maramer did a splendid job. The task of the production team was greatly eased when first the *Sunday Times* and then other leading London newspapers, such as the *Daily Telegraph*, *Independent* and *Guardian*, all gave permission for the new journal to re-run any reports which it cared to print, faxing it many stories free of charge. Even with this help, the paper cost £50,000 per issue, but in my view it was worth every penny, for it had a powerful effect both on morale and on communications, both up and down the chain of command.

One editorial about pay for reservists was so outspoken that it caused several servicemen to complain about its tone. The article also aroused the wrath of people in Whitehall, who found the leader too far out of line with official policy for their liking. The fact that we were being criticized from both ends of the spectrum seemed to me a striking tribute to the newspaper's editorial independence, which in my view was essential if the *Sandy Times* was to gain the confidence of the servicemen and be an organ which they trusted and respected, rather than just a glossy version of commander's orders.

An equally important project was the establishment of a broadcasting station specially for the Gulf Forces. Until we got one, the servicemen had nothing to listen to except American Forces' programmes and the fearful harridan known as Baghdad Betty, who, between pop music records, broadcast doses of crude propaganda from the Iraqi capital and from an unidentified building in Kuwait.*

A far more sinister form of propaganda was being beamed at the Saudis and other Muslim members of the Coalition in Arabic: allegations came over the air waves that infidel troops were billeted in the vicinity of the holy cities and, although these suggestions were quite untrue, they had an insidious, unsettling effect. Religious propaganda was something which the Saudis had never faced before and they took time to counter it with broadcasts of their own. The Minister of Information in Baghdad, on the other hand, was adept at it, having

---

* We made persistent attempts to pin-point this lady and eventually, when the air war started, managed to drop a bomb on her station, which put her out of business.

practised deceit on the Iranians for the past eight years, and for a while he had the better of the war of the air waves.

It was clear to me from the start that we needed a station of our own, so that we could keep our forces properly informed about what was happening and so that I myself could talk to them all from time to time. To me, a radio was essential – but to persuade London of the necessity was another matter.

Because the station would have to be mobile, we were going to need new equipment, which would cost between half and three-quarters of a million pounds. With Paddy Hine's help, I put together a case for the radio and submitted it to the Ministry of Defence. Tom King quickly appreciated the need and backed my request, but Whitehall failed to understand the importance of a radio station in such a widespread command. I gained the impression that the objectors considered the station a needless extravagance, and that they blocked our proposal on the grounds that we were not going to be in the Gulf long enough to justify such high expenditure.

Instead, they suggested, we should try re-broadcasting programmes through a transmitter which we already had in Cyprus. We knew quite well that we could not reach the whole Gulf theatre by this means and laid on a short trial to prove it.

After the dispute had rumbled on for several weeks, Alan Protheroe, Chairman of the Services' Sound and Vision Corporation – a Territorial Army officer and an old friend of mine – took a considerable risk in ordering the equipment before it had been officially authorized. Then, during a flight which Tom King and I made together in his VC10 while he was visiting the Gulf, I heard the Secretary of State give his private secretary Simon Webb a definite instruction that the system was to go ahead. Even so, it was again countermanded in Whitehall and I had to tell TK that his orders were not being carried out. The same thing happened yet again after a meeting at the Ministry of Defence, at which Paddy Hine pointedly raised the matter with the Secretary of State.

'How much will it cost?' Tom King asked.

'Up to £750,000,' said Hine.

'Do it,' said King. 'Go ahead and do it.'

Even then, for another two weeks, civil servants held out, refusing to sanction the expenditure. Eventually the front maintained by Paddy Hine and myself, and supported by the Secretary of State, carried the day: Protheroe's investment was saved and the new British Forces' Broadcasting Service station was flown out to us – but only after colossal and quite unnecessary expenditure of nervous energy.

Another medium of communication which I considered vital was the post. The bluey – the single-sheet air-mail letter form – is a war winner, nothing less. Handed out free to servicemen, it induces the warm feeling that at least the Government has given you something for nothing. It also has the advantage of offering limited space, so that you can fill it up quickly, especially if your writing is large. I myself wrote one to Bridget every day, and during the campaign as a whole phenomenal numbers of blueys were used. The cost was high – nearly £2 million – but again, the benefit to morale was incalculable. As British Forces' Commander, I put what some people might consider a disproportionate amount of time and effort into making sure that the post was as efficient as poss-ible. The Americans had immense problems with *their* mail and, to Norman Schwarzkopf's fury, a letter often took four or five weeks to come through from the United States. Ours took more like four or five days and I did everything I could to maintain this kind of service. When a postal strike seemed certain to take place in England, for instance, Paddy Hine arranged a special collection system in barracks in the United Kingdom and Germany, so that Forces' mail by-passed civilian post offices altogether.

All through October the men and equipment of 7th Armoured Brigade continued to pour into theatre. Once the men had been documented, kitted out and reunited with their vehicles and weapons, they drove off into the desert to start training. From the earliest days of the deployment, I made it my policy to go out into the field as often as I could. It was important not only that I should get to know my com-manders, but also that I should be seen by as many ser-vicemen as possible – and for me the most rewarding part of every visit was the time which I spent talking with the men. I always felt it important that I should tell them as much as I could about what was going on. Even if I said no more than their commanding officer had already told them, the fact that information came from the theatre commander gave it special authenticity and increased the credibility of the CO at the same time. Also, by asking questions, I was able to find out what the servicemen were thinking and worrying about — valuable intelligence, which often influenced my ideas and decision-making.

One officer whom I already knew was Lieutenant Colonel Arthur Denaro, Commanding Officer of the Queen's Royal Irish Hussars, one of the first army units to arrive.* On 26 October I found him sweltering in a hangar in Jubail, where his regiment were billeted until they could move out into the desert. Their living conditions were extremely cramped and the heat barely tolerable. As always, Arthur was resolute and cheerful, but he seemed sobered by the news which I brought of the Iraqi build-up in Kuwait.

One of 7th Armoured Brigade's most urgent problems was to find an adequate training area — an open space big enough for their tanks and artillery to manoeuvre and fire live ammunition. Saudi Arabia seemed to be square kilometre after square kilometre of absolutely nothing but sand and gravel. Appearances were deceptive, however. Investigation showed that even the most barren-looking stretch belonged to somebody and that much of the desert was highly valued as grazing for the racing camels maintained by Saudis of high military or social rank.

During October Patrick Cordingley put in endless hard work negotiating rights to train at Al Fadhili, immediately

---

* My connection with Arthur was curiously involved. His wife Maggie had first been married to Michael Kealey, who was under my command in the SAS battle for Mirbat, in Dhofar, during the 1970s. Michael's conduct was so outstanding that I would have recommended him for a VC, had it been politically admissible. As it was, he won a DSO while still a captain — only the second man of that rank to do so since the Second World War — but then tragically died from hypothermia on an exercise in the Brecon Beacons. Some time later, to the delight of all their friends, Arthur married his widow. So here we were again in Arabia, with myself once more in command of Maggie's husband in a desert war.

inland from Jubail. He needed a very large area – at least one thousand square kilometres – and, needless to say, the land he wanted turned out to be some of the best camel-grazing in Eastern Province of Saudi Arabia. To use it, he had first to persuade the Emir of Jubail, to whom the area belonged; then he had to tackle Admiral Bada, who ran the King Abdulaziz Naval Base; and finally he had to win over the Brigadier in the Saudi Air Force, Prince Turki, who had control of local airspace – for if a tank-round hit a rock, the ricochet might reach a height of twenty thousand feet and allied aircraft were continually flying over Al Fadhili on their way to patrol the border. At the same time, I myself was working to secure permission from the air controllers in Riyadh and our combined efforts eventually won through, although the victory was not total and the brigade were limited to firing for about five hours a day.

With official clearance obtained, their engineers set about building targets, markers and so on, and they christened the area the Jerboa Range, after 7th Armoured Brigade's mascot, the desert rat. Yet the practical problems of using it remained considerable. Because the area contained such good grazing, it naturally attracted the Bedouin, who had to be moved out of the way (with the Emir's blessing) before live firing could take place. Then, every day, the camels had to be driven off by low-flying helicopters: the animals were quite aggressive and would bellow and spit at the aircraft before starting to shamble away. Single Arabs were also liable to wander into the range to fly their falcons and they too had to be sent packing. The whole training area, in fact, had to be staked out by members of reconnaissance troops acting as wardens. Nor was the terrain by any means ideal, for the sand was extremely soft and fine: wheeled vehicles could make no progress across it, and tanks burnt an appalling amount of fuel churning through it. That part of the desert was also dotted with hundreds of stunted bushes, each with sand piled up against it, so that tanks and their crews were thrown about violently. Nevertheless, it was desert and all we could get for the moment.

Late in October Patrick himself had a lucky escape when

the Range Rover in which he was travelling through Dhahran was hit broadside-on by a Saudi vehicle and turned upside-down. Patrick was concussed and had to spend a few days in hospital, but he could have been very seriously hurt, or even killed. To have lost a key commander at that moment, just as our ground force was building up, would have been a major blow and the accident brought home to me the need to have replacements identified, trained and ready to take over all the posts in the chain of command, my own included.

At that same time, with Paddy Hine out on a three-day visit, I reported to Bridget: 'There are vital questions to be addressed. We have to decide if it is all to be long- or short-term. We have a window and, if we miss it, it will be long-term, and a different set of problems. It is becoming more apparent every day that possession of Kuwait is nine-tenths of the law.'

Those rather cryptic remarks reveal that, even then, we were beginning to realize that we might in due course have to turn from defence to offence. The window of which I wrote was the gap between the moment at which the Coalition's ground forces would be in position and ready to fight and the onset of Ramadan on 15 March. Already we were thinking that, if we were going to drive Saddam Hussein out of Kuwait, that was the time in which we would have to do it. The urgent necessity was to concentrate the minds of people in England and make them realize that far-reaching decisions had to be taken at once. Before he left for home, Paddy and I therefore discussed everything with Alan Munro and sent a strategy signal to the Foreign Office, outlining the critical dates by which decisions would have to be taken if our deployment was to be completed in time.

Already it was clear that we were facing a very large army and that the enemy forces were increasing every day. With the desert skies clear during autumn, information about the disposition of Iraqi troops came pouring down from satellites and surveillance aircraft in such detail that every time Saddam's men dug a new slit trench, we knew about it. What we desperately lacked, though, was 'humint', or human intelligence, for we had no live sources in Baghdad or any-where else in Iraq.

Such was the cold-blooded brutality of Saddam's regime that it was almost impossible for an enemy agent to function under it. Iraq was (and is) a state governed by fear. Every person of significance is watched by three other people and if that individual does anything unusual all three minders are required to report the deviation to the authorities. If two report some misdemeanour, and the third fails to, the latter will at least be thrown into gaol, probably shot. In the end even your own brother and sister have to report you – other-wise they too will be executed. There is no system of law or justice. The rule is, kill first and ask questions later, if at all.

After the war a senior Saudi prince and diplomat told me of the following conversation which he had had when he visited Saddam Hussein in Baghdad early in 1990:

SH   The one thing I value most in a man is loyalty.
P   Quite, but how do you know whether a man is loyal or not?
SH   Oh, I look him in the eyes. I can tell straight away.
P   What happens if people aren't loyal?
SH   In that case I kill them.
P   But what happens if you make a mistake?
SH   I don't mind if I make a mistake that way. I'd rather have an innocent man dead than a disloyal one alive.

In such a society, agents cannot operate and in their absence we were unable to discover much about the mood of Saddam and his government, the state of morale in the army, the degree of training, or the relationship between soldiers and their commanders. The result was that we could never assess accurately what sort of response we would get from the troops on the ground if and when fighting started.

Another problem which contributed to our shortage of humint was the fact that, until the air war began, very few deserters came across the front line. Not only was it physically difficult for soldiers to desert forwards through the barriers of mines and wire, but also, extraordinary as it seems, the Iraqi troops at first had no idea whom they were fighting, for their commanders deliberately kept them in the dark. Only when the Allied psychological warfare campaign swung into action did they realize that there were Western troops opposing them. Nor could men easily escape to the rear, since execution squads shot deserters on sight, without any question of bringing them to trial. Besides, the regime had a simple method of deterring would-be defaulters: whenever a serviceman did manage to escape, members of his family would be rounded up and shot. Such knowledge kept countless miserable conscripts in their holes in the sand.

A further constraint for us was the fact that the Saudis maintained very close control over any defectors who did come over. They would allow us to put questions which were to be addressed to the deserters, but they would never allow Westerners to interrogate Arabs directly. The result was that such information as we did obtain was always diluted and delayed, and we never got an opportunity to strengthen it by follow-up questioning.

Another potential source of information about the enemy was their communications network, but at first this was almost equally barren. This was partly because, at immense cost, the Iraqis had installed a country-wide system of buried and duplicated land lines, which were difficult to blow up or tap. Also their forward units in the desert maintained radio silence to an extraordinary degree. So little did they use their radios, in fact, that when the war finally started they could hardly remember how to communicate with each other. But for as long as they kept quiet, there was no radio traffic on which we could eavesdrop.

All in all, the intelligence position was fascinating but unsatisfactory and our shortage of humint was reflected most starkly by our lack of knowledge about the Western hostages whom Saddam was threatening to stake out as a human shield on sites of military significance. Our ignorance on this score made me thoroughly frustrated. I felt that if only we could find out where the hostages were, we might be able to do something about recovering them or at least find ways of not hurting them once the shooting started. I felt strong personal concern for them, and I did *not* want the RAF or any other Coalition air force to be responsible for blowing them into oblivion when attacking the bases to which they had been sent.

Thus I was keen to examine every conceivable means of rescuing the hostages before war broke out and I tasked the Special Air Service, who happened to be training in the United Arab Emirates, to examine ways of bringing them out. Paddy Hine agreed that this would be a reasonable task for our Special Forces and he set up a planning team of his own at High Wycombe to devise methods of springing as many of the prisoners as possible. The planners in England kept in close touch with the Foreign Office, whose hostage helpline was still highly active, and early every morning the World Service of the BBC would broadcast short messages recorded by relations and friends. These – we heard later – were a tremendous morale-raiser to the captives and were also eagerly listened-to by fugitives hiding in Kuwait.

Our main difficulty was that we knew where some of the hostages were, but not others, and that anyway Saddam kept moving them, so that no rescue operation could ever have been a complete success. With the help of the Foreign Office and the Ministry of Defence, the SAS worked hard to build up a picture of where the prisoners were being held. To have had any chance of success, they would have had to go in by parachute or helicopter and lift the hostages out to safe rendezvous in the desert – as the Americans tried to do in their attempt to rescue their people from the Embassy in Teheran in 1980. But at no stage did I feel that we could have recovered more than half the Britons, if that.

With every day that went past, our manpower needs grew. This did not surprise me – indeed, I regarded it as inevitable, for in any major deployment the commanders who have to make things work on the ground always discover requirements which could not have been foreseen at an earlier stage. Thus in due course we found we needed more engineering facilities, extra stages in the logistic train because all the distances were so huge, men to construct and guard prisoner-of-war camps, and so on. Yet what was obvious in theatre seemed to be far from obvious in London, which initially sought detailed justification for every increase, and only later allowed us a margin in which to work.

During the Falklands War Margaret Thatcher had let it be clearly known that her policy as Prime Minister was to give the Armed Forces everything they needed to recapture the islands. Her working motto was, 'If we've got it, they can have it.' As she herself told me after the Gulf conflict, she was under the impression that the same principle was being followed during the autumn of 1990. Other people in Whitehall, however, had other ideas and our requests for more men met such obstruction that Paddy Hine and I soon came to describe the Ministry of Defence's tactics as 'rate-capping'.

The trouble was that although, as the weeks went by, our operational concept changed fundamentally, the policy on rate-capping appeared to remain the same. From the Field Commander's viewpoint the fact that the Coalition was swinging round from defence to offence seemed to make no difference, and I had the impression that the arm-in-the-mangle policy was being rigorously implemented. When our ideas and aims did change, the civil servants, it seemed to me, retained an unacceptably high level of control over what the military were doing. In the Falklands campaign they had a far smaller say in military decisions: now, because the transition to war was gradual I felt that there was insufficient weight of military input in the decision making.

People in London seemed to become so obsessed with totals that they began thinking purely about numbers of personnel. In the initial stages, every request was analysed and challenged down to the last man, so that we had to spend countless hours justifying relatively small numbers of soldiers, all of whom were essential to our plans.

To some extent I sympathized with Tom King: clearly it was embarrassing for him to have to go back to Cabinet and admit that the Force levels which he had cleared earlier now seemed inadequate. Nevertheless, the delays caused by Whitehall led to some deplorable muddles. Servicemen would be stood up to go out to the Gulf and then be stood down again because their clearance had not come through. Then they would be stood up again. In one case we reached the ludicrous position of troops being flown out to Dhahran but then, because approval for them was still not forthcoming, they had to be told to re-board the aircraft and come straight home again – a humiliating experience, particularly for the commanding officer, who was one of the party.

Nor did we meet obstruction only in London. In Riyadh the continual increase in numbers excited grave suspicion: the influx of foreigners gave the Saudis valid reason for blocking requests to bring yet more people in. In self-defence, they could point to the disruptive effects which the invasion of Westerners was already having on Muslim society.

The result was that they became even more sensitive about new arrivals. They knew exactly what aircraft were coming in, because they kept tight control of their own airspace. At first, whenever we wanted to increase our Force levels, we had to follow a strict procedure. We, the military, would brief Alan Munro on what we wanted and he would go off to secure permission from the Saudi Defence Minister, Prince Sultan. If agreement was not immediately forthcoming, we would have to argue for it and in the early days there was at least one instance of reinforcements arriving before proper clearance had been obtained. Working in Riyadh, I could understand the Saudis' concern and I was prepared to take time and trouble to do things their way, but people in England found it very difficult to see why such a fuss was being made. Were the British not, after all, making an immense effort to help?

Later, things became easier and, as my relationship with Prince Khalid developed, I was able to clear reinforcements direct with him, while merely keeping Alan Munro informed.

For everyone in my headquarters, those first weeks of the deployment were a time of frantic activity. There was an immense amount of work to be done and no one knew how long we would have in which to do it. After I had called on Arthur Denaro in Jubail, he confided to a colleague that he thought I looked 'utterly exhausted' and I am not surprised. I was working on average from 0700 until midnight, travelling hundreds of kilometres every day, and getting no days off. I knew that it would be dangerous to allow myself to become worn out and then try to do something about it, after the process had already gone too far. Admonitions on this score kept arriving from Bridget. Spurred by her wise words, I tried to pace myself and make sure that I got a reasonable amount of sleep. I also issued positive instructions that everyone in the headquarters was to take time off: one day a week if possible, but half a day at least. Before I gave that order, people were working seven days a week, often until midnight or later, but still tended to feel guilty if they took any time off at all. I myself began taking Friday morning off – the Arab equivalent of Sunday – but although I repeatedly planned two or three days' leave, staying with Terry Finney, an old friend in Abu Dhabi, I never managed to take it.

This was easily the biggest command I had ever held in my life and I was by no means confident that my handling of its multifarious problems would be successful. In those early days everything seemed extremely uncertain, not least on the political front. In England, Mrs Thatcher was firm as a rock in her determination to see off Saddam Hussein, but apparently dove-ish noises were emanating from the Foreign Office, and the same sort of tune was filtering back to us from the United States. When Paddy Hine flew to Washington for discussions with Colin Powell, he came away much concerned by his impression that Powell was prepared to wait two years, if necessary, for Saddam to withdraw from Kuwait. Everyone in theatre knew that it would be physically impossible for us to keep our troops in the desert that long. If Saddam realized that, and developed a strategy which enticed us to stay on indefinitely, we were going to be in serious trouble.

CHAPTER 4

'MORE TANKS! MORE TANKS!'

At the start of November the weather began to cool down. We took to having breakfast on our terrace and on the second day of the month, writing to Bridget 'on my shady verandah', I described the morning as 'delightful, cool and summery, with butterflies in the bougainvillea surrounding the pool'. At the same time, however, the military climate was starting to hot up and the first two weeks of the month proved a time of rapid development as the mood of the Coalition shifted, and war began to look probable rather than possible.

Before I left England I had been thinking about the possibility of a substantial increase in our own ground forces; now, the more I saw of the Iraqi build-up and the Coalition response, the more certain I became that we, the British, would give a far better account of ourselves if we stepped up our land force from a single armoured brigade to a division. At the back of my mind was the memory of an unhappy experience in the Korean war when a British brigade had fought under American command. But, quite apart from that, my tactical reasoning was simple: whereas a brigade always fights as part of a division, and has relatively little freedom of manoeuvre on the battlefield because it has to conform with the divisional tactical plan, a division enjoys much greater autonomy, even though it is part of a corps, because it is usually given an area of ground in which to operate and can work to its own plan.

This was my purely practical reason for wanting more men, but it was strengthened by the political consideration that if the Americans brought in large reinforcements – about which they were already talking – our own contribution to the Coalition would begin to look very small. To have a division would both increase our prestige in theatre and give us more influence in the shaping of policy. With the help of Paddy Hine, I therefore put together the case for a division and submitted it to the Secretary of State.

My plan all along had been that I should chop, or hand over, tactical control of 7th Armoured Brigade to the Americans when I judged the moment right. The great strength of my position was that I had been given authority to place British servicemen under the command of the Americans. This meant that, provided I was happy with the role proposed for any unit of our Services, I could contribute in an uninhibited way to the overall plans being set up by Norman Schwarzkopf and his generals. Unlike in the Falklands, where the whole British Task Force had been concentrated on the same objective, our troops in the Gulf were spread out over a vast area and could not be coordinated in the same way. The RAF was flying in support of Coalition air defence; the Navy had been conducting embargo operations for some weeks; and the Army was training to join in the land war. But we did not have a British section of the front against Iraq and the most practical arrangement was to chop command of our armoured brigade to the Americans.

Before I did this, both Patrick Cordingley and I needed to be certain that our troops were ready and fully trained, and that the task to which they were going to be assigned was within their capabilities. Thus the timing of the hand-over was critical, and on 3 November I visited Walt Boomer to clear one or two conditions – among them that Patrick would retain the right to keep me fully informed of what was going on and that I, along with other senior British officers, would be able to visit the brigade from time to time, even though it was under American command.

Satisfied that all was well, I made the formal handover, after which I had to let Patrick get on and do his job. I did, however, retain what we called the yellow card, or power of veto, which would enable me to rescind the transfer of power and take the brigade back under my own command if I thought things were going wrong. This ultimate sanction gave me the opportunity to control what the British were doing, although rather remotely, and thereby still to have responsibility for them. To a layman I realize this may sound like opting out. In fact, as we were very much junior partners of the Americans, whose land and air forces were over ten times the size of ours, it was the best way of arranging things.

The deal which we struck was possible only because Schwarzkopf and I had come to such a close understanding. He knew that when I placed 7th Armoured Brigade under Walt Boomer, the British forces would work to United States orders, within the American system. I for my part was confident that Schwarzkopf would support our brigade with air power and extra artillery because he saw it as a valuable asset alongside the US Marines. Even so, at the end of the day I was still responsible for what happened to our brigade: if it got into trouble and sustained unacceptably high casualties, the ultimate responsibility would be mine.

At the same time as I chopped command, the Americans agreed that in due course they would put some of their own troops under *our* command, as part of our brigade. The idea was that everything would then look balanced and in the United Kingdom we would be able to show that the British were not entirely subservient to the Americans. In fact I never really wanted to go ahead with this arrangement, unless it was going to produce some tangible advantage for us: in my view, the small political gain would not be worth all the practical difficulties involved. I was therefore not sorry when, in December, Schwarzkopf told me that in the light of developments the arrangement would no longer make sense.*

The CinC was extremely robust about demanding re-

---

* In the end a Multiple Rocket Launch System regiment was placed under British command by the US VII Corps, but this was done out of pure expediency, not for political reasons, and the arrangement worked admirably.

inforcements of his own, and in particular ground forces large enough to deal with Saddam Hussein promptly. Outwardly he often gave the impression of being a bit gung-ho, especially when he appeared on television, but that was for the benefit of public opinion and in fact, if anything, he tended to be cautious. Deeply influenced by his experiences in Vietnam, he was determined that the battle in the Gulf should be fought on his own terms. These were twofold. First, he insisted that he should have sufficient forces to defeat Saddam Hussein without undue risk of sustaining high casualties, which he feared he would suffer if he became bogged down in a war of attrition. Second, before any ground assault went in, he proposed to rely on his Air Force to give the Iraqi army such a pounding as to reduce its operational effectiveness by fifty per cent. 'Both these conditions will have to be met if the President wants me to do it,' he had told Paddy Hine at a meeting in Riyadh during August. 'If they're not, he can find someone else.'

In the early days of the deployment, the outline plan had been that 7th Armoured Brigade should either be kept in reserve or act as a counter-attack force. For as long as our strategy remained essentially defensive that had seemed a good enough arrangement, but now that we were moving into an offensive frame of mind, many new issues arose.

By early November, ideas about the best way of evicting the Iraqi army from Kuwait were developing both in High Wycombe, where Joint Headquarters had a small planning cell, and in the US Central Command Headquarters in Riyadh. In both places – it soon emerged – people were thinking along much the same lines.

Nobody liked the idea of an amphibious landing at the head of the Gulf. With the sea and beaches mined, we all felt that such an operation would be unnecessarily expensive in terms of lives, much as the US Marines might welcome the chance to lead the assault.

If we set aside that option, the next broad alternative was a major, direct thrust into south-east Kuwait, straight north-wards in the direction of the city. This was evidently what

Saddam was expecting for he had built up his blocking force to an extraordinary degree: by early November some ninety Iraqi brigades were established in and around Kuwait, and at that stage the Coalition had only about twenty-five brigades with which to take them on.

The third major option was an altogether more ambitious manoeuvre: a wide left hook out into the desert to the west and back into Kuwait to the north of the city, where Saddam had positioned his strategic reserve, the Tawakkulna and other crack divisions of the Republican Guard. Our planning team in High Wycombe came to the conclusion that if we could engage and defeat this strategic reserve, the rest of the army would crumble and fall into our hands.

We discussed the two main options at a meeting in Schwarzkopf's headquarters during one of Paddy Hine's visits in early November. Schwarzkopf agreed with our analysis: he said that he too much preferred the left hook and that the Republican Guard was the target to go for. His main worry, however, was that he did not have the ground forces to carry it through. He saw Coalition troops becoming pinned down, first by the Iraqis' tactical reserve, and ultimately by their strategic reserve, and the battle turning into one of attrition, with heavy casualties – precisely what he wanted to avoid. 'We'd win it,' he said, 'but at far greater cost than I intend to pay.' For this reason, he went on, he had asked Washington for a huge reinforcement, including VII Armoured Corps, 24th Mechanized Infantry Division, an additional Marine regiment, three more aircraft carrier battle groups, extra air-craft and more amphibious forces. Altogether, this was a tre-mendous up-grading of the United States' strength in the Gulf, which in the end brought their contingent to more than 500,000 men.

Turning to Paddy Hine, Schwarzkopf asked if he, an experi-enced airman, thought that the Coalition air forces could achieve the fifty per cent degradation of Iraqi fighting power which he wanted. Paddy replied that he could not be sure: although plans for the campaign seemed well thought-out, there was a chance that the air forces might not be able to reach their objective, and what then? The Coalition forces would have to follow through on the ground, whatever the state of the Iraqi army. In other words, the Americans really did need the reinforcements for which they had indented. Schwarzkopf then revealed that there were differences of opinion in Washington about what the air campaign could achieve. 'Of course,' he growled mischievously, 'one of those guys in the Pentagon is Brent Scowcroft, President Bush's National Security Adviser. The trouble with him he's an airman and the worst kind of airman. He's a *strategic* airman!' It was clear that the US Air Force had been hard at work selling its ability to win this war single-handed.

Paddy Hine had naturally been doing everything he could to ensure that the RAF had a viable capability in theatre. Here at last was a campaign in which the Air Force was going to play a vital role and it was militarily important that it should do so: like the rest of the British armed forces, the RAF needed to ensure that its force levels were adequate for the task in prospect, at a moment when its future was being critically examined in the Options for Change review. Paddy therefore obtained ministerial approval for an increase in the RAF's contribution and moved two more squadrons of Tornado GR1s forward, one to Muharraq and one to Cyprus. He also considered bringing out a Harrier GR5 ground-reconnaissance squadron and raised the possibility of using Buccaneers as a precision back-up to the Tornados (although of considerable antiquity, the Buccaneers were the only British aircraft fitted with Pavespike thermal-imaging and laser-designating equipment, with which they would be able to guide bombs from Tornados on to pin-point targets), although this was only a daylight capability.

In view of the controversy which developed later, it is worth emphasizing that at this stage of planning, in November, the role of the RAF was clearly seen as one of runway destruction. The Americans had nothing like our JP233, the runway-cratering bomb, and for this reason they specifically wanted our Tornados to attack Iraqi airfields, thereby grounding Saddam's planes. Because the JP233 is designed to disintegrate into its component parts within seconds of leaving the aircraft, it has to be dropped from very low level and needs no electronic guidance.*

Early in November, while Sandy Wilson was still Air Commander and my deputy, he, Paddy Hine and I discussed air strategy at a meeting in my office. Paddy accepted that the RAF might spend most of the war attacking airfields, but warned that it might then have to move on to other roles. 'What if we decided not to hit airfields any more, because the job had been done?' he asked. 'What if we ran into very high attrition? We might have to go up and do something at medium level. The Americans might put us on to targets that needed laser designation or some kind of smart weapon.' He went on to suggest that the Americans would not be able to spare any designator aircraft of their own, 'And if we aren't careful, we'll find ourselves dropping bombs from medium level with no one to designate for us.'

In due course that proved a prophetic forecast. Meanwhile, however, Sandy Wilson was reluctant to have yet another type of aircraft based at Muharraq, with the large back-up team which it would need. Like everyone else, he was conscious of the need to keep numbers as low as possible and also was short of space. Besides, when he discussed the matter with Chuck Horner and his experts, he found that the Americans did not see the RAF performing in this way. They certainly would want the Tornados to attack airfields, at least for the first couple of weeks of the war, and then, if they switched the aircraft to different targets, they themselves would be able to provide laser designation. With some reluctance, Paddy therefore dropped the idea of bringing out Buccaneers for the moment – but he did not give it up altogether, and directed the crews to continue their training in the United Kingdom.

One vital question settled at this time was that of the supreme command of the Coalition forces. On 6 November, at an audience with King Fahd, the US Secretary of State James Baker

* The JP233 was regarded by other nations as a very strange weapon: when a dummy bomb full of concrete was lost over a training range, the event caused quite a stir and a search team had to find it to establish the cause of its premature release and to ensure that it had done no damage to marauding camels.

agreed that joint command of any offensive operations which took place would remain with the Americans: if it came to evicting the Iraqis from Kuwait, or launching an assault through Iraq, the United States would control the campaign and the Saudi forces would form part of the Coalition effort under Schwarzkopf's command. If, on the other hand, Saddam made a pre-emptive strike and invaded the Kingdom, a Saudi Arabian would be in command.

Until that point, it had not been clearly resolved who this commander would be. Prince Khalid was the most obvious candidate, but there were others in the wings, among them General Hammad, the Chief of the Defence Staff. It was up to the Saudis themselves to decide and we, the British, knowing that a debate was raging among the Arabs, made clear our view that Khalid was best qualified. Paddy Hine agreed with me that he offered by far the best prospect. We knew how to work with him. He knew us and our methods. To have brought in a new man at this stage would have upset the whole equilibrium of personalities which we had taken such trouble to establish.

Schwarzkopf was of the same mind and we agreed to lobby for Khalid individually. I called on him personally, telling him that we positively expected him to stay, and also sent messages to his father, the Defence Minister, Prince Sultan. I knew that Britain's long-established association with Saudi Arabia, and the fact that we stood as Number Two to the Americans in the Coalition, gave us strong influence with the King and his advisers. If we said that Khalid was the man for us, King Fahd and Prince Sultan would listen closely. It was with some relief that we heard, a few days later, that Khalid had been confirmed in his command.

All these changes emphatically confirmed the Americans' status as leaders of the Coalition. It was therefore exceptionally fortunate that in the first week of November I managed to infiltrate a British officer into the very heart of Schwarzkopf's headquarters, his central planning team. This was – as the Americans described him – Lieutenant Colonel (Promotable) Tim Sulivan, an officer in the Blues and Royals whose career had, paradoxically, been interrupted by the threat of war. Tim had already been nominated to succeed Patrick Cordingley as Commander of 7th Armoured Brigade, and in normal circumstances would have taken over from him in December, but because by then Patrick had established himself so firmly in theatre and done so much excellent training, we decided that it would be madness to remove him at such a critical moment and postponed his hand-over.

This was, of course, a bitter disappointment to Tim, but he saw the point of it and energetically sought some other way of joining the British forces in the Middle East. After commanding his regiment and going through the Higher Command and Staff Course at Camberley, he had been doing a fill-in job at the Ministry of Defence in London when the Gulf crisis broke. Gradually he realized that brigade and battalion commanders would not rotate until the campaign was over, so he began to make it clear that, if minds changed, he would very much like to take up his command; if not, he was keen to go out to the Middle East anyway, since he felt that if he missed the campaign entirely he would be at an enormous disadvantage when he did eventually take over.

In due course he was seen by Mike Wilkes who told him that there *was* a chance of his going out to Riyadh, as I was looking for a British officer to work on the American Staff. What had happened was that, quite by chance, I had met Tim while he was taking a German course at the Army Education Corps Language Centre. I had been impressed by his ability and now, when I heard that he was at a loose end, it immediately occurred to me that, with his background in armour, he would be extremely useful. I therefore asked Mike to have him transferred to Paddy Hine's small planning team in Joint Headquarters, so that he could gain some knowledge of what was going on; but he had been there only two days when I requested that he should proceed to the Gulf immediately.

To infiltrate him into Schwarzkopf's innermost sanctum was no easy task. For one thing, the American planners were pathologically secretive about their plans: they habitually classified documents 'Noforn' (not to be shown to foreigners), and at least once tore down maps from the walls when a

British officer entered the room unexpectedly. Another problem was that Tim, being six feet six inches tall, could hardly be called inconspicuous. Yet he soon solved the difficulties and got himself accepted, partly through his easy, laid-back manner, and partly through the brilliantly simple ruse of donning American uniform.

Arriving in Riyadh equipped only with British jungle greens, he soon perceived that whenever he went into an American briefing, he inevitably attracted notice: senior officers would look at him and start whispering to each other. When, after a few days, he said, 'Gosh, I stick out like a sore thumb,' one of the Americans said, 'Why don't you wear our uniform? You wouldn't show up so much.' Thinking this a good idea, because it would make him seem part of the team, Tim came and asked my permission to wear US uniform with British badges of rank. I gave it promptly and soon an amenable sergeant slipped him two sets, including boots, under the counter. The garments were a fairly ludicrous shape, barely meeting in the middle, and Norman Schwarzkopf was amused that Tim had bothered to acquire them at all; but they had the required effect of letting him disappear, chameleon-like, into the background. People soon began to forget that he was not an American and he became fully accepted as a member of the planning team.

As such, he was of incalculable value to me throughout the campaign, for he became privy to the Americans' innermost thoughts and was allowed to divulge them to me, although to nobody else. His presence thus strengthened still further our bond with the Americans and increased the mutual confidence which Schwarzkopf and I had in each other.

The team which Tim joined had been specially formed by Schwarzkopf to plan the eviction of Saddam's forces from Kuwait. Not trusting the competence of his own J5 tri-service planners to mount so complex an operation, the CinC had recruited a team entirely from the Army: three senior majors who were about to be promoted lieutenant colonel and one lieutenant colonel, Joe Purvis, about to be promoted colonel. Into this small and intensely rank-conscious cell came a strange animal whose own rank had them continuously worried.

When Tim arrived in Riyadh on 6 November, he was firmly billed as a staff officer and one of the planning team, rather than as a liaison officer, of whom, as a breed, most Americans hold a low opinion. His rank was lieutenant colonel, but his new colleagues were extremely polite to him, even overawed, for they knew that by some quirk of the British promotion system he was about to make a double jump, and that in the new year he was to become a brigadier. He was something they had never known before and something impossible under the American system: a lieutenant colonel about to become a brigadier. One of the junior members of the team could not bring himself to address him by his Christian name and when invited to do so, simply said, 'I can't do it.' To him, Tim was always 'Sir'. Then in December, as war approached and the Americans began to brief headquarters staff down to full colonel but no lower, it seemed expedient that he should move up a rank and so, on 10 December, he did. But when, on 31 December, he became a substantive brigadier, he felt he could not out-rank Joe Purvis, his team-leader, who became a full colonel on the same day. And so, in the New Year, Tim became a substantive brigadier, local full colonel – the only man, I daresay, who has ever held such a rank. He continued to wear colonel's rank until war broke out and thereafter, because he had a seat in the War Room, finally put up brigadier's rank because it gave him more clout among senior Americans.

By the time he arrived in Riyadh, I had already been moving towards another fundamental decision about the use of British forces: I did not want them to fight alongside the US Marines, to whom they had originally been assigned. My reasons were perfectly straightforward, even if they could not all be revealed at the time. The first was the fact that the terrain across which 7th Armoured Brigade would have to advance, if they remained where they were, was not at all suitable for the far-ranging, fire-and-manoeuvre tactics in which they specialized and for which they had been trained. In the south-west of Kuwait there were far too many man-made obstacles – principally oil installations – for their

armour to operate with the flexibility and mobility which
were its greatest strengths.

My second reason was secret. I had already got wind of the
fact that Schwarzkopf favoured the wide left hook above all
other forms of attack and that he intended to use his Marines
more as a diversion than as the main thrust. The Marines did
not yet know this, nor did Patrick Cordingley, and of course
I could not tell him. But I did believe most strongly that as
we British were making, in our terms, a very large commitment to the campaign against Saddam, we must at least be
given a chance to show what our armour could do in an
environment which suited it. The desert to the west of Wadi
al Batin, through which the wide left hook would be
launched, was perfect for our type of operations, being flat
and featureless for kilometre after kilometre. If we got the
division for which I had asked, I wanted it to be fully stretched
and employed, which would not be possible on the eastern
littoral.

These two reasons for wanting to move were sound in a
military and political sense. I thought so at the time and I
remain convinced now. Yet there was a third reason which
reinforced my conviction, and this was the question of casualties. Norman Schwarzkopf and I were very close on this point.
He, still haunted by hideous memories of Vietnam, was anxious to keep American casualties to a minimum. I felt the
same. Strongly as I supported the international crusade
against Saddam Hussein, I did not see that this war was worth
a lot of British dead. In general, then, our ideas were very
similar.

Even so, I was concerned by the idea of our forces going
into battle with the US Marines, for not only had they been
placed in the sector opposite the most heavily fortified Iraqi
positions, they also had the reputation of being exceptionally
gung-ho and the official prognosis put the amount of casualties they might suffer in an attack as high as seventeen per
cent. Further, we knew that the Marine Corps were nervous
about their own future − as were all the US armed forces −
and that they imagined the best way of avoiding cuts would
be to win the war against Saddam on their own. In America

their Commandant General, General Gray, was hammering away for a major slice of the action: in the desert, they were mustard keen to be the main thrust.

I was not scared of taking casualties. I knew that some were inevitable. But at the same time I was damned if I would allow the British, having put so much into the Gulf conflict, to take casualties out of all proportion to their numbers. Even if the Marines did suffer seventeen per cent losses, that figure would be watered down by the level of perhaps five per cent in the rest of the US contingent, so that the average loss for the Americans would come out respectably low. If, on the other hand, the whole British ground force were committed to the Marines, our casualties might *average* seventeen per cent – which in a fighting force of ten thousand men would have meant seventeen hundred dead, a figure totally unacceptable to me. I simply did not think this war worth that amount of lives to us and I did not believe that we should commit the main British effort at the point where the heaviest casualties were expected, especially with all the other arguments against it. Casualties were thus a factor of some importance in my desire to move our forces westward, but I did not mention it to Schwarzkopf because I felt that the military and political reasons were sufficient in themselves, and to have raised the casualty issue would have made us look chicken, which we most certainly were not. I am sure he realized casualties were at the back of my mind, but in this context he did not mention them either.

Ironically enough, 7th Armoured Brigade were getting on famously with the Marines and did not in the least want to sever what had become a mutually enjoyable and advantageous connection. The Marines needed our Challenger tanks, which were far better than anything they had, and they needed our engineers, because their own were less skilled. We needed the fire power of the Marines' artillery, because we did not have much of our own, and above all we needed their air power and support helicopters. The Marines also admired our expertise in manoeuvre warfare and saw that we were more practised than they at advancing across wide open spaces in tanks.

Because the Marines were not a NATO force, their procedures were very different from ours and to overcome the
problems which this caused I encouraged Patrick Cordingley
to integrate with them as much as possible. The British therefore put plenty of their people into American headquarters,
including their intelligence staff, and took fire-support teams
from the Americans into their own headquarters, at all levels,
so that if they needed an aircraft to put down bombs on a
certain grid reference, it would be an American in our own
headquarters who got through to the pilot on his radio net.
Altogether, the ties between the two forces had become very
close.

On a personal level, relations were extremely cordial. As
Patrick himself put it, 'We saw the Marines as splendid people,
who were wonderfully well trained and looked bloody
efficient and smart, and had the right spirit.' Goodwill
between the nations led to many exchanges, principally of
food and equipment. British Compo rations, which can be
heated, were markedly superior to the American MRE (officially Meals Ready to Eat, unofficially Meals Rejected by
Ethiopians), which are designed to be eaten cold, but the
Americans' cots, fairly luxurious camp beds, were the envy
of our servicemen, many of whom had to sleep on the sand.
Indeed, so many cots were swapped for Compo that later in
the campaign supplies ran out and the quartermasters were
utterly baffled as to where they had all gone. The Americans
did have one excellent supplement to their rations in the form
of pot-meals, designed to be heated in microwave ovens, but
they had no means of warming them up in their tanks and
whenever possible they would ask a friendly British crew to
pop a pot into their Challenger's boiling vessel.

All this created a powerful bond between the forces and
when I first mentioned the possibility of resubordination to
Patrick – without being able to divulge the real reason for it
– he was understandably not at all pleased.

The possibility of raising our forces to division level brought
to a head another simmering problem: roulement, or the
rotation of men and units. In recent years the Army had

become used to tours of duty lasting four months, a length pioneered by the SAS on its overseas assignments and taken up by all regiments serving on unaccompanied tours in Northern Ireland. Four months had become fixed in military minds as the norm, and any longer separation caused metaphorical raising of eyebrows, as well as loss of morale, for there is nothing that soldiers like better than counting off the days to their return home on their home-made charts.

The trouble with Operation Granby was that nobody could tell how long it might last and because many of the British formations had been specially tailored to take part, replacing them was going to be extremely difficult, if not impossible. To create the first wave of formations had been relatively simple, as we simply poached men from other units to make numbers up, but it was obvious that by the time we came round to forming a second wave we would already have done our poaching and would find ourselves in serious difficulties. Besides, everyone in the initial deployment had gone out at more or less the same time and clearly we could not roulement the whole lot simultaneously at a time when war might break out any day.

The uncertainty caused ripples of concern all through my time in the Gulf. Whenever I addressed groups of servicemen, I was inevitably asked when they would be going home and, as their commander, I felt obliged to try to give them some guidance. Paddy Hine, during one of his visits, did make some remarks about length of tours: the men read into his words what they wanted to hear rather than what he had said and before we knew where we were, they were all planning their return home on a date which had not been decided at all.

The problem was worst in the RAF, the earliest arrivals, who had gone out to the Gulf under the impression that their tour was no more than a demonstration of presence and intent, and that they would be home within four months at most. Because it was Paddy Hine's principle not to break promises, he quite rightly felt obliged to stand by what had originally been said, with the result that a lot of posting and unsettlement took place among RAF personnel during the critical days of December and January.

In the Army, no real decision on roulement was ever taken, because it became physically impossible to rotate everyone on a four-month cycle. We just did not have the men available. The Americans were equally extended, but they took a much more pragmatic approach from the start. When they first put people into the desert in August, they said, 'You come home when the job's done.' In retrospect, I believe this is the approach which we should have adopted and the one which we should use in future. If a soldier were to object that it is tough, my reply would be that this is what you're in the Services for and if you can't take it, you shouldn't have joined up in the first place.

For all his blindness as a strategist, Saddam Hussein must have realized how stretched we were and I reflected the uncertainty which we were all feeling when I wrote to Bridget on 10 November:

> I still think he will wriggle, but fight in the end. We are now getting to the position where even the USA cannot sustain its forces in theatre indefinitely, even if the alliance holds up. Thus the situation will *have* to be resolved by the beginning of Ramadan (15 March), either by political or by military means, which we shall have in place by January. The only message is: WATCH THIS SPACE.

In deciding to play the game long, Saddam was undoubtedly right. The longer the confrontation lasted, the more fragile our presence in Arabia became, the more difficult it would be for us to supply our ever-growing forces, and the more it would look as though we were simply squatting in Arab territory. Saddam clearly hoped that delay would destroy the Coalition and he was confident that he could keep his army at the front for as long as might be necessary. If some of his soldiers died from lack of water or food, that would not worry him in the least: he has never cared how many of his own people he kills in his pursuit of personal power.

Even though we had no doubt that we were faced by an exceedingly unpleasant enemy, our knowledge of his precise capability was patchy. We knew for sure that his nuclear programme had not yet reached the point at which he could construct a viable warhead, but we suspected that, unless checked, he would be able to do so in the near future. On the other hand, he certainly had chemical weapons, which he had used against the Iranians and against the Kurds, his own people. We fully expected that he would use them against us. We also knew that he had been developing biological agents, although whether or not he had the means of delivering them was another matter.

The possibility of chemical attack seemed to me more a psychological than a physical threat. It was one thing to kill static and defenceless people like the Kurds, or citizens in Riyadh or Tel Aviv, but quite another to take on a mobile army equipped for chemical warfare. An effective strike, with weapons exploding upwind of their target, and gas dispersing in the right direction, would be exceedingly difficult to bring off and in any case we British had the best chemical protection in the world. I was confident, therefore, that if Saddam did try anything with chemicals, our equipment would keep casualties relatively light.

Biological agents were more problematical. Even if the Iraqis' technology was primitive, it would in theory be quite possible for them to drop canisters upwind of our troops in the desert, or even for a truck to drive through Riyadh with an aerosol container spraying germs out of the back. Far-fetched though it may sound, the possibility was a thoroughly uncomfortable one to have hanging over us. Because one of the simplest methods of delivering gas or biological agents was from the air, it seemed all the more important, if war started, that we should ground the Iraqi air force as quickly as possible.

Further analysis of Saddam's character and record convinced us that, in digging in as he had on the frontier, he was making a colossal mistake. His strategy was governed by the experience of his eight-year war against Iran. There he had been fighting a second-rate army, poorly equipped and poorly led (for the Iranians had killed off most of their own generals). All they had been able to carry out was a series of entirely predictable frontal assaults, conducted without regard to loss of life. (The Iranians had gone as far as sending young children out across the mine fields to clear a path for the soldiers.)

Saddam had learnt how to deal with assaults of this kind and his policy was dedicated to holding hard against a frontal attack by infantry. He had no experience at all of a fast-moving battle of manoeuvre, in which enemy armour might swing round on him from an unexpected direction. Nor did he take account of the fact that he was faced with an air force of enormous power and sophistication – again, something which he had not encountered before. Altogether, in basing all his defence on what had happened in Iran, he totally failed to realize that he was about to fight a different kind of war.

The longer the confrontation lasted, the greater became our anxiety that the Iraqis would make a partial withdrawal to the north, vacating the city of Kuwait but retaining Bubiyan Island and the Raudhatin oilfield. Had they done that, they might well have got away with it. The world would not have gone to war, the Coalition would have broken up and with-drawn in confusion, and Saddam would have been free to develop his nuclear and chemical capability, with which, in a few years' time, he could again have started to wreak havoc on his neighbours. Luckily for us, he again made a huge strategic misjudgment, and stayed where he was.

On 10 November I had a long telephone conversation with Tom King, in preparation for the visit which he was to begin in a couple of days' time. So urgent was the question of reinforcements that, rather than wait for him to arrive in theatre, I put across in some detail my reasons for wanting a division. I pointed out that we were already involved up to our necks and might as well support the Coalition with all the resources we had, on the basis that the campaign simply must succeed. To go in with half-hearted measures, I said, would do nothing for our national credibility. To stay at brigade level would also put our forces at greater risk, proportionately. With a whole division, even though our total of casualties might be higher, the chances of fighting the war we wanted to fight, and in the way we wanted to fight it, would be greatly enhanced.

I went on to say that the level of influence which we had

enjoyed in theatre so far would be much reduced if we did not reinforce when the Americans did: we would have to do what we were told to a much greater degree. Furthermore, if we looked forward to the time when Saddam Hussein had been thrown out of Kuwait, we could not expect to enjoy the same credibility either in the Middle East or in the United States if we had not matched America in raising our force levels at the critical moment.

My most telling argument, I hoped, was that loss of influence would reduce my chances of placing the British ground force where I wanted it. Tom King, I knew, had already heard from Paddy Hine of my plan to move our armoured troops away from the Marines and into the main American thrust from the west. Now I explained that if we remained at brigade-strength, we would be no more than a small and subservient part of an American division, whereas to have a division of our own would give us tactical integrity. Furthermore, a division would give us the right to install British staff officers in the American corps headquarters; with only a brigade, we would have only a token liaison officer there and so would be unable to influence the planning and direction of the battle. Finally, I outlined my concern that if we stayed with the Marines, our forces might sustain far higher casualties, proportionately, than the troops of other Coalition members.

I emphasized that a decision on this issue was needed very soon. If the British Government felt able to back my request, I must know at once, because we were already short of time in which to deploy extra forces, acclimatize them and bring them up to the state of training required before committing them to operations. In this context, I assured the Secretary of State that the servicemen we already had in the Gulf were in a high state of morale and anxious to press on with whatever needed to be done. Their main object was to get home as soon as possible and the best way of achieving that aim (as they saw it) was to fight a swift and successful war.

As always, King frequently interrupted me to ask for further details. How would the division fit in with the Americans? How would it work? How did we propose to support it logistically? What sort of manpower would we need? Many

Storm Commanders: the close relationship
which General Norman Schwarzkopf
(*above*) and I established became the
cornerstone of British–American military
cooperation. Lieutenant General Prince
Khalid bin Sultan (*left*), Commander-in-
Chief of the Coalition forces, was the man
responsible on behalf of King Fahd for
coordinating the thirty-plus nations
deployed on Saudi soil. He held high
responsibility on behalf of his country and
the Islamic forces

Left: Air Chief Marshal Sir Patrick Hine, Joint Commander and my immediate superior, proved an inspiring leader. A staunch supporter of our forces in the field, he is seen here talking to British aircrew

Below: Brigadier Patrick Cordingley, Commander of 7th Armoured Brigade (the Desert Rats). I felt a special affinity with him and his men

Above: Air Vice-Marshal William (now Sir William) Wratten, my Deputy, planned and directed the British air campaign. His first loyalty was always to his aircrews

Below: Brigadier Martin White, our logistic wizard, masterminded the largest British support operation since the Second World War

Above: A formidable recruit: Commodore Christopher Craig, Senior Naval Officer, the Middle East, took over the Task Group on 3 December and soon produced what I wanted – plans for an offensive campaign high up in the Gulf

Above: Major General Rupert Smith was chosen at short notice to command the British Division. Refreshingly unorthodox in his ideas, he was always liable to seek less-than-obvious solutions to problems – very much a man after my own heart

A hands-on man: Tom King, Secretary of State for Defence, always wanted to see for himself so that he was fully briefed for Cabinet and the media, with Rupert Smith *(below)*

Right: A warm welcome for the new British Prime Minister from King Fahd, Riyadh, 6 January 1991

Below: Mr Major immediately struck the right note with the servicemen

Right: Desert parade, near Hafar al Batin: General Norman Schwarzkopf and King Fahd review Coalition troops on the eve of war. After the parade British service-men were invited to a sumptuous meal in the King's tent

Above: In my office with the Prince of Wales and Norman Schwarzkopf. At first I opposed the idea of Prince Charles's visit in December for reasons of security, but in the event it proved a remarkable morale booster

Right: As Sir Harry Secombe was coming ashore by helicopter from a Christmas show on HMS *Cardiff,* the alarm signalled that a hostile missile had locked on to them. When the pilot dived to wave-top level, the comedian announced he had reached the 'tuneless whistling stage'

Right: On board HMS *London*, Flagship of the Royal Task Group, the Captain, Ian Henderson, briefs me on plans

I give air and ground crews a last-light briefing, somewhere in the desert

Right: An ear to the ground. Today's servicemen have minds of their own and are ready to put over their views, regardless of the visitor's rank

Below: 7th Armoured Brigade's mascot, Patrick the Jerboa – a form of desert rat – was presented to me by a Saudi businessman. He survived the war and moved to live at Brigade Headquarters in Germany

Above: Serving Christmas lunch to the Queen's Royal Irish Hussars. The Army Catering Corps cooks had worked all night to produce turkey and plum pudding in the middle of the desert

The *Daily Star*'s headline 'Cheer up our boys with a taste of home' let loose a torrent of cakes, which I distributed to units in the field

of these questions could not be answered without detailed staff work, so I stuck to the main lines of my argument and assured the Secretary of State that Paddy Hine was working up a detailed brief for him.

When Paddy himself telephoned next day, 11 November, he reported that he had had two solid hours with the Secretary of State and thought he had convinced him that the division was a necessity. Although an airman, Paddy had taken immense trouble to think through the arguments I had put to him and, of course, when he came to present them, they sounded all the more convincing as laid out dispassionately by a former fighter pilot. He said he thought that Tom King had at last properly focused on the magnitude of the operation and had accepted the logic of our reinforcing in line with the Americans. The Chiefs of Staff had been instructed to prepare a working document for him by next day and a decision was expected within a week.

Meanwhile, with some foresight, Paddy had asked the Ministry of Defence to keep a lien on all the civilian cargo ships which we had chartered for our initial deployment. He was concerned that the United States would sign up every free merchantman in the world to transport their vast reinforcements and wisely made sure he had preempted any such move.

During that conversation we again discussed the possible use of Special Forces in an attempt to rescue the hostages. It had become increasingly clear that, in spite of American reassurances, our knowledge of their whereabouts was extremely thin and constantly falling out of date as they were moved around. It was also clear that any rescue operation would be hazardous and carry only a small chance of success. I found that attitudes in the United Kingdom were rather negative: people could not see how we were going to manage anything and seemed reluctant to grip the problem. All the same, I asked Paddy to keep his planners working on it, because I saw that even if full-scale hostilities did not break out, we would still wish to prise the hostages out and have their removal by force as an option. Paddy then asked if I could think of any better use for Special Forces and I said that at the moment I could not. Our technological capability on the battlefield and in the air seemed to be so overwhelming as to leave no gap which Special Forces could usefully fill. (In this, it turned out, I was wrong, for the SAS did later perform an absolutely vital role, that of destroying mobile Scud launchers, which proved to be beyond the powers of the air force, even with the overwhelming supremacy which it established.)

Another difficult subject for discussion was that of biological warfare. Paddy told me that a decision would soon be taken on whether or not vaccinations should be released for the British forces.* My view was that, if we had the vaccine, we should use it: to suffer casualties through not using it, just because other people did not have it, would be quite wrong. Nevertheless, the issue raised a range of awkward and sensitive political questions. What about the British expatriate community in Saudi Arabia, thirty thousand strong? Would they panic if they heard that our troops were taking precautions against, for example, anthrax attack? If they took fright and left, many of the country's essential facilities, such as water and electricity, would cease to function. What would that do for Saudi morale? The Saudi authorities wanted to buy vaccine from us, but there were not enough doses to go round the armed forces, let alone civilians.

The decision would cause problems in the United Kingdom as well. In spite of our efforts to keep the matter quiet, the Press would be bound to find out about it. What would the effect on public opinion be? There was a further complication, in that the attitude of the Americans was different from ours. We on the whole were in favour of vaccinating, they were not, because, in percentage terms, they had fewer doses available. If we went ahead, would it open up a split between us? In short, this one issue, with its unpleasant overtones, gave rise to protracted discussion and debate.

*   *   *

* It seemed possible that Saddam might try to use anthrax, because the spores are relatively simple to handle and disperse. The disease sounds exceptionally unpleasant: beginning with malignant pustules covered in black scabs, it progresses into a high fever and can lead to a collapse of the circulatory system or acute respiratory failure. If anthrax is not treated, it can cause death in two or three days.

In Riyadh Norman Schwarzkopf was under intense pressure from Washington, both to disclose his own plan (which he kept very close to his chest) and to consider other plans being dreamt up by amateur strategists in the Pentagon. As if he did not have enough ideas of his own to develop, wild possibilities kept being thrown at him. One such operation was to send a whole division way out into the western desert of Iraq to cut the Baghdad–Amman road. This would have been almost impossible to support logistically, because of the distances involved, and it would have diverted an immense amount of effort from the main thrust in the east, yet it did not suffice for Schwarzkopf to report back to Washington that this was not a viable alternative. He had to *prove* that it would not work, and this alone took a great deal of time and effort which should have gone into the plan proper.

The attitude of the British Government – luckily for me – was very different. British politicians rarely considered it appropriate to offer original planning suggestions and if they did, they were prepared to defer to military wisdom. Despite our problems in other areas, they genuinely tried to help, rather than to beat their chests as potential war-winners.

This divergence of approach closely reflected the difference in the way the two nations exercise control of the military. In the United States the generals are more directly responsible to Congress for what they do and have to answer personally to the politicians, who therefore feel they have a right to tell the generals how to run their campaigns. In Britain this is not so at all. In my experience, once the politicians decide that the military are to be let loose on a campaign, they settle the level of support which they are prepared to give the operation, then stand back and allow the military to get on with it. For this reason a senior general in the British Army feels much more able to delegate responsibility down the chain of command than his American counterpart.

Paddy Hine and I thus felt relatively free to plan as we saw fit. Nevertheless, we could not help but be aware of the intense political activity going on in the background: we knew, for instance, that London and Washington were trying to make sure that British and United States military objectives were the same and that the American strategy for using our troops remained unchanged. We realized that the best way of getting overall policy properly coordinated was through the London–Washington link and that regular communications between the two capitals must reflect the dialogue going on between myself and Schwarzkopf in theatre. Once we saw that, we had the key to the door. If Schwarzkopf and I wanted major decisions taken or changes made, our best way was to agree them in principle in theatre and then both work back to our respective bosses at home, to get their agreement as well. Alternatively, if I felt that I was going to have difficulty persuading Schwarzkopf to agree a particular point, I might arrange through Paddy Hine for it to be settled first between London and Washington, so that a directive came down the line from America to the CENTCOM headquarters in Riyadh.

This ploy was closely akin to the one in which Alan Munro and I together took trouble to play the Foreign Office and Ministry of Defence on closely parallel tracks and it brought home to me one of the basic principles of high command, which I was learning as I went along: that a senior commander must bring together everyone concerned, not only in theatre, but outside as well, and that often he must act almost more as a diplomat than as a soldier.

One evening I had dinner with Brigadier Nick Cocking (the senior British officer in the team advising the Saudi National Guard), Prince Mitab (a high-ranking Saudi officer) and several leading Saudi businessmen. One of them, Prince Abdallah bin Faisal, raised the matter of the desert rat, 7th Armoured Brigade's emblem. I said that it was not really a rat, but a local animal, and my neighbour confirmed that it was a jerboa, a sandy-coloured creature which looks a bit like a rat but is much more lightly built, with long, springy back legs and a tuft on the end of its tail. Jerboas live in burrows in the desert, he told me, and the Saudis go out at night with torches, nets and traps to catch them for food. When I asked if he could get me one, he said, 'Of course!' And sure enough, a few days later, three were delivered to my office in a single cage. Unfortunately one was soon killed by the others, but I sent the two survivors to brigade headquarters and that evening, at Schwarzkopf's component commanders' briefing, I was able to report that the British had already received reinforcements in the form of two jerboas, which had been deployed to strengthen 7th Armoured Brigade.*

Tom King's tour of the Gulf took place from 12 to 14 November. We usually had such a stream of visitors coming out that I could not possibly escort them all: I met VIPs when they arrived, briefed them, made sure their programme was in order and then sent them off accompanied by a staff officer, not seeing them again until I de-briefed them just before they left for home. The Secretary of State, however, was in a category of his own and I accompanied him on most of his calls. He was in good form from the start, even though he alarmed me by revealing the volatile nature of the political situation at home and agreeing that there was a real threat of a coup against Mrs Thatcher from within the Conservative party. For someone working all-out to plan a war, the news was extremely disconcerting. 'This is no time for uncertainty,' I told Bridget, 'just as the pace gains momentum out here.'

For Alan Munro and myself, a visit by a leading member of the British Government offered an invaluable means of opening doors and seeing people not generally available, from King Fahd, the Crown Prince and Prince Sultan down. On this occasion our audience with the King, at his palace in Jeddah, was particularly rewarding. It was after dark when we swept up to the palace — for Fahd likes to do business at night — but we caught glimpses of fantastically luxuriant gardens and the palace itself beggared belief. As I wrote to Bridget:

Unlimited money is spent on the most superb, Arab-style architecture — massive great buildings lined with marble, only the finest carpets on floors and walls. Chandeliers such as you've never seen, with a thousand lights on each, and all the mystical romance, the slow, inevitable pace of Arabia.

* At the time of writing, May 1992, the sole survivor, named Patrick, is alive and well at the brigade's headquarters in Germany.

After only an hour we were ushered into the royal presence. As always, the King was dressed in simple, traditional white robes and he came to the door to greet us. I saluted and bowed, and he showed us to the seats of honour – the Secretary of State on his right, the Ambassador next, then myself. On the King's left were three of his brothers and lesser figures of the court, including an interpreter and an official note-taker (Alan Munro had a habit of jotting notes on any old scrap of paper he could find in his pockets and was so addicted to the habit that he would refuse offers of anything decent to write on).

After the usual pleasantries, exchanged for the benefit of television and still cameras, the Press departed and we got down to business. The King, speaking in Arabic, welcomed Tom King with great warmth and thanked the British Government effusively for the help it was giving. He then gave a magisterial review of the political situation, and when we began to discuss Britain's role in the campaign, the Secretary of State raised our plans for bringing in major reinforcements and for setting up a forces' broadcasting station.

This last was a matter of some concern to the Saudis, who were alarmed by the idea of having the air waves over the Kingdom filled with Western trivia and sexual innuendo. Our aim was to run land lines across the desert to Bahrein, so that we could link in to the satellite there and pick up broadcasts from the United Kingdom. By skilful advocacy, Tom King obtained Fahd's approval, not only for this, but for the reinforcements as well. All in all, it was a most successful meeting.

It so happened that 7th Armoured Brigade were about to carry out a breaching exercise, for breaking through the Iraqi defences. I particularly wanted Tom King to see how difficult and dangerous such an operation was going to be. I wanted him to understand how breaching a mine field eats up troops and how vital it was that we got all the facilities we needed. We therefore let him take part in the exercise.

The Brigade had set up a dummy minefield, ditches which needed to be filled in, and so on. We put the Secretary of State in a Challenger and drove him tactically through the breach. From the flying sand and dust and chaos, from the violent driving across causeways, he got some idea of the scale and urgency of such an operation. He saw how, once you have blasted a hole in the enemy's defences, you must commit everything you have to going through it, because that is the moment at which he will hit you with artillery and chemicals and whatever else he has got, hoping to block you in the breach and bog you down, so that he has a sitting target. I wanted to convince Tom King that in our requests for extra manpower we were being realistic rather than extravagant. In fact I do not think he needed much convincing, but I felt that, after such an experience, he would be able to speak with unrivalled authority when he returned to the House of Commons and the Ministry of Defence.

Immediately after the exercise, he gave a Press conference covered in dust and sand, which in itself created an excellent impression. The rest of his tour was less violent but no less useful. Travelling with him in the private compartment of his VC10, I had plenty of opportunity for uninterrupted discussion and we did much good work in the air. Together we visited the United Arab Emirates, where the Ambassador, Graham Burton, gave a party for selected expatriates and King addressed them on the outline of the campaign, praising their own role in supporting it. We also spent one and a half hours on HMS *London*, which was beaten-up by four Jaguars firing live cannon in a thrilling low-level mock attack, and called on several of the Gulf rulers, among them Sheikh Zayed of Abu Dhabi, who was most anxious to know what form we thought the war might take, what would happen if the Israelis joined in, and so on. From previous visits, I knew he would give us every assistance – and so it proved. Like the Emir of Bahrein, Sheikh Isa, he wished to see an early resolution of the conflict; with clear perception, he appreciated that the size of the forces which Saddam Hussein had deployed into Kuwait meant that the Coalition would have to build up substantial reinforcements before it could go to war. He supported our efforts with vigour and enthusiasm, and promised us every possible facility.

At every port of call Tom King built up my own role in the

undertaking in a flattering but useful manner, pointing out that Britain was making a major contribution, that I was Britain's military representative in the Gulf, and that I was therefore a figure of some importance. I never asked him to do this, but he saw that it would be useful for me to have my status enhanced and did it of his own accord. There was one absurd incident at Jubail when the lift in the observation tower at the port jammed just short of the top and the Secretary of State became more nervous of what the Press might say about the mishap than about the fact that he might be stuck there indefinitely. Apart from this, everything went well.

'TK has left after a most successful visit,' I told Bridget on 14 November. 'We have won all the points we had with the Saudis and Americans.' I was confident that the Secretary of State had gone home persuaded of our need for reinforcements, but there followed a few anxious days as we waited to see whether or not he could carry the Prime Minister and Cabinet with him. Then on 22 November, to my immense relief, he announced in the House of Commons that the British force in the Gulf was to be increased to a division – not a full-scale division, but a light one, with a second armoured brigade (4th), and extra-strong artillery, logistic and engineering support. Norman Schwarzkopf was delighted with the news: insatiable for armour, he said, 'More tanks, Peter! That's what I want. More tanks!'

As I told Bridget, the division would make us the third largest Coalition force, after the United States and Saudi Arabia. 'If the Iraqis realize what is deployed against them, they must surely be having second thoughts,' I wrote. 'But we've got to destroy their chemical and nuclear capability.'

When I heard, on 29 November, that in New York the Security Council of the United Nations had passed Resolution 678, ordering Saddam Hussein to withdraw from Kuwait by 15 January or face the consequences, I knew we had moved into a new phase of the campaign. At first we had hoped to sort the matter out politically. Then we had warned Saddam that if he did not withdraw, we would use military means to evict him. Now we were putting together a force which would make our threat credible. Beside the immense American deployment, our own was relatively small, but it represented a major effort on our part, and in a letter home I sounded a warning note: 'The reinforcement will make large parts of BAOR non-operational, and it places a lot of responsibility on me to get things right. If I don't, governments will fall and our Services will be decimated.'

CHAPTER 5

BUILD-UP

Between these bouts of high-level military, political and diplomatic manoeuvring, I continued to visit units of all three Services as often as I could. For me, it was a relief and pleasure to escape from the continuous briefings and telephone calls of Riyadh, but visits were not merely jaunts. Far from it. I saw them as an essential command duty, indispensable for creating a sense of unity and purpose throughout my far-flung force and for gaining essential first-hand information. Calls on ships, on air bases and units in the desert enabled me to assess their morale and states of readiness for myself, rather than read about it in reports, and furnished me with the details which a commander needs if he is to gain a clear understanding of the capabilities of his force.

I knew from experience that as we moved nearer to war the tenor of life would change dramatically. Once the enemy began to prepare for battle, thinking and doing things for himself and trying to take the initiative, I would no longer be my own master. Events would be liable to happen very fast: we should have to be ready to react instantaneously to the unexpected and major decisions might be needed at any moment. I therefore made a point of travelling round the theatre as much as possible while the options were still fairly open. Occasionally I took my own Bergen (pack) and sleeping bag with me to spend a night in the desert – always a welcome reversion to an earlier way of life and a nostalgic reminder of earlier operations, old comrades in arms and other nights spent beneath the brilliant stars of Arabia. But I knew that this habit gave my staff concern, as they could not get hold of me. Although I had the fullest confidence in my deputy – first Sandy Wilson, then Bill Wratten – and was happy to leave matters in their hands, it was unwise to be out of touch for more than a few hours at a time. For this reason, and because there were so many different units to be seen, I generally kept my visits short and made sure that I was back in Riyadh in time for Norman Schwarzkopf's evening briefing.

My aim was never to stage any kind of formal inspection, always the reverse: I wanted to meet the men and women and their commanders at work, and I evolved a definite system for doing this. Having flown from Riyadh in the HS125, I would go on to a particular unit by helicopter. At the headquarters – perhaps just a couple of lean-to tents in the desert, with camouflage nets slung over them from the tops of armoured vehicles – I would meet key members and listen to a briefing, so that I gained a general feel for the unit and what it was doing. Then I would go round and meet servicemen at their work.

Meals in the desert were a particular pleasure. At a battalion headquarters there might be sophisticated facilities such as a table and a few chairs, and maybe plates, with proper knives and forks; but even when such things existed, I would help myself at the cookhouse counter and sit down with everyone else. If I had lunch with a tank crew, the cook of the day would brew up Compo sausages and baked beans, or maybe a curry with some rice, and slap it into mess-tins; somebody lent me eating irons and I ate with the men, sitting under a camouflage net beside their Challenger. There was never any fuss about rank or table manners. We returned to a basic existence: a group of soldiers making the best of things in an uncomfortable environment. In my experience there is no more effective way of getting to know people. Once you sit together on the sand and share conversation over a brew or a meal, you break down all barriers and reservations.

Usually I would lead the conversation, the value to me being that I gained a clear idea of what the servicemen were thinking. Did they feel they were being kept in the picture well enough? Was their equipment adequate? Were their complaints being dealt with? What were they concerned about? Did they understand the military and political objectives behind their deployment? Again and again I was impressed by their level of intelligence and education. The public image of a rough, tough, bull-necked sergeant bellowing obscenities at all and sundry is out of date. Today's servicemen have minds of their own and are ready to put over their views, regardless of a visitor's rank. Moreover, they are highly trained in technical skills and expect to be treated as human beings.

To me, every person in the Gulf counted as important and this made these occasions particularly poignant. To me, a unit or a ship's crew was not just a mass of faces, but rather a number of individuals, each of whom needed thought and consideration. Besides, I was always aware of the fact that I was going to send these people to war and that some of them might not return.

In the desert, they were always keenly interested to hear what I thought was going to happen, whether I reckoned there could be a political solution of the crisis or whether I expected that we would have to fight. So far as security considerations allowed, I always gave them my honest opinion. They were also eager to know when their tour of duty would end. Here I had to disappoint them and say that I did not know, but whenever I asked anybody if he would like to go home early, the answer was emphatically, No! To a man, they all wanted to be where the action was and to do their duty alongside their friends.

Whenever I spent a night out, I was impressed by the light discipline. Generally speaking, no lights were allowed at night and certainly in the forward areas no lights were allowed at all. This meant early to bed – in a sleeping bag on the sand – and early to rise: stand-to was at 0430 or 0500. The one luxury which I accepted with gratitude was exemption from sentry duty, which the soldiers did in two-hour shifts.

Visits to the Navy were particularly rewarding. On 16 November, for instance, I had a memorable day calling on the Broadsword-type frigate HMS *Brazen* and watching as she carried out an RAS, or re-supply at sea, linked to a Royal Fleet

Auxiliary by a cable carrying the fuel pipe. Later her captain, Commander James Rapp, cleared lower decks – that is, brought all the crew together – so that I could address them.* Then we flew on to *Argus*, a former container ship converted first into a helicopter-support vessel and then, for this operation, into a floating hospital, complete with a hundred beds, four surgical teams, nurses and a full range of equipment, including four Sea King helicopters specially fitted for casualty evacuation. Altogether she was splendidly kitted out and clearly would be of immense value if heavy fighting developed, but I felt sorry for the Royal Marine bandsmen, now acting as medical orderlies, who were having to live in cramped, squalid conditions below the waterline.

Whenever I addressed men in a group, as opposed to holding informal conversations, I stuck to a well-tried pattern. If the unit had just arrived in theatre, I would give them a quick run-down on local customs, explaining why alcohol was banned, why religious services had to be low-key and why there were restrictions on broadcasting. I also tried to offer the men readily comprehensible, worthwhile reasons for their presence in the Gulf. The principal one was that we were trying to safeguard Saudi Arabian oil, which furnishes more than thirty per cent of world needs. It was easy to explain that disruption of the supply would not just be a matter of concern to the Arabs, but would have a damaging effect on our economy at home. Flowing from this was the need to liberate Kuwait and prevent Saddam Hussein continuing his aggressive thrust down the Gulf. I also stressed that the British expatriate community in Saudi Arabia, thirty thousand strong, was the third largest in the world, after the Commonwealth and the United States. These expatriate Brits, I said, were all at threat and it was up to us to protect them.

---

* In 1985, when *Brazen* was in the Falklands during my tour of duty there, her Captain (now Rear Admiral) Toby Frere made her available to me as a Flagship, so that I could exercise my responsibilities to the islanders as Military Commissioner. He took me and Bridget on board (with special permission) and sailed round the islands, visiting far-flung settlements. Living in his cabin, which he had given up to us, we had three fantastic days, entertaining islanders on board and feeling like monarchs of the far South Seas.

Next I would explain briefly how we were working within the Coalition, how our operations fitted into the United Nations' remit, how important it was that we should co-operate with all the Allies and give our full support to the Coalition cause. Then I would outline the role which I expected the ship or squadron or troop to play.

Matters of personal interest were always high on any unit's agenda: there was the endless saga of allowances, the unanswerable question of roulement. Also of burning interest was my opinion of whether or not we would go to war. In giving this, I would relate it to the political background, both in the United Nations and in the world as a whole. I always tried to talk at a strategic level, because I reckoned that what the men wanted was their theatre commander's view on theatre problems, and not what they would normally hear from their own commanding officer. At the end, I tried to leave the men on a high note by giving them some praise and encouragement for the way they were carrying out their role.

All this would take fifteen or twenty minutes. Then I would ask for questions, which always gave me an excellent impression of the unit. In general, the bigger the audience, the harder it was to get them started: if two or three hundred men were gathered round an aircraft, with myself standing on the wing, shyness was often thoroughly inhibiting and some groups asked no questions at all. Others would begin with a few faltering queries and then open up into a full-scale discussion. For occasions on which nobody would break the ice, I had several ploys up my sleeve. One was to tell an individual to come up with a question and another to ask the whole group to think about a particular subject, with the warning that I was going to ask somebody to comment on it in a moment. I always took care never to make anyone look foolish, or to have a joke at the expense of someone who had asked a question, however stupid it might have been, because that would have killed the chance of further participation stone dead. Altogether, I found such occasions hard work but rewarding, because they stimulated that essential element of command, communication, not only down the chain, but up it as well.

*   *   *

On the evening of 16 November, after our visit to *Brazen* and *Argus*, we held a farewell dinner in Riyadh for Sandy Wilson. As his tour came to an end, he behaved impeccably, standing back except when needed and keeping out of the limelight. His successor was Air Vice-Marshal Bill Wratten, another former fighter pilot. Tough, stocky and balding, he was an outstanding expert in his own field and a good man with whom to discuss a problem of any kind, as he would always give frank comment based on common sense and sincerity. He and I had met on the same course at the Royal College of Defence Studies and he had served in the Falklands as the first commander of the detachment at RAF Stanley, so we had some background in common. But Bill had never been to the Gulf before and so had a great deal to learn.

His professional knowledge and experience stood him in good stead. He had flown Vampires, Lightnings and Phantoms, and as Officer Commanding 11 Group RAF he was already in overall command of the Tornado F3s deployed in theatre, so he knew the aircraft and their crews in advance. He had also kept a close eye on events in the Middle East, before coming out, by regularly attending briefings at Joint Headquarters in High Wycombe. In theatre, he was briefed by Chuck Horner and Brigadier General Buster Glosson, architect of the air campaign, and then immediately began visiting his squadrons, so that he could tell at first hand if British assets were in the right places and be sure that they had everything they needed. I myself took him down to 7th Armoured Brigade and introduced him to Patrick Cordingley, for I considered it most important that Bill, a tri-service officer, should be accepted by all three Services, not just his own. This may sound obvious, but it was something which needed positive effort on my part, to break through the inevitable inter-service suspicions and differences of approach. In any tri-service operation it is essential that senior commanders not only get to know but also learn to like, trust and respect their opposite numbers, and I put much time into giving new arrivals a push so that their position was well established right at the beginning.

*   *   *

One long-running battle which I did *not* win was my attempt to secure the services of the aircraft carrier *Ark Royal*, known as the CVS, or Carrier Vessel (Support). SNOME – first Paul Haddacks, then Chris Craig – was based *faute de mieux* on HMS *London*, a Broadsword-class frigate not ideally suited to acting as Flagship because of her lack of space and of suitable communications. Now that the Navy's role had expanded so widely from that of the original Armilla patrol, which had been restricted to the waters of the Gulf, senior officers were keen to have the *Ark Royal* as Flagship, mainly because the carrier had excellent communications. When I arrived in theatre, I found that they had already put up a case for her to be sent out, but that their request had been rejected on the grounds that her usefulness would be outweighed by the high cost of preparing her for the role. Since I felt that the presence of a British carrier, with her Harriers and helicopters, would be distinctly advantageous to the Coalition, I took the matter up with Norman Schwarzkopf, only to hear him observe wryly that he already had more ships in the Gulf than water to float them on. A more enthusiastic response came from the American naval commander, Admiral Mause (pronounced 'Morse'). I explained to him that we needed the CVS mainly as a command facility and that if we kept her in the Red Sea, as I then thought we might, she would be able to give additional air-defence support to the US fleet in those waters, freeing American aircraft for other operations. At my suggestion, Mause worked up a case for having the CVS, which Schwarzkopf (by then) supported with reasonable enthusiasm. Washington, however, found little in its favour and, although the request was passed on in the direction of London, it mysteriously failed to arrive for a long time, becoming delayed, I was told, in Switzerland. By the time we raised the subject yet again with the Ministry of Defence, it was too late: people had made up their minds that the carrier was not necessary and HMS *London* continued to act as Flagship throughout the war.

One vital element in our preparations for war was the medical plan, and on 19 November I called a conference of my medical advisers to review arrangements for handling casualties. If war came, our basic requirement would be to transfer casualties back from the battlefield to the United Kingdom as rapidly as possible, and to make sure they were alive when they reached home. Because wounded men cannot be moved at various stages of treatment, it was essential to have hospitals all along the line which would be capable of holding casualties for limited periods and teams of medical staff to patch people up at each level, some as far forward as brigade headquarters.

The number of field surgical teams (FSTs) we would need depended on the number of casualties which we were expecting and the number which each team could deal with in a day. Based on the experience of the Second World War, it seemed reasonable to allow for five per cent casualties. With British forces numbering about thirty thousand, this would mean fifteen hundred casualties overall, twenty-five per cent of them killed and the rest wounded.* The worst possible scenario might produce four hundred casualties a day and, working on the supposition that each surgical team could deal with nine or ten a day, we deduced that we would need no fewer than forty-nine FSTs. Each of these would consist of four specialists and would include at least two surgeons, an anaesthetist and one other.

Soon it became clear that our requirements could not be met from military resources in the United Kingdom, nor yet from civilian ones, without serious detriment to our country's peacetime services, especially when we took into account the fact that we would also have to provide medical attention for very large numbers of prisoners-of-war, as we were required to do under the Geneva Convention. As a first step, the Government therefore put out a call to reservists, men and women: it was loath to issue compulsory call-up orders when we were not in a state of war and hoped that enough volunteers would come forward.

But people proved slow to offer their services because they

---

* Thirty thousand seemed our probable ceiling in November. In fact, by the end of the deployment, British forces in the Gulf totalled over forty-five thousand.

were afraid of losing their jobs – unlike men and women called up compulsorily, volunteers are not guaranteed their jobs back when they return. Compulsory call-up was therefore instituted but this still left a gap, and in the end Tom King had the novel idea of soliciting help from a whole range of friendly nations. The response amazed me. Within a few days we had offers of field hospitals from Sweden, Canada, Norway, even Rumania, which was trying to make its mark on the international scene. Belgium, Denmark, the Netherlands and Singapore promised to send field surgical teams, New Zealand a medical team. Welcome as they were, these offers of help created their own problems, for they threatened the Saudis with a fresh influx of foreigners. Who was going to clear the arrival of all these aliens? The British? No, Alan Munro was perfectly clear that all nations must make their own arrangements. Some of them, however, had no diplomatic representation in Saudi Arabia and this in itself produced further problems.

Then there was the question of what to do with bodies. In most past wars it had been British practice to bury the dead in the land where they fell, but again religious restrictions made this impossible in Saudi Arabia and our only way out of the difficulty would be to fly bodies back to the United Kingdom. For practical reasons of transport, and because we felt it would be detrimental for morale at home if a trickle of coffins arrived while fighting was in progress, we decided that we would have to store bodies until the war was over and we hired a number of freezer wagons for this purpose. Yet the exceptionally unpleasant nature of Saddam Hussein's arsenal added further complications to our plans. What if people died from chemical or biological attack? Would their bodies be contaminated? And even if it proved possible to decontaminate a corpse killed by gas, what about the bodies of people who had died from exposure to biological agents? Would they have to be burnt? Such questions demanded urgent study.

I knew all along that the subject of casualties was highly sensitive and needed careful handling, My general policy was to excite as little apprehension as possible and, in public relations terms, to play the matter down, for I thought that to alarm people unnecessarily would do more harm than good. For one thing, I knew that everything possible in the way of medical facilities and support had been laid on by Tom King and the High Command at home. For another, I myself did not believe that we would have *that* many casualties.

I knew, as Norman Schwarzkopf did, that if we were able to amass the ground forces which we considered militarily essential, and if we secured the logistic back-up to enable them to fight, we would be able to crush the Iraqi army far more quickly than if, for political reasons, we were pitched into war before we were ready. Schwarzkopf was determined not to launch the land offensive until he was fully prepared and I supported his stand entirely. I was therefore confident that we would win an overwhelming victory, without excessive losses. At the same time, my experience told me that if the Iraqis fought at all, we would be bound to suffer *some* casualties in taking on an army of half a million men. My personal estimate, which I had kept very much to myself, was that we might lose four hundred dead.

Then, towards the end of November, some rather unguarded remarks made by Patrick Cordingley to the Press suddenly revealed just how emotive the subject could be. A group of defence correspondents – a kind of First XI among British journalists – had been sent out from London and billeted on Patrick for thirty-six hours. Since he is a thoroughly affable man and his visitors were intelligent and well-informed, he inevitably talked to them a great deal during the time they were with him and could not stick to the formality of a routine Press conference.

Patrick's ideas about casualty levels were rather different from mine. My own estimate of four hundred dead was, to me, a fairly small total: considering the example of earlier wars and the size of the forces now assembling against each other, a total of that kind seemed inevitable. But to Patrick, a man of a younger generation, not even born when the Second World War ended, it seemed an enormous amount. Furthermore, having lived and trained in the desert for weeks on end, he had become acutely aware that the confrontation in which we were involved was 'by no means a vicarage tea party', and that there were 'some thoroughly unpleasant weapons around'. He also felt that although he and his colleagues had faced the problem of casualties squarely and did not mind talking about it, the British public had not yet given it serious thought.

Thus, when one of the defence correspondents said to him, 'I understand that if you go into the attack now, you think casualties will be light,' he was taken aback. As he recounted later, he was astonished by what seemed to him the stupidity of the remark: 'I said that what was abundantly clear was that a lot of people were going to die. Not necessarily Brits or Americans, because we were much better equipped than the enemy; but if two armies that size met, there must inevitably be a large number of casualties.'

The reaction was immediate and explosive. During the night he was four times woken up by callers demanding clarification of what he had said. Whitehall went up in smoke. Speculation raged and possible totals of men killed soared into the thousands. The *Evening Standard* published an article headed 'BLOODBATH IN THE GULF'. In the *Mail on Sunday* Sir John Junor demanded that Patrick be sacked. Such was the pressure put on him that for a while he believed he really was going to be relieved of his command.

In fact there was never the slightest question of that. He had my full confidence as a commander and, if anyone in authority had called for his dismissal, I should have defended him vigorously. As it was, I was furious when I found that people in England had begun to telephone him direct, breaking my fundamental rule about not communicating with field commanders over my head. Through Paddy Hine, I had that stopped immediately and did what I could to defuse anxieties. I did not by any means agree with what Patrick had said, but he believed it, and in any case his remarks had been exaggerated out of all proportion in the reporting. If he made a mistake at all, it was in not establishing clearly that he was talking off the record, but it is almost impossible to maintain such distinctions if one is continuously in the company of Pressmen for a day and a half. The fault really lay in the arrangements made for the media, and in the fact that the defence correspondents had been dumped on him for so long. I told Paddy Hine that I wanted everything possible done to protect him and let him get on with his job. Paddy entirely agreed and did his utmost to defuse the situation.

The episode, though uncomfortable at the time, particularly for the soldiers stuck out in the desert, who had a great deal of time to brood about possible loss of life, had an extraordinarily beneficial effect. Until then many British officers in the Gulf, and Patrick especially, had felt that interest and support from the British public had been no more than luke-warm. Now the outcry about casualties woke the country to the reality of what was about to happen and let loose a flood of sympathy and affection, which built up towards Christmas like a tidal wave.

Countless citizens suddenly felt that they wanted to do something, anything, to help. Letters and parcels began to pour in, first by the hundred, then by the thousand, many addressed simply to 'A British Soldier, The Gulf'. To cope with this sudden deluge, Tom King announced the creation of a new post-box number, BFPO 3000, to which people could forward mail without a specified recipient. Everything going by that route was handled separately from the personal post, which otherwise might have been drowned in the flood. The scheme was such a tremendous success that, in spite of the most strenuous efforts at delivery, some twenty container-loads of parcels remained undistributed at the end of the war and had to be forwarded to other operational areas such as Northern Ireland and Belize.

In the Gulf, we tried to pass envelopes or blueys lacking a name to men who had no regular correspondents at home, with positive instructions to answer them, and most of the soldiers responded willingly, as they always do when some-body needs help. Often the goodwill messages came from people who themselves were looking for some kind of solace: many reflected loneliness, emotional emptiness or other prob-lems in the life of the sender, who was delighted to receive a reply, even from someone of whom he or she had never heard. Exchanges started up and many lasting new friend-ships were forged in this way.

*   *   *

A spate of technical problems added to our preoccupations. Helicopter engines were found to be suffering severe wear from sand-ingestion. Even with sand filters fitted, the average life of a Lynx engine came down from its normal twelve hundred hours to only one hundred (without a filter it lasted about ten). The power-packs of the Challenger tanks – engines and gear boxes combined – were failing so often that 7th Armoured Brigade's training had to be severely curtailed. The wheeled vehicles which had been designed for war in Europe, and which in Germany were perfectly adequate for bringing up supplies of fuel, ammunition and food, sank into the sand when loaded. The container trucks designed to run on tarmac roads were particularly ineffective and, to improve our mobility, we borrowed a lot of M453 tracked vehicles from the United States and hurriedly shipped them out. The wheeled vehicles then ferried supplies as far as they could before their loads were transferred to the tracked vehicles and taken on into forward areas.

As if we did not have enough local problems to grapple with, we began to get highly disturbing news of a revolt among leading Conservatives at Westminster, where Michael Heseltine was making a bid to take over from Mrs Thatcher as Prime Minister. Already, during his visit, Tom King had dropped hints that all was not well among the Conservative leadership and, on 14 November, after travelling with him, I had noted: 'I'm very concerned about the situation at home and feel that Michael Heseltine is letting us all down for the benefit of his career.' The servicemen, getting wind of the tussle, were much concerned about it and had asked the Secretary of State some probing questions about the backing they were likely to receive if things changed.

Now, on 20 November, with leadership ballots in progress at Westminster, my feelings burst out in a letter home:

> They do not deserve our vote when they shenanigan about while the young men are out here to risk their lives. As a party they're guilty of indolent neglect.'

On 21 November, talking to Tom King on the telephone, I told him how worried we all were about what was happening at home. He assured me that while the Conservatives remained in power, he would guarantee me support, whatever happened. 'What a mess!' I wrote to Bridget. 'I have got TK's confidence, and I like and respect him. But if Maggie goes, he may well lose his job.'

Next day came the news that Mrs Thatcher had indeed been forced to step down – a thunderbolt which sent shock waves through the entire Coalition. Her fall was a shattering blow for Arabs and Americans alike: they all had the highest regard for her and simply could not understand how it was possible for a leader of international stature, who had done so much for her country, to be evicted from office by a vicious party squabble just as Britain was preparing to fight a major war. To our allies in the Middle East, this seemed the most extraordinary behaviour from a government securely in power. 'What the hell are they *doing* in England?' demanded Norman Schwarzkopf on the evening of 22 November. At the end of one air-force brief, Chuck Horner announced that he had some good news and some bad. 'The bad news', he said, 'is that Margaret Thatcher has been forced to resign. The good news is that she's joined 7th Armoured Brigade.' But even though he made a joke of it, I think he too was worried. The Gulf rulers were not merely pro-British, but even more pro-Thatcher. They were great admirers of her style of strong government, which was very reminiscent of their own, and whenever I called on them after her departure, they always asked after her before anyone else. 'Where's all this democracy you keep talking about?' they wanted to know. 'How can the Prime Minister be deposed if the people haven't even voted?'

For us Britons, her demise was extremely unsettling. It distracted us from the business of facing up to Saddam Hussein and created a damaging sense of uncertainty. We did not like the way in which the leadership struggle had been conducted, for we felt that it had lowered the standing of the whole Conservative party and we feared that it would weaken the resolve of the British Government, which was vital to everyone in theatre. We were very careful about what we said at the time, because the Press was on the look-out for disparaging remarks, but we felt the loss of Mrs Thatcher deeply. Her fall put a premature end to the arrangements – never announced – which had been made for her to visit the Gulf in two weeks' time. There is no doubt that, had she come, she would have received the most tremendous reception from rulers, commanders and servicemen alike.

Now, on behalf of the British forces I wrote her a personal letter saying how sad we in the Gulf all were that she had had to step down. I thanked her for her support and decisiveness in setting up the whole deployment, and told her that she had held the respect of every man out there. 'Everywhere I have been amongst the Arab rulers,' I wrote, 'and the many Americans, senior and junior ranks, you are held in the highest possible regard, and your departure from office will leave a void, difficult to fill, in their esteem for Britain ... My purpose in writing is to wish you the very best of luck in the years ahead, to thank you for what you have done for our country, and to tell you we shall miss you. You did indeed put the Great back into Britain. Let's hope we shall now keep it there.'

When I heard that her successor was John Major, I was pleased and relieved, even though no one knew much about him, for he had been my choice among the candidates. It was a disappointment to learn, as we did at first, that he would not be visiting the theatre, since he wished to concentrate on Europe, leaving Middle Eastern affairs in the hands of Tom King. But very soon Mr Major realized that it was imperative for him to come out, to meet King Fahd, to see and be seen by the servicemen, and generally to forge for himself the links which had bound Mrs Thatcher so closely to her forces. One of his first actions in office was to reaffirm our reinforcement package to the House of Commons. This, of course, was more than welcome and I sent a signal to our troops saying that the new Prime Minister was strongly behind what we were doing in the Gulf, and that there would be no change of policy.

In the middle of this distant upheaval we had a crisis of our own, when I suddenly heard that Tim Sulivan had been thrown out of the American planning team. The news, if true, would have been disastrous, because he was in an uniquely valuable position. Luckily it turned out to be nothing but a misunderstanding. Tim had still been trying to obtain the green pass which would admit him to the intelligence section of the CENTCOM headquarters, known as the Skiff. High Wycombe had telexed Washington for clearance, but it had not yet come through and Tim urgently needed the pass so that he could go in and collect some documents with which to brief Paddy Hine, due to arrive for a visit on 24 November. When he told a British intelligence officer, 'If I don't get this pass, I don't get in,' the message had somehow become distorted and it emerged from the circuit suggesting that he had definitely been sent packing by his American colleagues. It was a very great relief to find that nothing of the sort had happened. Soon the pass arrived, he gained access to the Skiff and all was well.

Much on our minds at this time were psyops, or psychological operations, which embraced both strategic and tactical deception. The Americans had a whole group working on the subject and, although we had only one man assigned to it, we were very keen to join in. A certain amount could be achieved informally if senior officers now and then discussed a bogus plan: such talk, we knew, would quickly spread through the Saudi and Arab world — for if you pick the right listener and tell him one really deep secret, you can be sure that he will pass it on, as readily as a confidant of any other nationality. A more positive task was that of creating alarm and dissension among the Iraqi troops dug in along the border. This we proposed to achieve, as war drew nearer, by broadcasting through loud hailers and dropping leaflets.

Already small radios and audio tapes were being smuggled through Jordan and Iraq into occupied Kuwait. The tapes were mainly of popular Arab music played by leading entertainers and so were worth listening to in their own right, but they also contained factual yet seditious messages, telling listeners how Saddam Hussein was ruining their country, how he had violated Islamic principles by his invasion of Kuwait, how Kuwait was not worth dying for and how the

Allies would crush them unless they gave themselves up. Altogether some fifty thousand tapes were smuggled in, apparently to good effect.

Like any other form of attack, these activities needed careful planning – as we realized when the draft of what we proposed to put on the leaflets was condemned by our Arab colleagues as being quite unsuitable. The Saudis naturally wanted to keep tight control of psyops: they were afraid that if the information carried an offensive tone, it would bounce back in their faces when the war was over. The general aim of the Coalition was to encourage Iraqi soldiers to surrender: we pointed out the flaws in their leadership, highlighted the immense power facing them and suggested that it would be better to pack up and call it a day. But unless the message was couched in precisely the right terms, it would have no effect. The Arab mode of expression is much less direct than ours and in any case, Iraqis were more likely to surrender to other Arabs than to Americans, who they had been made to believe were evil ogres liable to slit their throats on sight or eat them for breakfast before they had been in captivity a single day.

New faces brought new sharpness to our preparations and none more so than that of Major General Rupert Smith, who had been chosen to command the British Division. Goodlooking, very dark with aquiline features, and with grey already streaking his hair, Rupert had been selected with a unanimity that reflected his exceptional qualities. In Germany, the Commander-in-Chief of BAOR and the Commander of 1 Corps, when asked to nominate a man to take over the Division destined for the Gulf, had both simultaneously come up with his name, even though he had been in command of a division in Germany for only two weeks and many officers of greater seniority were available.

Meeting him for the first time on a working basis when he arrived in Riyadh for a reconnaissance on 23 November, I was immediately struck by his originality. Although possessed of an exceptionally logical mind and most professional to do business with, he was also refreshingly unorthodox in his ideas and liable to seek less-than-obvious solutions to the problems which confronted him. I soon found that he was a man after my own heart, in that, when given an order, he liked to go away and get on with the execution of it and did not expect his commander to interfere with what he was doing. In fact he carried this trait to such lengths that it might have worried somebody who wished to maintain close control – but I knew at once that he and I could work well together.

When he arrived, I arranged for him to receive a full briefing from my staff and then had a long private talk, explaining my command philosophy and my methods of working. After a day and a half of this kind of background introduction, he went on to look at the environs of Jubail and the Al Fadhili training area just inland. With Norman Schwarzkopf's permission, I had told him in confidence that the US Marines, with whom 7th Armoured Brigade were still training, were destined to be only a diversion in any attack which the Coalition launched on the Iraqi forces in Kuwait and that I hoped to detach the British ground forces from them, so that we could take part in the main action to the west. This information was still absolutely secret, but it was essential for Rupert to know it so that he could begin to formulate a realistic plan of action, and I was pleased but not surprised when he said that he entirely agreed with my proposal for the resubordination of the British Division.

When he compared the forces which he had been allotted with the task on the ground, he at once detected major shortages, both in formations and in overall numbers. As soon as he returned home, he therefore put in for the additional units which he reckoned he needed to do the job properly. Paddy Hine and I once more found ourselves enmeshed in the numbers game. Paddy, being in England, bore the brunt of the bureaucratic onslaught. The civil servants had been charged by ministers with ensuring that every demand was properly justified, with the result that Tom King, having just set a new ceiling, became very reluctant to go back to the War Cabinet and give them a higher figure. Instead, as Paddy put it, he started to 'dine *à la carte*' and dealt with each request man by man, as it came along, sitting as chairman of a small committee with advisers round him.

In our view, this was a crazy way of doing business, because the commanders on the spot were not out there to amuse themselves or aggrandise their positions: only they could tell what they needed to do their job properly and minimize risk to human life. Eventually Paddy became so exasperated that he enlisted the support of the Chief of the Defence Staff and confronted Tom King with the reality of the situation, pointing out that we were almost certainly going to war and that we positively needed all the men we had asked for. 'If it does mean your going back to Cabinet,' said Paddy, 'that's tough. But we don't want to fall flat on our face when we come to meet the task put upon us.'

When January came, and the haggling was still in progress, Paddy eventually arranged that the Secretary of State would allow him a margin of five hundred men on top of those already authorized and he operated within this for the rest of the campaign. Yet the arm-in-the-mangle attitude persisted among civil servants right to the point at which war broke out.

Curiously enough, while all these arguments went on over people, I was never inhibited by financial constraints. At one point in November I noted that I had £160 million immediately available for contracts in certain key areas, and another £224 million for ammunition contracts. Whenever we wanted to rent property or equipment, such as flat-bed tank transporters, a phenomenal amount of haggling went on, but often it was between the Saudi firm which owned the building or the vehicles and the Government or armed forces, since the Government had generously agreed to meet our in-theatre costs and it was the Saudi administration which would pay in the end.

In Jubail Martin White found much the same – that money was no object. Thus when he wanted to hire an enormous cold store at the rate of six million riyals for six months, nobody in the United Kingdom raised any objection. It was partly because of the storage capacity of this building that our troops ate so well. Finding that he could buy a surprising amount of food from local contractors, Martin and his staff did wonders in supplementing Compo rations with fresh eggs, vegetables and fruit (bread and rolls were baked every day in the force's own bakery). Buying supplies locally exposed us to another risk: that the food might be deliberately poisoned. Counter-intelligence suggested that the chances of this were quite high and we therefore made frequent checks – without ever discovering evidence of contamination.

The arrival of the Divisional reconnaissance party in Riyadh threw my own catering arrangements into turmoil. Gloria, our Filipino housekeeper, had done her best, but she was a pretty moderate cook at the best of times, and to produce an adequate dinner for fourteen visitors was beyond her. So, at the suggestion of Mark Chapman, I brought up Sergeant Martin, an Army Catering Corps chef, from Jubail. He proved both skilful and efficient, and when, after making inquiries, I found that he could be spared without penalty from the task which he had been given in the Force Maintenance Area, I kept him on. He possessed the great advantage (in Mark's eyes) of having to obey orders: instead of being obliged to go before Gloria on bended knee and beg her to stay on late because we were not going to be home till 2300, Mark could simply tell Sergeant Martin to have dinner ready then. Gloria stayed on, doing her other duties, but our catering was greatly improved.*

Another considerable boost to my morale was given by the arrival of a new Chief of Staff. There had been much debate as to which Service the new man should be drawn from. Because the Army element of our force was so large, there was a case for sending an Army man; but in a signal to Paddy Hine I pointed out that the Royal Navy was weakly represented in my headquarters and that once the air war began, my deputy, Bill Wratten, would be completely taken up by

* Gastronomically speaking, Bill Wratten and Ian Macfadyen, who shared a house in the same compound, had better luck. Tensa, the Eritrean woman who looked after them, was a brilliant cook and produced the most delicious, exotic meals. She also ran the house with outstanding efficiency. As Bill remarked, it was the only period of his life in which he went to bed with knife-edged creases in his pyjama trousers.

that, so that a case for another Air Force man could also be made.

Eventually the choice fell on Air Commodore Ian Macfadyen, who arrived on 24 November and proved an immediate success. His experience and background made him an ideal man for this job: he had already worked as a staff officer both in the Headquarters of the Northern Army Group in Germany and in the Falklands. Now, as a one-star officer, he escaped from his predecessor's impossible position of being *primus inter pares*: he had full authority to issue instructions on my behalf and to act for me when I was out of Riyadh. His energy and all-round competence freed me from office routine and gave me more time to travel, to meet people, to stand back from day-to-day detail and concentrate on policy.

A good Chief of Staff becomes the voice of his commander: he reflects his commander's views, carries out his orders and interprets them in detail. If I had suddenly said to Ian, 'We're going to move the Division to a new location next week,' it would have been his responsibility to interpret that decision in the form of specific orders and to set the whole move in motion. A Chief of Staff has a responsible and demanding job, but also one of considerable influence: he needs to be a man with experience and judgment. Ian, having both these essentials, became a very great asset.

This was just as well, for my headquarters had grown haphazardly as the situation developed and no one had had the time or authority to sit back, think its organization through and sort things out. After a few days touring the theatre to meet key commanders, Ian did just that.

His other problem was that the headquarters kept growing inexorably. It seemed paradoxical that, while Tom King and others were doing their damnedest to keep down the numbers of men in the deployment as a whole, more and more personnel were pouring into my headquarters not only unasked-for but frequently unannounced. Everyone in the United Kingdom wanted to join in on the act, often with the best intentions. Someone in London would say, 'Oh, he's bound to need support in this or that branch of engineering.' So, without my being consulted, an engineer lieutenant colonel would appear, together with a captain and a bevy of clerks to run his department – and suddenly I found I had another staff branch. After a while I became so annoyed by these excesses that I began putting people on the next plane home, just to make the point; but even that rather drastic action had only a limited effect and the headquarters continued to swell until it again overflowed its accommodation and we had to search for new premises.

Already the RAF headquarters was in a separate building, with the headquarters of the USAF, and it made sense that they should stay there, as the coordination of the air campaign was so immensely specialized and complex. Our naval headquarters, on the other hand, was housed in the Saudi navy's building and, although we could talk to people there on the telephone, we had only a few lines on which we could exchange classified information, so that if we wanted to discuss sensitive matters, we had to walk over to see them, and vice-versa – a cumbersome process which slowed communication and tended to create misunderstandings. The only solution, as I saw it, was to find a building big enough to house us all, and in mid November I initiated a search for something suitable.

Thus Ian had scarcely started work when, apart from all his other preoccupations, he had to start house hunting. Without too much difficulty he identified a suitable building: the former head office of British Aerospace, which had been standing empty for four years, though the business of haggling over the rent with the owners, through the medium of the Saudi army, proved so long-drawn-out that we could not take possession of it until the first week in January.

The day that Ian came out, 24 November, proved a red-letter one for me. 'The best day since I arrived,' I told Bridget, for I had exceedingly helpful talks with both Norman Schwarzkopf and Prince Khalid. 'NS bared his heart and told me all his plans,' I reported home. 'I now feel much happier with everything.'

First I had a long and friendly interview with Prince Khalid, who was warmer towards the British than ever. By now he had almost stopped querying every new draft of reinforcements which we wanted to bring in and was inclined to agree our requests *en bloc*. Then, in a still more crucial private meeting, Norman Schwarzkopf and I had a frank and thorough exchange of views. I was flattered that he took me so fully into his confidence and I was particularly glad when he confirmed that I would have a seat alongside his in the War Room if the shooting started. Seizing the opportunity, I put to him, fair and square, my reasons for wanting to move our Division away from the Marines. Over the past couple of weeks I had tried to soften him up on this point, and indeed Paddy Hine had also mentioned it to him, but we had deliberately not fed any hint of it back to Washington, since I felt that this was a matter which Norman and I would have to decide between us. Now he listened carefully to my arguments, though without enthusiasm. He was sensitive enough to see the political and military imperatives behind what I was asking, but at the same time found it very difficult to accept my proposal, for to him the resubordination issue was nothing but an unnecessary logistic problem. If he did allow us to move our Division, it would mean breaking up the successful partnership which 7th Armoured Brigade had formed with the US Marines: he would have to find another armoured brigade to support the Marines and fit our Division into the plan for his main attack. For the time being he would not give me any straight answer, but at least the matter was now in the open and the ball in the CinC's court.

One major question which remained unsettled was that of our policy if military circumstances changed. What would our response be, should Saddam Hussein decide on a partial withdrawal? What if he pulled back to Kuwait City, leaving the rest of the country free? What if he withdrew to Bubiyan and Raudhatin? We were continually discussing these possibilities, but Schwarzkopf badly needed a directive from Washington. It was not for us, in theatre, to determine to smash Saddam: that was up to Washington, London and the United Nations. Of course, we would all have been extremely disappointed if, after we had created such a huge military organization, the whole confrontation had collapsed like a house of playing cards. If Saddam had goaded us into building up our forces, lured us to the brink, and then suddenly packed up and gone home, we should have found it a terrible anti-climax. After vast expenditure, we should have been left absolutely flat, unable to make any effective riposte. We too should have had to go home, because the Arabs would not have wanted us hanging around. Furthermore, we should not have been able to return to the Gulf in the near future, as the over-stretch of our logistic system would have made it impossible for us to return quickly, even if political difficulties had been resolved. Saddam, had he so wished, could have walked straight back into Kuwait.

The lack of any clear political objective was a constant worry, and yet, with every day that passed, I felt more certain that we were going to have to fight. 'We now move into a sensitive period,' I wrote home on 29 November. 'I do *not* believe Saddam Hussein will withdraw, and I think war of some sort is more likely. He will be defeated, but at what cost in lives and in further disruption in the Middle East, spilling over into the rest of the world?'

CHAPTER 6

BATTLE OF NERVES

At about 0800 on Sunday, 2 December 1990, a metallic American voice suddenly crackled out over the loudspeakers in my headquarters with the warning, 'Scud launch! Scud launch!' Infra-red satellite sensors had detected the heat generated by a short-range ballistic missile taking off from a site near Basra in Iraq. We spent the next two minutes in a state of some anxiety, fearing that the Scud might have been fired at Israel, with all the consequences which that might entail. Then other sensors gave us the bearing of the rocket, and we were relieved to discover that it had only been launched as a test firing, east to west, down Iraq's range in the western desert. Two more Scuds travelled the same path later in the month and it became clear that Saddam Hussein was deliberately stepping up the pressure in our protracted war of nerves. He knew from worldwide Press reports that the Coalition was reinforcing its troops on a massive scale and this was his answer: far from preparing to withdraw from Kuwait, he had begun launching rockets as a demonstration of bravado.

'We are into a very sensitive period,' I told Bridget, 'Anything could happen virtually without notice.' President Bush had offered to send his Secretary of State, James Baker, to Baghdad for talks, but that seemed to me no cause for optimism. Far from it – the thought slipped through my mind that Saddam might seize Baker as an extra-valuable hostage and so precipitate hostilities, rather than avert them. 'We must not feel secure just because talks are planned,' I wrote. 'Saddam is quite capable of using them as a deception for pre-emptive action and he knows we are not ready at present.' (In the event, Baker did not go to Baghdad. Contact between America and Iraq was established through Geneva.)

Even though we had been in direct confrontation with Saddam for more than three months, we continued to underestimate his stupidity. If he saw war coming, as evidently he did, why did he wait? Further delay was to our advantage. Why did he not make a first strike when he knew our preparations were far from complete? If he *was* proposing to try something, this was the moment. There were several options open to him. He could have launched an air strike, either against shipping or against our land forces – the endless convoys on the one and only Tapline road running north-westwards across the desert from Jubail were an obvious and vulnerable target. He could have launched Scud attacks on Riyadh, Dhahran or even Israel. He could have made a cross-border strike into Saudi territory, as he later did at Khafji. The Coalition forces were by no means ready to fight: large numbers of our troops were in transit round the world, or had not even left their peacetime bases, and those established in theatre were in a defensive posture. American plans for the air war were still in preparation: we were not yet in a position to cut off the Iraqi forward troops from their supplies by bombing or to sever their communication with rear echelons. In short, the Allies were in considerable disarray and would have been seriously embarrassed if Saddam had chosen that moment to force the issue militarily.

If he had struck, I believe we would have held him and then dealt with him, but our problems would have been enormous, and our casualties substantial. In retrospect, I am not surprised to find that I was feeling the strain of ever-increasing responsibilities, and that on 3 December I wrote home:

> This job could be the one that pricks the de la B. reputation! There is so much to go wrong, with the most severe consequences, and at times I wonder why I took it on. Most times, however, I know I could never have considered *not* taking it on.

With every day that passed, the strength of the Coalition was growing. Alan Munro returned from leave in the United Kingdom with a letter from John Major to King Fahd, assuring the Saudi ruler that, notwithstanding the change of Prime Minister, the British Government remained fully committed to the cause. On a visit to the port of Jubail I got an awe-inspiring glimpse of the military power which the Americans were assembling. 'For the next thirty days the Allies will unload twenty-four hundred vehicles a day, and seventy kilometres of convoys will leave the port every day,' I reported home. 'Sixty per cent of the US armed forces will be out here – about half a million men – and the largest air force ever assembled in history, with up to three thousand aircraft and the most modern technology.'

Another formidable recruit joined the Coalition in the form of Commodore Chris Craig, the new SNOME, who arrived in theatre on 1 December and took over his command two days later. A former naval helicopter pilot and instructor, Chris had won a DSC for his outstanding service as commander of the frigate HMS *Alacrity* during the Falklands War. A big, solid, dark man, with a fine square jaw, he arrived with the reputation of being aggressive and go-ahead at sea and very few days passed before I saw that he would be a real asset on the Coalition's right flank. I told him I wanted plans for an offensive campaign by the Navy high up the Gulf and he immediately set about working up the ideas laid down in my directive and outlined by the team from the Maritime Tactical School.

The scare raised by Patrick Cordingley's remarks about casualties coincided with a sudden collapse in Whitehall's resistance to my demands for a forces' broadcasting station, and for telephones. At first we had hardly any telephones at all and the few that existed in transit camps attracted vast queues. When the Ministry of Defence finally agreed arrangements, Mercury came up trumps, beat British Telecom out of sight and installed fifty extra telephones at key points. Later we developed mobile telephones, so that calls to home could be made from right out in the desert.

My own existence continued to be fast-moving and widely

varied. For instance, I spent the night of 4 December in the desert with A Squadron of the Queen's Dragoon Guards, commanded by Major Hamish Macdonald. I learnt something of their tactics by going on a short patrol in one of their Scimitar armoured fighting vehicles, which was good fun, interesting and useful in that it gave me a detailed understanding of what armoured reconnaissance could achieve in the desert. Driving across the sands at night, listening as the commanders kept up a running commentary, gave me a feel for the problems of manoeuvring in the dark and for the difficulties of controlling air support. I could see all the more clearly the potential for blue-on-blues (accidental attacks on friendly forces), particularly from the air, and made a note to improve our procedures for avoiding them.

Talking to the servicemen in the desert that evening, I said that there was not, after all, going to be a visit to theatre by the Prime Minister, only to wake up in the morning and hear on the radio that John Major *was* planning to come out in January. The men were impressed to find that even their Commander did not know what was going on!

Next day, in Dhahran, I called on Prince Mahommed bin Fahd, a son of the King and Governor of the Eastern Province of Saudi Arabia. A most friendly man, strongly Anglophile, he was to have visited the United Kingdom, but had been told by his father that he must not leave home at such a critical moment. Together we went to a very grand lunch party given by a leading businessman in a house full of marble, priceless carpets and the inevitable chandeliers – the whole place, as I told Bridget, 'glittering with wealth such as only an Arab can create'.

That same evening, back in Riyadh, I had a long private discussion with Norman Schwarzkopf, partly over the vexed issue of biological warfare agents and inoculation, and partly over the resubordination of the British Division. No decision about immunization had yet been taken in London: I was still in favour. 'I strongly support we use the vaccine,' I noted. 'I cannot see that we should possess it and not use it. We should be entirely blameworthy if we didn't use it and Saddam delivered biological.' If we did use it, the question was, in which part of the theatre? Some people felt that if Saddam resorted to biological attack at all, he was most likely to aim at Riyadh and try to spread panic there. Others thought he would hit troops in the front line.

Our difference of opinion over resubordination ran even deeper. My plan to move our Division did not suit Schwarzkopf in any way and I could well understand his opposition. From the military point of view, it would offer him no advantage and would simply cause administrative and logistic upheavals. When I had first brought the matter up, several weeks earlier, he had made no particular comment; perhaps he had hoped that I would not follow it through. But since then, I guessed, he had come under pressure from the US Marines, who possessed a powerful lobby in the Pentagon, to leave our armour where it was. Now he had begun to resist my request on the grounds that if our Division did join the wide left hook, we would not be able to support it logistically, as the length of our supply lines would be too great. I felt certain that we would manage and I determined to fly out a small team of experts to prove it. Afterwards, in a secure telephone conversation, I asked Paddy Hine to make sure that Tom King backed our request very firmly, so that no gap should be visible between British military and political aspirations.

On 5 and 6 December Colin Powell, Chairman of the US Joint Chiefs of Staff, visited the theatre with Dick Cheney, the Defence Secretary, and I gave them a seven-minute briefing on the British role. I found Powell approachable and articulate and, although I did not have much to do with him, he was courteous and friendly to me. I was also glad to see that Norman Schwarzkopf held him in high regard and that a happy relationship existed between the two. Powell made it clear that Baker was going to take a robust stand with the Iraqis on the question of withdrawal from Kuwait. He would tell them that partial withdrawal had never been an option: they had got to pull out altogether.

I was glad to find Powell and Schwarzkopf acting in concert, but concerned that they still seemed to lack a clear plan for offensive action. By then it had become clear to me that the CinC had no written directive as to how he should proceed.

He had an oral directive of sorts – to plan the recovery of Kuwait – but no precise instructions as to whether he was to attack Iraq as a whole, march on Baghdad, capture Saddam, or what. This lack of definition concerned me, as did the disparity between British and American rules of engagement.

Rules of engagement (ROE) are not normally of much interest to civilians, but to sailors, soldiers and airmen they are literally a matter of life and death, for they govern one's response to hostile action and lay down the circumstances in which one may or may not open fire on the enemy. Their purpose is essentially to ensure that nobody starts a war by mistake; but although their aim is simple, their application has been rendered more and more difficult to manage by the ever-increasing range and complexity of modern weapons.

Consider, for example, a warplane armed with stand-off missiles which are launched from a far greater distance than conventional bombs or bullets. It is no longer adequate for ROE to lay down that your pilot may not fire at another aircraft until it is within a certain range. Distance has become largely irrelevant. Time is more important, but also you have to take into account whether or not the enemy aircraft has shown hostile intent by locking on to your own plane with its weapon-launching radar. All this produces dire complications, especially as, in every case, potential military response is governed by the political policy of the country to which the armed force belongs.

In the Gulf we knew that, if hostilities broke out, we would immediately move on to full wartime ROE, which would give our commanders maximum discretion within geographical boundaries: inside these, we would be able to use any of our weapons against the enemy whenever he threatened. Before hostilities began, however, we were constrained by more restrictive ROE, and these varied from one nation to another, those of the Americans, for instance, tending to be freer than ours.

This divergence of ROE within the Coalition concerned me greatly. Of course I did not want to precipitate war accidentally: an incident like the shooting down of the Iranian airliner by the Americans in 1988 would have been explosive in the last month of 1990. On the other hand, the RAF Tornados, which were flying continuous combat air patrols, were potentially at risk every day and so, to a still greater degree, were the Royal Navy ships deployed in the Gulf. In my own view and that of my senior commanders, the ROE which we had been given were too restrictive to afford them adequate protection. But then perhaps every commander feels this when responsibility for his men and equipment is in his hands.

A Type 42 destroyer such as HMS *Gloucester* had three hundred men on board and cost some £120 million. Had the Iraqis found a chance, they would have attacked her with low-flying jets and Exocet missiles, which can be launched from a range of up to eighty kilometres. Our standard ROE forbade our ships to engage hostile aircraft until they were within a few kilometres – far too late. For Britain, essentially a maritime nation, it would have been a devastating blow, both morally and materially, to lose so vital an asset either early in the war or even before war had started – and yet our ROE seemed to me to increase the risk of such a disaster.

It is hardly surprising, then, that ROE were a matter for constant debate and argument at both national and international level. In my headquarters I had two lawyers working on the subject, but I felt that back in the United Kingdom people were taking a cool, detached attitude and worrying more about the possible legal consequences of making our ROE too generous than about the chances of our losing a ship or aircraft to a pre-emptive Iraqi strike. At the same time, I realized that a balanced attitude was necessary, and that any over-reaction could have provoked a war.

On 6 December Saddam did make a move of a kind, by suddenly releasing the Western hostages he had been holding. As he set them free, he made the fatuous remark that they were no longer needed and could go home for Christmas, but his motive remained unclear. He may have thought that he could win points in terms of world opinion, or simply that there was nothing to be gained by hanging on to them any longer. Later, King Hussein of Jordan told me that he tried to convince Saddam that the hostages were doing him more harm than good and this advice may well have played a part in pushing him to a decision. Perhaps, also, James Baker had made it clear to the Iraqi dictator that the presence of hostages would not deter us in any attack we might make. As I wrote in a letter to Bridget, 'We do not know what to make of the news. He is a very devious person. I suspect he sees the hostages as an increasing liability and he hopes their release may put the alliance's cohesiveness in question. One thing is for certain: the release is *not* a gesture of goodwill.'

Friday, 8 December, brought me the rare luxury of a day off. Brigadier Peter Sincock, a long-standing friend from Staff College days, and now Military Attaché at the British Embassy, organized a trip out into the desert south of Riyadh, to visit the dramatic Tuwayk escarpment which runs some nine hundred kilometres roughly north-east/south-west, with very few routes up and down its rocky face and most of them negotiable only by donkeys and people on foot. After motoring out in a four-wheel-drive vehicle, we set up some picnic tables and chairs at a spot on the lip of the escarpment and Peter expertly barbecued some delicious steaks, which we ate gazing out over a fantastic view, with kites and vultures wheeling below us. Short as it was, the break did me good and gave me a chance to think about the position in which the Coalition found itself.

By then, I realized, we were almost at the point of no return. Both the United States and Britain had committed themselves so heavily – in military terms, as well as in political reputation – that if we did not succeed in securing Saddam Hussein's withdrawal from Kuwait, the entire deployment would look like an extremely expensive failure. Besides, as our forces built up, we became impatient to complete the job which we had been sent out to do: having brought out so many thousands of men, we did not want to find that all they were going to be able to do was sit in the sand and then go home. Our worst fear remained that of Saddam staging a partial withdrawal, leaving us stranded, and my anxieties on this score came out in a letter home:

He has a really evil collection of chemical and biological weapons, and he could cause substantial casualties in a last-ditch or revenge attack. We shall rely on our overwhelming air superiority to destroy this capability if push comes to shove.

But partial withdrawal is a nightmare politically and I feel sure it is a game he will consider playing. We've put such political capital into his total withdrawal that anything less will be a substantial setback to us and honours to him. Only today the Saudis told me they would not be able to keep their people on side if Saddam did make a partial retreat. We still plan to put the Islamic forces into Kuwait if that happens, to occupy the territory vacated, but there will be no fight and in offensive terms it will be very difficult for us and the United States to go it alone.

In retrospect, I can only surmise that Saddam was so blinded by his own conceit that he simply could not see what was coming to him. He knew quite well what forces were massing against him. Not only had the world's Press carried news of our reinforcements, as part of our efforts to make him withdraw we ourselves had sent him information and photographs. His staff may well have deliberately misinformed him about the capabilities and resolution of his own troops, but even if they did, only the blinkered self-confidence of a megalomaniac could persuade him that they would have a chance when it came to war.

Dictators are driven not by reason, but by their own egos. Rather than modify their policies in the face of overwhelming threats, they do not acknowledge setbacks and keep going along the lines they have chosen. Saddam was determined to consolidate his invasion of Kuwait, regardless of the consequences: he was confident of the fact that the boldness and viciousness of what he had done would be enough to stun the rest of the world into inaction. Even when he saw other nations preparing to react violently, he could not bring himself to withdraw or start to negotiate his way out of the mess which he had created.

On 10 December the new elements of 1 (BR) Division began to arrive at Jubail, and their commander, Major General Rupert Smith, was faced with the formidable task of having the whole Division assembled, trained, integrated with the Americans and ready to fight within a period of six weeks at the most – and all this in an environment totally new to his men and to their equipment, which had been designed primarily for northern Europe.

During his reconnaissance in November, he had immediately seen that the Iraqi desert offered him the chance to develop a novel concept of armoured operations. In Europe, where the British Army normally trains, the terrain has a profound effect on tactics. Movement of the front, fighting part of any large force is largely constrained by the many features of the landscape, such as roads, rivers, bridges, bogs, forests, villages towns and cities, all of which canalize armoured vehicles and restrict their mobility. The result is that a commander keeps having to alter his formation as he advances. Unlike a flotilla of ships or a flight of aircraft, which can forge straight ahead, armoured vehicles cannot advance steadily in the formation of most value to them. Furthermore, because they are constantly having to shift their relative positions, the commander keeps being obliged to rearrange his force so that his various weapons are in the most effective positions.

At the back of the force, in contrast, the logistic tail can travel almost at will. The countryside of Europe is covered with concrete and asphalt, along which trucks can move with ease, and there are facilities everywhere. Thus although the front end is constrained by the ground, the back can roam where it wants.

In the desert, Rupert saw, exactly the opposite was true. Tanks at the front would be able to motor on at will, maintaining their formation, and there would be no need for commanders to keep changing their weapon mix. At the back, however, there *were* going to be constraints: trucks bringing up fuel, ammunition, spares and so on would have trouble finding their way across flat, featureless expanses. They might also become bogged down in sand and exposed to attack. It was the back end which was going to become canalized and vulnerable.

He further saw that there was no point in fighting for a piece of sand. As he put it, it would be 'rather like a sailor fighting for a wave or an airman for a cloud.' A patch of sand, he decided, was an irrelevance. If some foolish Iraqi wished to dig a hole and sit in it, the best way of defeating him would be to go round behind him and deprive him of his water. As long as the Iraqis chose to defend sand, he reckoned 'they had neutered themselves', and he set about training to fight a fast-moving battle in depth, as he put it, 'fundamentally to alter the way we did business, to accommodate the reality of the circumstances.'

For the men now pouring in, there was everything to learn, but for the soldiers who had already spent two months in theatre, the big enemy was boredom and many units found this period of enforced waiting a severe trial. Whereas in Germany or elsewhere everyone had been working to a fixed programme, with events laid out ahead for days, weeks and months on end, here they were suddenly thrust out in the desert with no certainty about the future. On the one hand they were being trained and worked up for war; on the other, they had little to do and felt starved of definite information. There was a great deal that they would have liked to know. Were they going to fight or not? If war did break out, when would it be? Where would they go?

The combination of inaction and uncertainty had a damaging effect on morale and I instructed my subordinate commanders to grip the problem through commanding officers, telling them that their competence would be judged on their ability to manage this period of waiting. All war, after all, is ninety per cent boredom and ten per cent terror, and hanging around is always part of the game; but I had to rub it into commanders that it was their responsibility to keep life interesting and worth while for their men.

In 7th Armoured Brigade Patrick Cordingley had evolved a system of rotation, whereby men did sixteen days in the desert and then came in for three days' rest and recreation at Camp Four, a collection of Nissen huts originally built for Filipino workers on the outskirts of Jubail, which we had taken over. To a newcomer, Camp Four looked pretty bleak, but with its beds, air conditioning and showers, it made a luxurious contrast to life in the sand and proved an invaluable asset.

Out in the desert there was the insidious problem of loneliness. Outsiders tend to think of army life as a hugger-mugger existence, with everyone piled in together, but in the sands it was not like that at all. Every night there were about eleven hours of darkness to be lived through. Patrick was always very conscious that men were alone during that time, dotted around beside their tanks and armoured fighting vehicles, or huddled in trenches, staring out over flat, black desert beneath a sky full of stars. Strenuous efforts were made to overcome the sense of isolation which this existence produced: tents were blacked out extra thoroughly so that men could have some light, write letters, read and chat to each other. Later, they enjoyed sophisticated facilities such as television sets and occasional film shows from the mobile cinema sent out by the Services' Sound and Vision Corporation.

Loneliness, however, remained a constant enemy. An indication of the stress which people were feeling came one night when, after a row with his troop-sergeant, a man walked off into the desert. Next day there was no sign of him. Fellow soldiers found nothing but a line of footprints leading away across the sand and they feared that he had become lost in the desert, where he might survive at most for four or five days before he died of thirst. In fact he had kept walking due east, towards the sea, until he hit a road and hitched a lift down into Jubail, where he gave himself up, but his disappearance had given his unit a nasty jolt.

No one saw the need for positive leadership more clearly than Arthur Denaro, Commanding Officer of the Queen's Royal Irish Hussars. After the war he identified three distinct phases of his regiment's stay in the desert: the first a time of arrival and training, the second a period of waiting, and the third the battle itself. The first phase, which he described as 'an exciting, adventurous time in which professionalism was honed', proved relatively easy to manage. In the second, he found that 'a different, more personal and compassionate form of leadership was required by all to take us through those tense days as a team, a group, a family'. The third phase, the battle itself, was very short.

Like many units, the QRIH had been built up to full strength by the drafting in of men from other regiments. Of the hundred-odd reinforcements, the majority were individuals, but four formed troops came from the 17/21st Lancers and, rather than keep them all together, Arthur blistered one troop on to each of his own squadrons, to strengthen the new-comers' sense of identity with their foster Regiment. As he said, 'Although they remained strongly and staunchly 17/21st Lancers, they were definitely Irish Hussars throughout the conflict.' He made a point of personally welcoming every new arrival and took enormous trouble to see that all their families were treated the same as those of his own men: for instance, on St Valentine's Day, at the height of the air war and two weeks before the land assault went in, every wife of every man serving in or with the Regiment had a rose delivered to her home, whether in England, Ireland, Germany or any-where else, and later every one of them received a brooch in the form of a desert rat in gold.

In this period of waiting, Arthur decided that he must bring the Regiment down from the high peak of readiness which it had achieved, but at the same time 'keep it bubbling along'. He therefore devised a regime of three days' squadron training, three days' regimental training, and three days' relaxation in a collection of tents known as St Patrick's Camp, with regular visits to Camp Four. He also set weekly goals and paid particular attention to communication 'to break the rumour chain', start-ing a regimental *Desert Newsletter* as a complement to the *Sandy Times*. As he recorded afterwards, it was a tiring but immensely rewarding time for the commanders, who made great efforts to see that they 'daily walked and talked amongst the men, stop-ping for a brew, lending a hand and cracking a joke. There was time for the men to relax, play sport, put on skits and write home.' But as all this took place miles from anywhere, every recreational initiative needed imagination and drive.

Along with fellow COs, Arthur was profoundly glad of the universal ban on alcohol. Some drink got through – often in shampoo bottles – when men realized that parcels were not being opened by the authorities, but because it was forbidden, and everyone knew that if he got caught he would be sent home – the ultimate disgrace – it caused little trouble and there was no drunken fighting in the evenings. (When a contingent from 7th Armoured Brigade went down to Bahrein for the

Christmas carol service, they immediately fought any RAF personnel they came across, tribal jealousies being sharpened by the fact that some of the Air Force men were living in luxury hotels while they were stuck out in the desert.)

As the units of our Division arrived and American reinforcements poured in, the CENTCOM planning team was refining a succession of schemes for a major assault on the Iraqi forces, should it come to a land campaign. Every few days the planning team would submit their latest proposal to Schwarzkopf: often it was thrown back at them to be reworked, but gradually ideas were developed and refined in a process of progressive and constructive improvement until the wide left hook became the preferred option. In broadest terms, working from right to left, the plan was that the battleships of the US Navy should bombard the Iraqi positions on the coast and offshore islands of Kuwait and that the seaborne US Marines should make either a feint or an actual amphibious landing from the Gulf. The Arab elements of the Coalition forces would attack up the littoral, aiming straight for Kuwait. Next to them, to the west, the US Marine Corps would engage the Iraqi forces due north of them, in a major diversionary battle. To the west of the Marines, the Egyptians and Syrians would push to the north and then swing right-handed, to come into Kuwait City from the west. The main allied assault would start from far out in the west, well beyond the Wadi al Batin, and after driving north would also swing right-handed, sweeping in behind the Iraqi defences to attack the elite divisions of the Republican Guard and cut the front-line troops off from their communications and supplies. No Western forces were to enter Kuwait City until it had been cleared by Islamic troops. When Tim Sulivan, in the heart of the American planning team, privately asked his colleagues whether or not they thought the British were right to move their armour away to the west, where the main action was going to be, they all agreed that, militarily, this was the right solution.

Working in the midst of the Americans every day, Tim got to know them much better than I did and saw more of their strengths and weaknesses. In particular, he saw how autocratic was the exercise of command and what an inhibiting effect this had on the free thinking of the staff. He saw how often Norman Schwarzkopf bawled out members of his staff, but he also observed with admiration the special tactics which one man had developed for dealing with the CinC's outbursts. Brigadier General Arnold, the G3 from Third Army, an exceedingly good-natured and efficient officer, who did a great deal for Anglo–US relations, had evolved a perfect method of coping with Stormin' Norman: whenever the CinC went ballistic and machine-gunned one of his proposals, Arnold would stand his ground and say with perfect dignity, 'Thank you, General, for giving me your guidance.'

In the middle two weeks of December, the question of resubordination became a major issue for me. When Paddy Hine and I gained the impression that Schwarzkopf, under political pressure to leave our land forces where they were, was playing for time before he gave us a decision, I tried to force the pace by insisting that we should carry out a reconnaissance among the high command of the US VII Corps before committing our Division to them. At the same time I decided to apply political leverage of our own through London, and was disappointed when the Chief of the Defence Staff, Marshal of the Royal Air Force Sir David Craig, told Paddy Hine that it was up to the commander on the spot to decide what he should do, and that he had said the same not only to the Secretary of State, Tom King, but also to Colin Powell, who had come over from Washington on a flying visit.

My view was that I needed full support from the entire British chain of command. Without it, my position was potentially dangerous, for if the Americans gained the impression that it was only I who wanted the Division to move, and that I had no backing in London, they would seize the opportunity to drive a wedge between us and defeat my proposal in detail. Luckily for me, Paddy was typically robust on the issue and gave way to no one.

'Life here is getting tenser by the day, as we all ponder what will happen next month or sooner,' I reported home on 13 December. 'Saddam Hussein has removed the bulk of his ground forces from Iraq and piled them all into the KTO

[Kuwait Theatre of Operations], leaving only the minimum needed for security.'

Over the past few days aerial reconnaissance had detected a disturbing innovation: instead of merely building up his main defensive barrier inside Kuwait, Saddam was extending it westwards into his own territory, on his forces' right flank, and we became concerned that he might somehow have gained knowledge of our plan to attack with a wide left hook. Very few people knew about the plan at that stage, but there had been Press speculation which was not far wide of the truth and it looked as if Saddam might be reacting to it. Certainly he was reinforcing an area in which we wanted him to be weak, so that we could cut through rapidly and come in behind his main forces. I discussed with Norman Schwarzkopf the possibility that there had been a leak, but we decided that the Iraqi moves had been coincidental.

The issue of resubordination was building to a climax. The team of logistics experts which I had sent for had arrived and were due to make their presentation to Schwarzkopf and his generals that evening, 13 December, and I felt that for me, personally, a great deal was at stake. 'I now present my case to Norman Schwarzkopf and all his generals tonight,' I wrote home. 'I've outlined my arguments forcefully to Paddy, requesting the support of the CDS and TK. This is the most important and far-reaching decision of my tour.'

That same evening, I used a telephone call to Tom King to gain the Secretary of State's unequivocal support and I put the matter straight to him. When I asked, 'Are you backing me on this or aren't you?' he responded enthusiastically and said that he certainly was. He then told me that the last of the British hostages were safely home, reunited with their families, and that the new Prime Minister was very keen to learn about the deployment in the Gulf. Altogether, the call did much to reassure me.

Our key logistic briefing took place in Schwarzkopf's upper conference room, where there was a large table surrounded by chairs, with a podium, projector and screen away in one corner. Apart from the CinC, the audience included the Deputy CinC, General Calvin Waller, the Army Commander,

Lieutenant General John Yeosock, the Senior Operations Officer, Lieutenant General Bert Moore, and other senior commanders. Several of them, I am sure, began the meeting in a sceptical frame of mind. Our own team consisted only of Brigadier Simon Firth, with Lieutenant Colonel Philip Taylorson and Major Peter Sharp supporting him.

Having introduced the team, I gave a short introductory talk. I said that the logistic capability which I had been given was the best ever granted to a British Divisional force and that, since we had this support, we should use it to the full. If we stayed with the US Marines, our logistic capability would not be stretched. I was confident enough to say that in some respects I thought that we, the British, were better equipped logistically to support our national effort than the Americans were theirs.

I stressed that the team about to make the logistic presentation did *not* know the strategic plan, so that the scenario which they had worked out was based on a hypothetical situation. I also emphasized that, if we did resubordinate our Division, we would need no American help in bringing forward its supplies. Far from being a burden to the Americans, we might even be able to help them in some areas. On the other hand, I also made it clear that time was already running short. If we were to have the Division moved, trained and ready to fight by the time the Americans wanted it – which I understood was the middle of January – we needed a decision as soon as possible.

'Our Division is tailored for manoeuvre operations,' I said. 'It's most important to us that it should be used for operations of that kind. If we *don't* use it for that, not only will we be under-employing it, we'll be employing it in a type of battle for which it's not trained or rehearsed. If we move and fight with VII Corps, we'll have plenty of room to manoeuvre. If we stay where we are, that opportunity will not be there. Our troops will give a good account of themselves in either situation, but if you want the best out of the British, they must be deployed into an area where they find themselves on familiar ground.'

To close, I made the point that there was nothing new in

what I was asking: I had raised the subject of resubordination nearly two months earlier and indeed, the fact that we had succeeded in getting a Division was itself related to the question of resubordination. 'This presentation,' I concluded, 'is therefore not so much to justify the redeployment, which I believe is fully justified anyway, as to prove to you that logistically it will not be a burden on US forces. In fact, we want to prove to you that our Division is perfectly capable of standing on its own two feet.'

With that I handed over to Simon Firth, who proceeded to give a brilliant exposition, only twenty minutes long, of how we would support the Division with our own resources, even though its supply line would be up to five hundred kilometres long. The Americans heard him in silence, asked one or two questions about minor details, and that was it. Norman Schwarzkopf said, 'OK, Peter. That's fine. I'll let you know tomorrow.' Clearly the Americans wanted to discuss the matter further and we British left the meeting with nothing decided. But I was confident that we had won the day, for the logic of the presentation had been irrefutable. Simon Firth and his colleagues had shown beyond doubt that we could look after ourselves in logistic terms and I therefore felt that the Americans had no further grounds for objecting to our move.

Norman did not give me an answer next day, as he had promised. Instead, I spent three and a half fascinating hours listening to his corps commanders go through their plans. This made me more certain than ever that I was right to insist on having our Division moved and I wrote a strong letter to Paddy Hine explaining why I needed support from the CDS and from Tom King, and asking him to forward copies of the note to both. To Bridget I wrote, 'I've now heard General Walt Boomer's plan for the Marines, and I like it even less.'

At last, on 16 December, in a short discussion, Schwarzkopf gave me his agreement, but he made it clear that the move did not have his whole-hearted support and that he would sanction it for political rather than military reasons. He also said that as he would now have to strengthen the US Marine division with an extra American formation, to make up for the loss of British armour, he could not now honour his earlier assurance that he would place American troops under British command.*

This reservation did not worry me, as I had never wanted American troops under our command for operational reasons, only for the political advantage which they might bring. I had discussed the matter at length with Rupert Smith and we felt that to put an American brigade into our Division would implement in reverse the very situation which I had tried to avoid in removing our brigade from the Marines. We felt it would be far easier to fight the Division one brigade down than to bolster it with an American brigade and so introduce all the complications of liaison, communications and different operational concepts.

I was delighted from every point of view that Norman had come round, even if he was not best pleased, for I felt that to achieve what I so badly wanted was worth a temporary loss of credit with the United States. For weeks I had worked hard to be as cooperative as possible, building up a fund of goodwill with both the Americans and the Saudis, against the day when I needed to ask something which might not be very popular, but which was of paramount importance to me. That day had now come. I knew I had spent much of my credit forcing through this major decision, but I also knew that the breakthrough was many times worthwhile.

Soon I came to realize that Norman's decision reflected strongly to his own credit. The move did cause him problems and I suspect that he had been under heavy pressure to prevent it, not least from the high command of the Marines in the United States; but when he saw how important it was to us, he accepted my arguments.

Walt Boomer felt the loss of British armour keenly. Knowing this, in January, when our Division was beginning to form up with VII Corps, I wrote to thank him and the Marine Corps for the 'very great support and encouragement' that they had

---

* In the event, as noted earlier, when Rupert asked for additional fire support, he was given a Multiple Launch Rocket System regiment under command by General Fred Franks, the Commander of VII Corps.

given our troops since arriving in theatre and to say that it
was 'a matter of personal regret to my commanders to break
the close professional ties and happy rapport' which had
grown up between the nations. In conclusion I wrote: 'As we
move towards the land battle, let me end by wishing you and
your Marines good luck and Godspeed in the days ahead. You
have a fine command, and we are proud to have been a small
part of it.' This letter went unanswered and I am afraid that
Walt remained less than happy with our arrangement.

In the last few days before the resubordination issue was
resolved, many other developments took place. The Foreign
Office, reflecting our belief that a major war was in prospect,
told the Embassy that wives should be advised to leave Saudi
Arabia. Alan Munro felt that this advice was alarmist: he
thought that it was wise for wives to move out to places like
Jeddah, beyond missile range, but that if they all went home,
it would undermine the resolve of expatriates and also indicate to the Saudis that we lacked confidence in our ability to
defend their capital. I disagreed with him. I had little doubt
that Riyadh would come under missile attack, possibly with
chemical warheads, and I feared that if the situation deterio-
rated suddenly, air transport would become very scarce and
evacuation difficult or impossible. 'Better a complaining wife
at home,' I told Bridget, 'than one dead in Riyadh.' On reflec-
tion, however, I believe that Alan's arguments were right and
mine wrong: the choice was by no means as stark as I had
made out and it would have been bad for morale to have
initiated the evacuation of Riyadh.
  On 11 December I had an inspiring day with Commander
Philip Wilcocks on board his destroyer HMS *Gloucester*. I saw
the ship at action stations and tasted the peculiar, claustro-
phobic atmosphere in which the crew of a modern warship
train to fight within their gas-tight citadel. I was also pleased
to be granted the privilege of clearing the lower deck. I came
away with the heartening impression that Chris Craig was
gripping his Task Group with drive and enthusiasm. Many of
his senior officers had already served on at least one Armilla
patrol, so that they had an excellent working knowledge of

the Gulf; but now he was conducting an energetic work-up to war and at the same time forging close links with the US Navy, alongside whom he would have to fight.

The British outline naval plan covered three specific areas. The first was forward air defence, in which our Type 42 destroyers would join American vessels out to the north ahead of all other ships, to form a shield against attacks by the Iraqi air force. The second area was mine warfare, in which our five little Hunt class MCMVs, or mine counter-measure vessels, made us the leaders of the Coalition. (The Americans had no MCMVs of this kind, but relied on heli-copters. These had been specially developed during the Viet-nam war and although they may have functioned well enough in the Mekong Delta, they were not very effective in the open waters of the Gulf.) The third area was forward logistic and operational support, in which we also played a pioneer role. Unlike other navies, which leave their supply ships well to the rear, the Royal Navy likes to take its Royal Fleet Auxiliaries with it, so that replenishment and repair facilities are constantly available to the ships in the front line.

At the same time as working up their skills for war, the Task Group was continuing to enforce the embargo against ships bound for Iraq, for a few merchant vessels were still plying up and down the Gulf, albeit with their captains in a highly nervous state. For this role, the Navy had a clear and robust set of rules of engagement, which allowed them to go through the full escalation of oral challenge, formal caution, consolidation on that, warning shots and, if necessary, dis-abling. (During the crisis as a whole sixty ships and a million tons of cargo were turned away – a significant deprivation to Iraq, not counting all the ships which lurked in ports like Aden without attempting to run the gauntlet.)

In general, however, Chris Craig felt particularly exposed to a pre-emptive strike because the Americans wanted him to place his key destroyers close up against the coast of Iran, which he regarded as the most likely source of a break-out by enemy aircraft. In theory a jet could come straight off the coast at ultra-low level, without warning, and because the ship would not be able to engage it in Iranian airspace, she would in effect have about a fifteen-kilometre or thirty-second warning before she could counter-attack an intruder armed with lethal Exocet missiles, which were used with such devastating effect against HMS *Sheffield* and other ships during the Falklands campaign. There was also the further problem of identifying strange aircraft immediately.

I assured Chris that I and Paddy Hine were doing all we could to have naval ROE improved and at least brought in line with those of the Americans. Here at sea, even more than on land, I saw the almost unbridgeable gap between the needs of the military, who must have the power to protect their key assets, and those of the politicians, whose foremost aim is to prevent the triggering of Armageddon. The question constantly being asked was, 'Have we got the right compromise?' The answer, at that moment, in my view, was 'No'. Uncertainty on this score was not only a worry to SNOME: it was also likely to have a corrosive effect on the morale of his command teams.

Partly because I had full confidence in Chris, and partly because communications between his Flagship, HMS *London*, and my headquarters were less than perfect, I delegated a high degree of authority to him, so that he could direct normal operations without constantly referring back to me. This meant that he had tactical control of all his ships, and the ability to hand off tactical control of some of them to the Americans, whenever he saw fit. The arrangement gave him what he called 'a refreshingly long piece of string' on which to manoeuvre and gained him credit with the Americans, who saw that he was able to take decisions for himself.

Back on land, with the hostage problem solved, I instructed the SAS, now available for other projects, to plan classic operations deep in Iraq and to keep an eye on resistance in Kuwait. My hope for Kuwait was that, as soon as the confrontation was over, a team of British civilian advisers would appear on the scene to seize the initiative in offering help and advice on the rebuilding of the city, thus promoting British business and British arms sales. As I noted, 'If we don't move fast, the Americans will hog it.'

On 13 December we decided to up-armour all our Challenger tanks and Warrior armoured fighting vehicles; that is, to bolt on plates of extra armour over the outside of their tracks, to give them better protection against enemy tanks and artillery. This was a major decision, taken at the last moment after urgent studies in the United Kingdom. Special teams were flown out and all the vehicles were up-armoured in the field by their crews, with help from the Royal Electrical and Mechanical Engineers, who did a magnificent job. As the plates were some nine inches thick and extremely heavy, we were afraid that the vehicles might sink into the sand under the extra weight, but in fact they worked better after the modification than before, partly because the new armour channelled the sand downwards and reduced the amount being ingested by the engines. Such was the weight of the plates that they ate up carrying capacity in aircraft, and other less urgent cargo, even mail, had to wait until we had flown out enough plane-loads to keep the engineers busy; the rest of the armour was then despatched by sea.

On 14 December, when we learnt that, after further reinforcements, the Iraqis had up to forty divisions in the Kuwait theatre, Norman announced that the offensive which the Coalition was planning would be called Operation Desert Storm. 'That's what the name of this operation's going to be,' he said, 'and that's what I want everybody to call it.' That was the conference at which, for the first time, senior commanders were first formally briefed on the outline plan.

The approach of Christmas was an ever-increasing headache and I was particularly concerned to make sure that the Western forces in the Coalition were not caught off guard on Christmas Day, an obvious date for Saddam to make a pre-emptive strike in the hope that we might all be distracted by religious services and parties. I therefore sent out a message to all ranks, exhorting them to be especially aware of the need for security and on their guard not only against possible attack by Iraq, but also against terrorist incidents.

It was fortunate that in the run-up to the holiday period, after many delays and setbacks, all the welfare arrangements for which I had been campaigning suddenly fell into place. On 16 December the Forces' Broadcasting Station was at last up and running, and the BBC had managed to have a satellite reorientated so that we could receive their television pro- grammes at certain times of day. Galvanized by Patrick Cordingley's remarks on casualties and by Tom King's announcement of BFPO 3000, the British public had responded with staggering generosity, donating no fewer than eight hundred tons of Christmas parcels. At the same time, more than £1 million in cash poured in from every kind of source, private and public. To deliver the parcels, we hired three giant jet transports and with the money we bought essentials like satellite receivers, television sets, video players and radios (equipment of this kind could be powered by the generators built into fighting vehicles).

A further boost to morale was brought by General Sir Edward Burgess, President of the British Legion, who arrived in Riyadh at midnight on 16 December with twenty-six thou- sand free telephone cards, each worth £10, given by Mercury, and the first two pallets of Christmas presents, from the Legion and the *Daily Telegraph*. Having formally handed over the presents at the airport and received a briefing from me, the General re-boarded the same aircraft and flew home again – a real Santa Claus, if ever there was one.

Visitors like Sir Edward, who had a definite and beneficial purpose, were thoroughly welcome; but so many people wanted to come out that we and the Americans had a constant struggle to keep numbers down. At one stage the tide of Americans became so overwhelming – politicians, civil servants, senior officers – that Norman Schwarzkopf found his work-time severely curtailed and the American Ambassador in Riyadh, Chas W. Freeman Jr., sent a signal to Washington expressing his concern about numbers. The influx of observers, he said, made him wonder whether the Pentagon did not see the whole of Saudi Arabia as one immense game park, of which General Schwarzkopf was the Chief Game Warden, with nothing to do but receive visitors and show them round.

On the British side, we had nobody with the specific role

of handling visitors, so that the job usually fell to Ian Macfadyen or Mark Chapman, both of whom were grossly over-
worked already. I did not increase my own popularity by
taking a stand and issuing an instruction that colonels of regiments were *not* to be allowed to visit their troops. As war
approached, I saw a need to take an even tougher approach
and after discussion with Paddy Hine obtained a directive
from the CDS laying down that no visitors at all would be
allowed after a certain date, when hostilities were imminent.

One who had a positive need to tour the theatre was the Hon.
Archie Hamilton, MP, Minister of State for the Armed Forces,
who came out for a brief official trip on 18 December. He
proved excellent at talking to the servicemen, and he covered
a great deal of ground in a short time, not only visiting units of
the Army and Air Force, but also flying out to meet Chris Craig
aboard HMS *Gloucester* and inspect our hospital ship *Argus*. His
visit served to emphasize how different the problems of ROE
appeared when viewed from in-theatre and from Whitehall,
and I was glad to learn from him that in London the Ministry
of Defence was negotiating with the Pentagon to bring our
rules into line with those of the Americans.

In Bahrein there occurred a ridiculous scene which would
have fitted easily into a television soap opera, but which the
Minister handled with his customary good-natured tolerance.
Our party stayed for one night in a hotel and just as I was
going to bed Colin Ferbrache knocked on the door, with a
towel round his waist, and dripping with water having just
leapt out of his bath, to say that someone was trying to reach
me on the telephone from London, but that by mistake the
call had been put through to the Minister's suite. I hurried
along in my pyjamas, past the bodyguards in the corridor
and found Hamilton reclining on his bed, also in pyjamas,
watching television, quite unperturbed by the interruption.
The caller turned out to be Major General Sir Christopher
Airy, the Private Secretary to the Prince and Princess of Wales,
on the line from St James's Palace, wanting to finalize
arrangements for a visit by Prince Charles. As it was impossible to talk sensibly from where I was, I rang off and called
the Palace back from my own room.

In Riyadh, meanwhile, there took place an important change in the line-up of the Coalition. When Pierre Joxe succeeded Jean-Pierre Chevenement as Minister of Defence in Paris, he immediately authorized a change in the French command arrangements. Until then French forces had been obliged to report back to Paris before they could initiate any action; now they came under the operational control of the Americans. So far the French had been very much out in the cold, on the western flank of the Allies, but now, with characteristic decisiveness, Norman immediately brought the French in on his plans and found them a real role in the Coalition line-up, so that instead of being very much on the margin, they had a genuine role in Operation Desert Storm (by the end, their contingent numbered ten thousand men).

Another significant innovation was the first in a series of weekly briefings attended by the commanders of all the main forces in the Coalition, including France, Egypt, Syria, Kuwait and the United Arab Emirates, besides Saudi Arabia, ourselves and the Americans. Both Schwarzkopf and Prince Khalid appreciated the importance of bringing the leaders together, so that we got to know each other and gained an overall view of the problems facing the Allies. In Khalid's view, weekly conferences would help produce a front of unanimity and demonstrate that the Coalition really was working as a team. The first meeting took place in the Saudi operations room, which was bigger than the American one. Proceedings were in English and Arabic, with translations for those who needed them, and the whole occasion was formal and carefully orchestrated. I arranged for the RAF to highlight one particular problem – the control of hand-held air-defence weapons, which I knew was inadequate – and although little was achieved in military terms, the occasion undoubtedly strengthened our general sense of purpose.

By now I was so wrapped up in preparations for war that I found it hard to concentrate on details of life at home. I did feel mildly disappointed if my copy of *Farmers' Weekly* arrived late and I sent back dutiful hopes that the sale of potatoes was brisk, but my mind was firmly fixed on the multifarious problems confronting us in the Middle East. Nevertheless, I was delighted to get a letter from my farming partner Simon Cutter, which included the riddle: 'How do you get thirty Iraqis into a phone-booth?' Answer: 'Tell them they can't go in.'

CHAPTER 7

ONE EYE ON THE HOLLY

Emotionally and practically, Christmas was an extraordinarily difficult time. On the one hand, we wanted our servicemen to celebrate the festival as best they could, and natural feelings of nostalgia and homesickness were inevitably reinforced by the immense outpouring of support, praise, confidence and love which surged over to us from Britain – not only from our own families, but from the public as a whole. On the other hand, we had to repress the natural tendency to relax, to avoid giving offence to our Saudi hosts, to keep everyone very much on guard against the possibility of a pre-emptive strike by Iraq and to remain ready for immediate war. As Chris Craig aptly put it, we all had one eye on the holly and the other on Baghdad.

Anxious that there should be no ambiguity about our attitude to Christmas and wanting to be sure that everyone understood the rules, I instructed my headquarters to produce a policy statement, and in due course this rather stark document was issued to all commanders. Its stated aim was 'To ensure we enjoy Christmas to the best effect within the constraints imposed', and its introductory paragraphs set the scene with characteristic military precision:

1 Christmas is a joyous occasion in which all ranks will wish to participate.
2 The celebration of Christmas will take place, bearing in mind the overriding need to maintain an operational profile.

In laying down policy, the statement went into considerable detail, but individual commanders were left to ensure that they were discreet in making their own dispositions. For those way out in the desert or on board ships in the Gulf, it was relatively simple (although Chris Craig made it his policy that every ship should have a brief break alongside, either at Christmas or at New Year). Problems were liable to arise in places like Riyadh and Dhahran, where we were working among the civilian population.

It was a particularly difficult time for our new Force Padre, Lieutenant Colonel the Reverend Basil Pratt, who arrived from the Guards' Deport, Pirbright, in mid December. I wanted him to act as my personal envoy in taking the emotional pulse of the force. At our first meeting I explained that what I would like to hear from him was his view of how things were going, because he, the padre, would pick up vibrations which nobody else could detect. Without going into individual cases, he would be able to give me an idea of what servicemen were really feeling, as opposed to what they might be saying to their officers, and report where morale was strong and where there was a problem. His assessment would enable me to give a touch on the tiller here or there, and maintain a more sensitive degree of command than would otherwise be possible.

I myself found it hard to adjust to a comfortable emotional level. I knew that at home, as in other years, my family would be congregating in traditional fashion, that there would be church going, present giving and feasting; but now the only sensible thing to do seemed to be to shut my mind to what was happening in England. I felt that the place for me was out in the desert, among our servicemen, so I declined the many kind invitations emanating from the British Embassy, which was outstandingly generous with its hospitality, and other expatriate centres in Riyadh, and deliberately arranged the busiest possible programme of visits. Letters to Bridget summed up my feelings:

> Things are becoming increasingly taut as Saddam Hussein stab-
> ilizes his forces and maintains diplomatic hostility at a high

level. The tension is bound to increase in the days ahead, and this alone could lead to an outbreak of hostilities, as it is not easy to stop the great machine of war preparations rolling on into conflict.

Hundreds of thousands of tons of ammunition, stores and equipment pour in on ship after ship. One vehicle every fifteen seconds on the Tapline road, and breakdowns bulldozed aside. I now feel that we have put so much into this that there can be no stopping until it is resolved.

This was for me the heart of the matter: although Norman Schwarzkopf insisted that he would not go to war until all his troops were fully prepared, a sense of inevitability had spread through the Coalition – a feeling that after such a tremendous build-up we could not simply dismantle our forces and go home. We all tacitly assumed that we were going to sort Saddam out, sooner or later, whatever he did. For the time being, to our ever-increasing incredulity, he sat there like a boxer in the ring, with his hands down by his side, waiting to be hit on the chin. What we expected was that he would sock us one as we were still climbing into the ring and unable to respond effectively. We could hardly believe that he would not have a go and it seemed likely that he would choose the Christian festival as a good period in which to catch the infidel forces unawares.

I did manage to give myself a Christmas break of sorts, a few days before the festival. Until then, apart from the odd half day, I had had virtually no time off in ten weeks; but now, on 19 December, I escaped for two days to the small house which served as the British Ambassador's residence in the old Embassy compound at Jeddah and which Alan Munro, with typical generosity, had made available to me. Even there work did not stop, for I had a useful meeting with Alan and Ian Blakeley, who was First Secretary at the Embassy in Kuwait and now had set up a diplomatic out-station with the Kuwaitis-in-exile. Our purpose was to work out how we might develop our role in Kuwait and Saudi Arabia after the liberation: we were anxious that there should be a planned transition from war to peace and that the British should miss no opportunity of maintaining their influence in the area, but should build on the reputation which we had gained for ourselves during the war. We therefore sat down to draft a strategy paper, so that our views could be included in plans already being prepared in the United Kingdom. We were anxious to make sure that we played the biggest possible part in the reconstruction of Kuwait and also in helping the Arabs, when we were asked, to rebuild their forces with the provision of training facilities and equipment.*

Next day, 20 December, brought a wonderfully refreshing change. Thanks to the initiative of Hugh Tunnell, Consul-General in Jeddah, and his wife Margaret, and to the generosity of Mobil Oil, I spent the day aboard the company's seventy-foot motor yacht, which took us out to the barrier reef forty kilometres offshore in the Red Sea.† Together with the Tunnells' two little girls, Camilla and Olivia, we swam, sunbathed and lazed. In a letter home I described the yacht as 'a real gin palace' and so it would have been, had it had any alcohol on board, for it possessed every luxury, including baths, and was driven by an extrovert called Fred from Barry, in South Wales.

'There were servants on board,' I reported, 'and drinks all day (no alcohol) and a superb, slap-up lunch of cold salmon and a delicious chocolate pudding called Mississippi mud pie. The coral is fantastic, better than the Barrier Reef in Australia. We saw a giant stingray, and I chased it!'

That night, back on land, I slept for nine and a half hours and then at lunchtime next day had a further nap of ninety minutes, making eleven hours in all, the greatest luxury imaginable. In between I opened my Christmas presents from home: a volume of Kipling's collected poems from Bridget, a splendid yachting cap from Edward, a compact disc of Beethoven's Choral Symphony from Nicola, and a collection of

---

* Our Christmas conference eventually bore fruit in two ways. First, Peter Sincock did not leave the Middle East when his time at the British Embassy was up, but went into Kuwait to write a report outlining how the country's defences might be rebuilt, and his paper formed the basis of the reconstruction which began early in 1992.
Second, the Department of Trade and Industry sent out a delegation, accompanied by top-level industrialists, within two days of the war ending, to make an assessment of the potential business available in Kuwait.
† Hugh Tunnell later became British Ambassador to Bahrein.

Sixties pop hits from Phillida called 'Golden Favourites', which was designed to cheer me up, but somehow did not quite match my mood. A better bet was the fudge which Phillida herself had made and some expensive chocolates sent by an old friend, Pixie Newnes. These last were especially welcome, not just because I have a weakness for chocolate, but because of the boost it gave to the energy levels of my body, something I had learned in my physically more demanding days with the SAS. All in all, I had a most valuable break: hard as it was to relax immediately, I returned to Riyadh with my batteries well charged up.

This was just as well, for we had a very important visitor. 'Prince Charles arrived safely and was met by the Crown Prince, Prince Abdullah bin Abdul Aziz, then whisked off to 1 Div. Headquarters, where he was briefed,' I told Bridget on 22 December. Earlier, when it had been proposed that the Prince and Princess of Wales should visit the theatre together, I had advised against the idea, for it seemed to me that the presence of the Royal couple at such a dangerous moment would create an unacceptable security risk and that, if we arranged for the Princess to make public appearances among servicemen, it would cause acute difficulties with the Saudis. To my relief, but to the unbounded disappointment of the troops, the idea of the Princess coming had been dropped and soon I had reason to change my view about the value of Prince Charles's visit. Although he looked tired and was suffering pain in his arm, which had been operated on after he had injured it playing polo, he was clearly glad to be in theatre and communicated his enthusiasm to everyone he met. As he had set up the visit at very considerable personal inconvenience and given up what little spare time he had before Christmas, we felt all the more appreciative.

After a first-class briefing from Ian Macfadyen, he visited the port of Jubail and then the Force Maintenance Area, where Martin White gave him a run-down on logistics. Then he flew out into the desert for a picnic lunch with the Queen's Royal Irish Hussars, whose Commanding Officer, Arthur Denaro, he knew well. There, as always, he showed a sure touch with the servicemen. As he was eating a sandwich with one group, he said to a young soldier, 'What sort of a Christmas are you going to have, then? Any chance of turkey?' To which the soldier instantly replied, 'No, sir. We're hoping to go to Iraq.' The Prince loved that. He and Arthur had a fifteen-minute, heart-to-heart talk alone under a camouflage net, discussing possible casualty rates, among other things, and he then asked, unprompted, if he might say a few words to the men. Surrounded by five hundred soldiers sitting or leaning on their tanks, he spoke most movingly about how impressed he was by their morale and training, and how people in England were right behind them. When he wished them Godspeed, he himself had some difficulty bidding Arthur farewell.

After a call on the Scots Dragoon Guards, whose pipers played as he left in the evening light, he flew on to spend the night aboard HMS *Brazen*, whose Captain, Commander James Rapp, had once been a ship-mate of his. Next day he visited the RAF base at Dhahran. Then, after a formal lunch in Riyadh, where, in the absence of the King, he was royally entertained by the Crown Prince, he came to my office, met Norman Schwarzkopf and toured my headquarters before leaving for home. Although short, low-key and fast-paced – he was constantly changing from one uniform into another – his visit did a colossal amount to raise morale. Afterwards, in a long, hand-written letter of appreciation, Christopher Airy told me how much the Prince had enjoyed his trip, how uplifting he had found it, how glad he was to have met 'the indomitable General Schwarzkopf' and what a sense of pride he had felt in the whole British deployment.

On the night of his departure we received information to the effect that the Iraqi ambassadors to Washington, London and Paris were being recalled to Baghdad. The news caused a flutter, even though its implications were ambiguous. Was Saddam preparing to pull out after all? Or was he simply trying to stiffen the sinews of his envoys and reaffirm that there was no question of giving way?

On Christmas Eve I had what I described to Bridget as 'a full and satisfying day'. First I flew to Dhahran in the 125 to meet General Fred Franks, Commander of the US VII Corps, who had just arrived from Germany. My aim was partly to make his acquaintance myself, but also to introduce to him Rupert Smith, who would be working under his command.

Physically, Franks was the exact opposite of Norman Schwarzkopf, being small and quiet, and limping slightly on one artificial leg – the legacy of a severe wound received in Vietnam. But he resembled Norman in being intelligent and likeable. With the Americans still in their dark camouflage uniforms designed for Europe, we met in the Portakabin which was serving as his office and quickly established certain basic principles of Rupert's attachment. I said that, although I guaranteed not to interfere, I must know what the American plans were, to see how they suited British capabilities, and also that I must always have access to Rupert, who would report to me outside the normal chain of command. Franks was entirely cooperative and accepted my proposals without reservation. He then outlined his plans in broad terms and we discussed the problem of how to maintain security: it was going to be at least three weeks before we could move 7th Armoured Brigade to join him and already an article had appeared in the *Sunday Times* speculating that we might be going to transfer our ground troops from the Marines to VII Corps. Our aim was to cover the move by deception, maintaining continuous broadcasts of signal traffic recorded when the Brigade was on exercise. I left Franks and Rupert together, confident that they would like each other and jointly develop a concept of operations which would suit our forces.

My next stop was the RAF Tornado squadron at Tabuk, the airfield in the far north-west where in early days we had had difficulties with the Saudi base commander. Now relations seemed excellent and, as I told Bridget, the men were 'making the best of a pathetic Christmas'. They had put up a few decorations in their overcrowded living accommodation and piled parcels round the centre points in the Portakabins. It was all as cheerful as it could have been, but I did not feel able to wish anyone a happy Christmas, so I just said, 'All the best for tomorrow.' As I told Bridget, '"Merry Christmas" and "Happy New Year" seem out of place and not very sincere or appropriate, when I consider that some of these men may well be dead by the end of January.'

My own programme for Christmas day was as full as I had been able to make it. After a quick breakfast at our house in Riyadh, I set off for the airport and flew in the 125 to Jubail, where Rupert met me and drove me to his Divisional Head-quarters. An hour's briefing there reassured me that he felt able to work with Franks and I went on by car in mid morning to the tented transit accommodation known as Blackadder Lines – another reference to the TV series – in which 4th Armoured Brigade were temporarily living. After a further hour's briefing and conversation with the Brigade Com-mander, Brigadier Christopher Hammerbeck, I flew by heli-copter for a quick visit to the headquarters of 7th Armoured Brigade.

The day's first highlight was lunch with the QRIH at St Patrick's Camp, out in the desert. My schedule promised that I would fly there, but because a sandstorm had blown up, reducing visibility to a hundred yards and grounding all helicopters for the rest of the day, Arthur Denaro himself came to fetch me in the Japanese Toyota Landcruiser recently presented to him by the Saudis, of which he was inordinately proud. To the unbounded delight of my staff, who were fol-lowing in another vehicle, we had gone no more than a couple of hundred yards when we became bogged in soft sand. That little episode finished up with me having to push him out of trouble, and some telling pleasantries were exchanged. Thereafter, I felt able to advise members of his Regiment, no matter what rank they held, that they would do well never to let their Commanding Officer take the wheel again.

I found that Arthur had brought his whole Regiment in for lunch. The tanks were drawn up facing each other in groups of three, with their barrels raised and pointing inwards. From the camouflage nets slung over them hung a mass of decor-ations – cards, ribbons, balloons. Having talked individually to as many men as possible, I helped serve out a full-scale Christmas lunch. It was, as I told Bridget, 'a very spirited performance'. Some of the men sat at tables with their weapons slung about them, the rest on the ground, and we all ate turkey and plum pudding, laced with grit from the sandstorm, which was still blowing, washed down by six hundred bottles of Falkenstein alcohol-free white wine given by Eldridge Pope, the Dorchester firm whose chairman, Christopher Pope, was also an Irish Hussar. To produce such a meal in the middle of nowhere was an amazing achievement on the part of the Army Catering Corps cooks, who in typical British fashion had worked through the previous night to have everything ready. After we had eaten, the whole battalion gathered round and I gave them my Christmas message, such as it was. I reckoned that Arthur had taken some operational risk in bringing in all his men except a few sentries and I told him so, but I also said that I thought he had done the right thing and that the risk had been well worth while for the benefit to morale. The soldiers were extremely cheerful and clearly sparked up by the change in routine.

I would have liked to stay on, but by then, because helicopters were grounded, I was running late and it was a major disappointment to me that I had to cut out a planned visit to the Scots Dragoon Guards. Instead, with dusk already coming on, I made my ninth and last journey of the day, to spend the night with the 1st Battalion of the Royal Staffordshire Regiment and was greeted by their Commanding Officer, Lieutenant Colonel Charles Rogers. They too were thoroughly hospitable and presented me with one of the pottery mugs which manufacturers at home had specially made and sent out to them.

The second high spot of my day came last and unexpectedly. By the time A Company of the Staffords gathered on a sand dune, together with their Commanding Officer, Major Chris Joynson, for me to address them and answer questions, full dark had fallen, so that the men could not see me, nor I them. Instead of a three-star general, I became just a voice in the black desert night. The result was that the men were completely uninhibited. Obviously their own NCOs could identify individuals by their voices, but being invisible gave the soldiers the confidence which springs from anonymity and their questions amazed me by their number and quality.

Out rolled all the usual concerns about length of tours, post, the serviceability of vehicles and so on, but also many intelligent inquiries about Saddam Hussein's intentions and the political situation in the Middle East as a whole, both before and after the conflict. For me, it was the most rewarding question-and-answer session of the campaign.

After it came a film, shown by one of the three excellent mobile projector units sent out by the Services' Sound and Vision Corporation, then supper and a brew of tea cooked in the back of a Warrior, and the chance to talk to many people, among them a platoon of Grenadier Guards, who had been blistered on to the Staffords to make up manpower shortages. The Grenadiers had tremendous pride in their own Regiment, of course, but they had fitted themselves into a strange unit with typical application. One of their non-commissioned officers told me that, far from settling for a second-class job, they were doing things the Brigade of Guards' way, which naturally was better than the Staffords' way and in fact they were showing the Staffords how to carry on!

I did not let on that I was in the middle of a dogged exchange of correspondence with Major General Simon Cooper, who was then commanding the Household Division, and had become much exercised by the need, as he saw it, for guardsmen attached to other units to wear brigade insignia, either in the form of cap badges or as red-and-blue armbands. Simon was an old friend, but I could not find much time or sympathy, at a moment like this, for the Household Division's obsession with sartorial detail. In my last letter I had pointed out that 'the core of cohesion in battle has always lain in group loyalty at brigade and battalion level', and concluded that in the desert the problem of regimental identity was being 'quietly resolved without recourse to formal and distracting action at a time when there are more pressing issues to be getting on with.'

By the time I crawled into my sleeping-bag and lay down on the sand in the lee of a vehicle, I had been on the go for some sixteen hours and I reckoned that very few minutes of that time had been wasted.

*   *   *

'If only I was younger!' I wrote wistfully in a letter begun on Boxing Day. 'Stand-to at 0515 and a walk round the weapon pits as the sun came up. A cold-water shave and a good breakfast cooked by Driver Jones.'

After the storm, the weather was clear and the temperature much like that of a fine spring day in England, cool in the early morning, but warming up as the sun rose. Again, I had many calls to make – on 33 Field Hospital, on the British Forces' Broadcasting Service (where I gave a Press conference and made a broadcast), on HMS *Cardiff*, on the RAF in Bahrein, on 22 Field Hospital – before returning to Riyadh in the evening. Altogether that day I made ten separate journeys, by car, helicopter and 125, and gave six addresses. 'Throughout I put across a straightforward message – no frills and fairly sombre,' I told Bridget. One of my most enjoyable encounters was with Cathy Bland, whom Bridget and I had got to know as a theatre sister in the Falklands. Now I found her with 22 Field Hospital, which was about to move deep into the Saudi desert, though for security reasons I could not tell Cathy where she was going.

Afterwards, I was sorry to miss the carol service held in the open air in Bahrein. Brilliant television engineering linked my Gulf forces live to services in Germany and the United Kingdom, and the result (which I later saw and heard on a video recording) was exceptionally moving. The sight of Trish Austin, reading one of the lessons as she held in her arms her baby girl only two days old, whom the father, in the Gulf, had never seen, left countless watchers in tears.

Back in Riyadh, my Boxing Day was still not at an end, for the Chief of the General Staff, General Sir John Chapple, had arrived on a visit and I talked profitably to him until 0230. Like me, he had felt unable to spend the holiday period relaxing while his men were in the desert and had made the highly creditable effort of coming out. An incident next morning left him in no doubt about the volatile atmosphere in which we were living. At 0830, just as he was arriving at my office, the sirens sounded a Scud alert. The Iraqis had launched a missile and, until we could determine the direction in which it was heading, we had to assume it might be coming for Riyadh. For a moment the CGS seemed taken aback and asked whether this was an exercise. Only when somebody sharply told him, 'No! It's live!' did he struggle into his NBC suit – the first time in history, I daresay, that the most senior officer serving in the British Army had been obliged to do so for real. The launch turned out to be either a test-firing or a demonstration, or both, and the missile flew harmlessly into Iraq's western desert, but it gave us a salutary reminder that Saddam might launch the pre-emptive strike we feared at any moment.

Looking back on the festival that hardly was, I felt upset that I had failed to attend any church service, but glad that I had seen and been seen by so many of our servicemen and women. In leaving my headquarters at such a militarily sensitive time, I had taken a risk, rather as Arthur Denaro had in bringing in his men for lunch. But by then everything was running as I wanted it and I had full confidence in the ability of my colleagues. In Bill Wratten I had a Deputy Commander who I knew would take correct decisions without waiting for me to reappear, should a crisis blow up, and in Ian Macfadyen I had a Chief of Staff whom I could trust completely to handle routine matters. In any case, I could have returned from almost anywhere in theatre within a couple of hours.

'I did the right thing in going into the desert,' I wrote home. 'The expats have been very generous, especially in Riyadh, Dhahran and Jubail, and every soldier in Riyadh who wanted a home had one – but I didn't want to be involved in parties.'

In the event, there were no outbreaks of religious discord and everybody behaved with commendable restraint. The only servicemen who suffered a severe disappointment were some members of the RAF who, hearing that a detachment of Canadian nurses had arrived in theatre, invited them to a Christmas party. The Canadians were delighted to accept but, to the consternation of their hosts, they turned out to be large, hairy and exclusively male. I felt particularly grateful to the selfless professional entertainers who came out to put on shows, not least the magician Paul Daniels and the singer-comedian Sir Harry Secombe. Nobody on board the helicopter which brought Sir Harry ashore after his visit to HMS

Cardiff will ever forget that short flight: suddenly there burst into life the raucous klaxon which warned that hostile radar had locked on to the aircraft. Instantly the pilot dived to wave-top level and began to jink about. Down close to the water, the alarm ceased, but as soon as the pilot climbed, it came on again, and he flew the rest of the trip to Jubail like a stone doing ducks and drakes, with no explanation of what had triggered the alarm system. Discussing the incident afterwards, Sir Harry revealed that he had 'reached the tuneless whistling stage', and when Alan Munro asked him who he thought had been persecuting him, he replied, 'Probably someone who can't stand Songs of Praise'. In a letter of thanks I suggested that the words 'locked on' would 'evoke fond memories in days to come'.

One particularly un-festive event of the Christmas period was our decision to go ahead with immunization against one of the more likely biological agents, even at the risk of provoking a mass-exodus from Riyadh. So many non-British expatriates had already left the city that the operation of essential utilities such as power stations and desalination plants was threatened. (The Brits, in contrast, had stood by their posts and gained special kudos from doing so.) Nevertheless, my view prevailed, that since we had the vaccine, it would be irresponsible for us not to use it, whatever the political and social side-effects might be.

Unpleasant doubts persisted. The authorities had made the injections voluntary, I told Bridget, 'without yet answering essential questions such as those about long-term effects. Have humans had them before? What side-effects are there? We are hoping to keep the matter quiet, but it is bound to leak out in the Press.' (In fact vaccine had been tested by and on veterinary surgeons for more than a decade, without ill effect, but I did not discover this until some days later.)

In spite of these uncertainties, soon after Christmas thousands of doses were administered to volunteers (myself among them) in the British and American forces, boosted by shots of whooping cough to make the vaccine take faster. As predicted, the jabs made me feel extremely ill. I should have gone to bed, but pressure of work made it impossible to do

so and I carried on as best I could. Bill Wratten was alarmed
to see that for the first time ever I could not manage the half
bar of chocolate which he put out for me when I went for
our private review of the operational situation and for a cup
of coffee in his air headquarters.

To the men out in the desert, the jabs were one more cause
of stress. Already they were taking NAPs tablets, designed to
reduce the damaging effects of gas in the event of a chemical
attack. These gave many people diarrhoea and, scarcely less
worrying than the threat of gas – especially to young men –
they were said to contain eighty-five per cent bromide. Then
men were also given the biological vaccination at the same
time against whooping cough, which knocked them out for
twenty-four hours. Then, rumour had it, they were also going
to be immunized against plague, which no one had heard of
since the Dark Ages.

At least, if Saddam attacked with gas, our soldiers would
be better off than the Americans, for we had more NBC suits
per man . . . but all this was more than enough to prey on
the minds of troops with not enough to do.*

Christmas neither began nor ended anything. The atmosphere in Saudi Arabia was exceedingly volatile, as though
one struck match could cause a major explosion. Planning for
war continued inexorably. On 27 December I had a meeting
with Norman Schwarzkopf, trying to sort out differences
between us and the Americans over strategy, rules of engagement and targets.

Again, if Saddam did make a pre-emptive strike with Scud
missiles, under American ROE Norman had authority to
retaliate immediately and attack Iraqi air bases in Phase
One of the air war. Our own rules definitely did not allow
us to do this, so we were faced with the probability that

---

* The fact that we had anti-gas agents available at the right moment demonstrated
the enormous value of the work done over the years by the Chemical Defence
Establishment at Porton Down, on Salisbury Plain. At the same time, it exposed the
folly of the peace protesters who campaign against it. Far from seeking means of
spreading noxious chemicals and diseases, Porton Down devises ways of combating
them. The number of countries which possess a chemical capability is continually
growing and since many of them have unstable and unpredictable regimes, the
importance of the work done at Porton Down can only increase.

we would be stuck in an impossible position. I noted to Paddy:

> Our ROE are out of line with those of the USA. I cannot get ministers to see that war may start at any time and that they must delegate authority to respond if we are attacked. At present we sit and wait while ministers muse. I'm putting the greatest possible pressure on the system and will raise the matter with John Major when he comes out. [The Prime Minister was due to visit the theatre on 6 January.] NS can retaliate fully, so we shall be out of line. Our aircraft smoulder on the ground while the USA get on and win the war.

My frustration was well founded. By the rules that remained in force, the Americans were allowed to take on a bogey (enemy aircraft) if it was making a hostile approach, which might mean that it was still forty kilometres away. We, in contrast, were still not allowed to take action until it locked on to our plane with its weapons radar. By then it might already have launched an air-to-air missile and the time for retaliation would have gone. One morning Chuck Horner said to me, in a matter-of-fact way, 'Look, if your boys can't take on hostile-approach aircraft, I really don't want them up there. We'll deal with things ourselves, because you'll be too late.' The situation was still worse at sea, where we were not allowed to engage enemy aircraft until they were within a few kilometres of a ship.

For day after day the discussion ground on, with Paddy Hine hammering away at the Ministry of Defence to release the ROE we needed and Bill Wratten doing much good work in theatre (it was he who fought the detailed battle, on my behalf). In London ministers seemed astonishingly reluctant to face reality or to understand the predicament we were in. Clearly they were afraid that we might start a war prematurely and nobody could deny that the chances of an explosive incident were high. Every day Iraqi aircraft were flying down towards the border in aggressive mode and turning away to the east just short of the frontier. The Americans were tracking them continuously and directing aircraft to engage them if they came any further south. One mistake by a nervous pilot could have provoked the most devastating consequences. The Coalition air forces were mounting ever-larger combat air patrols twenty-four hours a day, backed by AWACS electronic intelligence-collection and target-identification aircraft, which could vector the fighter bombers on to any bogey appearing on their radar screens. On the ground eighty or ninety more warplanes were standing by fully armed at ten minutes' notice or less. Tanker aircraft were also flying round the clock. As I wrote in a letter home, 'The war here can be in full flow within two hours of *go*, which is all it takes to load up the massive air force.' Later, when I returned to London, I realized that strenuous efforts had been made in the Ministry of Defence to iron out the anomalies between British and American policy on ROE. At the time, however, this was not apparent in theatre and my over-riding concern was that we should be able to react adequately in an emergency.

On the evening of 27 December my mind was taken off ROE for an hour or two by a curious diversion, an invitation to a party given out in the desert by Prince Abdallah bin Faisal. We drove out in the middle of a freezing afternoon to his farm, a real showplace, where a thousand sheep and two hundred camels were beautifully kept. When offered camel milk, I took a cautious sip and found it delicious. Next I helped to select a most handsome sheep, which was promptly slaughtered, hung up, skinned and barbecued. We then adjourned to a scene straight from the Arabian Nights: a log fire blazing in the middle of a tented compound, with camel seats and rugs set out round it, and were served with a sumptuous meal. In writing to thank the Prince afterwards, I was able to say without exaggeration that, as a fellow farmer, I had been particularly struck by the splendid condition of the animals and that the barbecue had been an entirely new experience for me and my fellow officers.

Next morning was *Juma* – Friday, the Arab day off – and I planned to spend it catching up on my mail. But hardly had I sat down to write home when there was a Scud alert, so I struggled into my NBC suit and finished the letter in full gear except for gas-mask. By the time it had been established that the launch was another test firing, half the morning had gone. Already life in Riyadh was becoming jumpy and I was not surprised that many expatriates were sending their families away, either back to the United Kingdom or down to cities such as Jeddah in the far south, out of missile range. Arabs also were starting to leave the city, with the welcome result that traffic had become a great deal thinner.

On 29 December I was still fretting at our lack of progress and my frustration came out in a note which I made that morning:

> The level of ministerial indecision and looking backwards is appalling and desperately time wasting. There is every likelihood that we shall stay behind while the Americans go to war and our ministers dither over their decisions.

We had plenty of problems on the ground as well. On average, one tank power pack could be expected to fail every time the entire fleet moved five kilometres, and we restricted 7th Armoured Brigade's Challengers to fifteen kilometres a week in an attempt to conserve them for war. All our Warrior armoured personnel carriers had to be halted for modifications to their engines, which were ingesting sand in damaging quantities. It seemed incredible that factors such as these could constrain the entire Division more than the logistic problems, formidable though those were, but our vehicles and equipment had not been designed for use in the desert, so problems were only to be expected.

On the last day of 1990 we took Bill Wratten out to dinner, to celebrate his award of a CBE in the New Year Honours. We had an agreeable evening, but nobody felt in particularly festive mood, for we all knew that war was coming, and soon.

CHAPTER 8

SECONDS OUT

The old year went out with a jolt. On 31 December the Syrians announced that they would not take part in offensive operations. That evening, at the weekly multi-national meeting, Norman staged a protest by refusing to attend and detailed his deputy Cal Waller to stand in. The Syrians' action sent shock-waves fluttering through the Coalition, because everyone knew that a weakening of this kind could have a pernicious influence: if one country decided it would not go to war, others might easily do the same. It was not the loss of the Syrians' fighting power that we minded so much as the possibility that their withdrawal might start an irreversible slide.

'This will cause problems and upset all our carefully laid plans,' I wrote home. Fortunately the Syrians did not opt out any further, though they retained their non-combative stance throughout the war and followed up behind the Egyptians, who did all the fighting in their sector, so that Syria's presence was limited to a defensive deployment. But for a few days we and the Americans were nervous that other nations might pull out and the Coalition might start to crumble.

The approach of the 15 January deadline seemed to galvanize the politicians in London. Via Paddy Hine, I was told to pledge our unwavering support to the Americans, which of course I was delighted to do. 'At long last ministers are taking decisions to get things done,' I told Bridget. 'Either John Major has got a grip or there's been an exchange with

Washington at highest political level. Whatever the cause, everything has become more positive.'

It was as if people in England belatedly realized how close we were to war. For months the feeling had persisted that the Coalition forces were doing no more than staging a political demonstration, which in the end would resolve the crisis; now at last the message had got through that we were not in that game any more, but about to fight. All at once messages coming down the chain of command gave us full support: I got the impression that the British Government was extremely keen that there should be no wavering on our part, but that we should remain totally committed to the Coalition and the way the Americans were running it.

This is not to say that anyone in London had yet taken the decisions which we desperately needed on Rules of Engagement. I spent most of 2 January trying to sort them out and I got Air Marshal Kip Kemball, Paddy Hine's Chief of Staff at High Wycombe (an old friend from the Falklands, where he succeeded me as Commander, British Forces), to tell ministers straight that unless they increased the flexibility of our ROE, we would have to withdraw our aircraft from the American and Saudi plans. I wrote home:

> The politicians are ducking and weaving, and trying to avoid the real decisions they are there for. They love section-commander type decisions, like organizing uniforms or deciding on the British Forces' radio. ROE matters, where the future conduct of the war and their own and their Government's position could be in question, they avoid if at all possible.

That same day, 2 January, I got another unwelcome surprise when I heard on the news that in England Wing Commander David Farquhar, Paddy Hine's Personal Staff Officer, had lost secret documents and a lap-top computer containing an outline version of the American war plan. It was all the more of a shock that this information came not through official channels, but over the BBC. The implications of the loss were unnerving, to say the least: it seemed that our whole plan might have been compromised and Coalition lives put at risk.

At the first possible moment I telephoned Paddy to find out what had happened. He told me that on 17 December, soon after his own return from Riyadh, he and his PSO had gone to London with Mike Wilkes to brief the Prime Minister on the plan. Afterwards they had separated and Farquhar had set off with the documents and computer in the direction of High Wycombe. On the way, at Acton, in West London, apparently acting on impulse, he had asked his driver to stop so that he could look at a car in a second-hand showroom. Before leaving his own blue Vauxhall, he transferred the computer and briefcase to the boot, locking them in. Evidently an opportunist thief saw him do that, for when Farquhar and his driver returned after a few minutes, the boot had been forced and both were gone.

In the briefcase, apart from documents, was £1000 in cash, which Farquhar had drawn from an imprest account. Naturally the thief pocketed this. Neither the papers nor the briefcase appealed to him, however, so he threw them away into a rubbish skip in the car park of a supermarket, close to where he had seized them, but he kept the computer, as it was obviously of value. Within minutes the papers were found by a doctor. Having once been in the Services, he saw what the documents were and handed them in to the police. A check showed that all but four sheets were present and the missing pages, which had blown away on the wind, were recovered in the next two hours. That same evening, therefore, all the papers were back in safe hands and the circumstances of their return made it clear that they had not been copied. (Fortunately Mike Wilkes had himself retained papers relating to the ground campaign, so that part of the plan was never at risk.)

The computer, however, was missing. Next day in the Ministry of Defence Paddy had what he described as 'an agonizing discussion' with the Chief of the Defence Staff and the Secretary of State. It seemed highly improbable that the thief himself could be an Iraqi agent, but there was every chance that he might realize the value of the information on which he had stumbled and try to sell it in high places. The *ad hoc* committee did inform the Prime Minister and, because the

Press had got wind of the incident, a D-notice was slapped on it to prevent any mention of it in the newspapers, but just after Christmas the story was blown by the *Irish Times*, which was not subject to British rules.

By then experts had sifted through the evidence on what information there might or might not have been in the computer. Farquhar was confident that he had erased the highly sensitive outline plan of how the air and ground war would be fought, but specialists familiar with that particular piece of equipment concluded that he probably had not been able to remove it all and that anyone who really knew how to access the computer might be able to extract what remained from deep in its memory. The experts were split over the issue and, although it seemed unlikely that the basis of the brief had still been present in the memory, doubts remained.

This news put me in a devilishly awkward position. What was I to tell Norman Schwarzkopf? If I said nothing, he would certainly hear about the theft from somewhere else. I suggested that as the matter was of such crucial importance, Paddy himself should fly out to brief the CinC personally and this he agreed to do. At the same time, the Vice Chief of the Defence Staff, General Sir Richard Vincent, flew to Washington to brief Colin Powell, so dangerous did the whole incident seem and so potentially destructive of Anglo-American relations.

While Paddy was on his way, I broke the bad news to the CinC and apologized. Norman seemed fairly relaxed, but I was anxious that the confidence which had built up between us might be undermined by this piece of gross negligence, and that the Americans might not go on trusting us with classified information. My embarrassment came out clearly in a jumpy letter home:

Now NS and Prince Khalid want details which I don't possess, so I have to give a wet 'Don't know'. Are the plans compromised to the point where lives are at risk? What was in the package? I don't know. Major loss of confidence all round, and Brits look stupid. I have told UK that Paddy should come out and explain it all, and he is on the plane tonight.

Cock-up No. 2 is when I'm told to tell NS we are with him

all the way, whatever happens, and he finds out Brit ministers
will not delegate ROE for me to release aircraft for rapid
response to a pre-emptive Iraqi strike. More egg on British
face . . .'

Prince Khalid was justifiably upset over the loss of the computer and over the fact that he learnt of it in a roundabout
fashion. What concerned him particularly was the fact that
Iraqi troops had just started to move again, further strength-
ening the right flank of their defences. Was this a coincidence
or was it a response to information gleaned from the
computer?

Again I found myself apologizing and doing my best to give
reassurance, undermined by the knowledge that I was not
sure of my ground and by the nasty feeling that there might
somehow be a connection between the theft and the Iraqi
reinforcements. Khalid accepted my reassurances, but in general he was more apprehensive than I had ever seen him and
he talked over the situation at length. He was most anxious
that the air attack should be unleashed on the sixteenth, the
moment the United Nations deadline expired, but he was
also looking further ahead and was worried about the future
internal security of the kingdom. He wanted to be sure that
the Americans and British would leave Saudi Arabia as soon
as the war was over and he accepted that the Saudi forces
would have to be rebuilt, possibly with overseas advice and
training. The long-term menace of Saddam Hussein was much
on his mind and I came away from the meeting convinced
that, whatever else happened, we must destroy Iraq's nuclear,
chemical and biological capability while we had the chance.

In the middle of this turmoil King Fahd suddenly
announced that he wished to demonstrate the political
cohesion of the Allies by conducting a review of the Coalition
forces out in the desert near the border. Whether or not this
idea came in response to the Syrian move, the Americans had
some initial reservations about diverting troops to a multi-
national parade. What were we, the British, to do? We were
anxious not to offend the Saudis, but we were also aware of
US feelings.

After I had discussed the matter with Alan Munro, he and I both referred back to London on our separate nets for directions. Whitehall took a relaxed view and said that if we wanted to be involved, we should go ahead. I decided that it would be churlish to stand down and so set in motion the business of collecting together a hundred representative men and arranging their transport to the airfield at King Khalid Military City, three hundred kilometres out in the desert, north-west of Jubail.

The parade, held on 4 January, was an extraordinary event, never to be forgotten by those who took part. It was a motley crew that we assembled, including men taken from RAF ground crews, the Royal Army Ordnance Corps, the Royal Engineers, the cavalry and even two token naval officers. A group of bandsmen, conscripted for the day from various units, had hastily laid aside their medical-orderly gear and shaken the sand out of their instruments to provide some music. I described the scene in a letter home:

Today we set off into the blue for Hafar al Batin. We had not been able to find out the exact time or location, so I with a hundred servicemen arrived at King Khalid Military City. There we were met by a very nice Saudi brigadier general and for one hour we drove out to a piece of open space with nothing in sight except a couple of tents for VIPs and a long line of posts saying 'Brits', 'Czechs', etc. There were seventeen nations on parade, which must have been unique.

Our contingent, with a large Union Jack and a desert rat flag, went on parade at 1030 and stood there till 1250. The band played gallantly throughout and, as they launched into traditional marching tunes like 'Rule Britannia', great applause went rippling down the polyglot ranks. The Americans, having declined to join us, were holding their own parade a short distance away, but NS and I sat together as we waited. At last, after a number of dignitaries had arrived, a cavalcade of about twenty cars swept up, with King Fahd in one. He drove past the soldiers, Americans first, and then there were speeches lasting one and a quarter hours, all in Arabic, about the importance of keeping the Coalition together.

Afterwards we adjourned for lunch and all our one hundred

servicemen were invited to a giant fuddle.* They arrived late,
having got lost, at this lunch spot in another piece of desert:
a vast tent and carpets sinking into the sand with the weight
of food, whole roast goat, lamb, fish, rice of many kinds, *khubs*
(bread) and such. As in all Arab meals, people got up and left
as soon as they had eaten, so some of the senior guests had
already left and, with typical Arab classlessness, our men were
waved to the empty places, irrespective of who they were.
REME craftsmen and Ordnance Corps privates sat next to ministers and three-star generals at the King's carpet, some within
one place of the King himself. I sat next to NS, opposite the
Crown Prince and we had the whale of a feast.

Whether or not the parade did anything to cement the
Coalition together at that difficult moment, I cannot say, but
certainly no more cracks appeared and everyone pressed
ahead with the business of preparing for war. At the top of
my own agenda was the visit by John Major, due in theatre
on 6 January. When asked what he should talk about to
the servicemen and women, I sent back the message that all
the regiments in the Gulf were desperately anxious about the
Government's White Paper, 'Options for Change', which had
proposed far-reaching defence cuts. Men were worried that
when they arrived home after the war, they would find that
their regiment had disappeared, amalgamated with others. I
advised that the Prime Minister should be very positive and
that he should not try to prevaricate, as people would not like
it if they felt they were being given half truths.

On 5 January I met Michael Weston, the British Ambassador to Kuwait, who had gallantly held out in the Embassy
long after Saddam Hussein's troops had seized the city, before
eventually leaving, with Iraqi permission, via Baghdad.†
Since then he had been living in Geneva (where his wife

---

* A corruption of the Arab invitation to a meal *ta-fadhal*, meaning 'be my guest'. The
word has passed into the British Army use to mean a meeting in which the participants
huddle round in a circle, sitting or squatting on the ground.
† By the end he and the few remaining members of his staff were down to their last
half-hundredweight of rice, besides some tuna fish and tasteless chicken sausages. They
had, however, found a useful supply of water for washing and so on by digging down
beneath the Embassy compound. Their excavations began as a grave for an old lady
who, they feared, was about to die; but when they heard that the American diplomats
had struck water at a depth of twelve feet, they carried on digging and did the same.

worked with the Disarmament Commission), and now he had come out to meet John Major, who was going to visit the Kuwaiti Government in exile. Michael still looked thin and drawn after his ordeal, but we had an enjoyable time swapping notes on the rescue plans which we had put in hand, in case things had become really unpleasant. (We had plotted a joint Anglo-American operation, in which helicopters would sweep in from the sea and lift out the remaining members of our two missions.) Now we began to discuss ways of reoccupying the British Embassy as soon as possible after hostilities had ceased and of organizing future British representation in Kuwait.

It was by no means an ideal moment for the Prime Minister to arrive. As I wrote home,

> There's a tension building up which is coming through in small ways and individual, personal relations, and there is a requirement for everything to be done by yesterday. We are moving on to a higher state of alert, as there is intelligence that terrorists may be planning to attack. Embassies are particularly at threat and I'm having to have special arrangements made to look after them.

In spite of the all-round anxiety, John Major's first visit to the Gulf was eagerly awaited, both by members of the British forces and by the Saudis, none of whom had ever set eyes on the new Prime Minister. The shock and astonishment which had greeted Mrs Thatcher's deposition six weeks earlier had given way to frank curiosity about her successor and on the morning of 6 January he arrived to a five-star welcome: band, guard of honour and all the Saudi Council Ministers, from the Crown Prince and Prince Sultan downwards, lined up to greet him on the tarmac at King Khalid International Airport. When the ceremonial introductions had been completed, we drove off to the British Embassy, where Alan Munro had arranged an excellent buffet lunch in his private garden. Moving around freely, Major met members of the British expatriate community and then, in an admirable short address, told them how much people in the United Kingdom respected them for sticking to their posts. All round us were reminders that war was imminent: as we drove into the Embassy courtyard, we passed tables laden with gas-masks being issued to British civilians and a specially detailed soldier kept the Prime Minister's chemical warfare kit close to him all the time.

'Quiet, sincere and interested in people,' I reported to Bridget, and I had no cause to change this, my immediate impression of John Major. I soon saw that he was very much his own man and that he had come out on his own initiative. Soon after his takeover, word had reached us that he planned to concentrate on Europe and that his other commitments would prevent him from visiting the theatre. Clearly, developments had changed his mind.

After lunch, he and I drove alone to my headquarters. On the way he said he wanted to know 'the truth' about how things were going and I did my best to tell him. We discussed the nightmare of the lost documents and he seemed confident that no damage had been done. I told him that in general all was well, except that I doubted if our initial air attack could prove as successful as we hoped in reducing the ability of the Iraqi army to fight. I explained that, according to the traditional theory of battle, one needed a three-to-one numerical superiority to be sure of victory. Here we had, at best, one-to-one parity and so were going to rely heavily on what the air forces could do to lower the enemy's capability on the ground before our land forces went in. Our aim was to reduce Saddam's fighting power by up to fifty per cent, but I wondered if that could ever be achieved and, if it were not, how well the Iraqis would fight. In short, I warned the Prime Minister that in my view the answers to these questions would decide whether or not we were in for a difficult and bloody battle.

As we went into my headquarters, groups of American men and women who were on sentry duty and had got wind of the official visit, waylaid us with snapping cameras and cries of 'Hi! Prime Minister!' Major's response was to shake hands and chat to them in the friendliest fashion. There followed a detailed discussion between the Prime Minister, myself, Bill Wratten and Ian Macfadyen, and an excellent briefing on the plan from Tim Sulivan. Putting himself in Saddam's place, Major asked, 'What pre-emptive action might I take? How could I fight if I'd lost all my air support?' I discussed the alternatives open to the Iraqi dictator and emphasized the need for the Coalition to launch the air assault as soon as possible: otherwise Saddam might begin a token withdrawal, unsettle the allies politically and undermine their will to fight. But since our land forces would not be ready until well into February, the air war would have to continue for several weeks. Would British and American politicians stand the moral strain, I wondered, if allied aircraft hammered Iraq day after day, night after night?

Major quickly took everything in and made a real effort to understand our ideas and feelings about the war. Then he asked me to clear the room. With everyone except his Private Secretary gone, he said, 'Peter, I can tell you, although you're not to pass it on, that we'll probably go in on the fifteenth or the sixteenth.'

I was surprised to find that, ten days before the event, he had such a clear idea of when the war would start. Evidently he and President Bush had been in close touch. The news came as a relief to me and took a heavy weight off my mind: from that moment I could plan with certainty in the knowledge that we were going to attack, no matter what last-minute manoeuvres Saddam Hussein might attempt.

Next Major toured the headquarter cells, talking to individual servicemen and women – something at which he excelled. Everyone responded enthusiastically and he got a strong impression of their morale. Then we collected all the staff in a large room downstairs so that he could address them on the importance of their work and tell them how grateful people in the United Kingdom were for what they were doing.

Again he spoke well, but this time his talk ended abruptly and in chaos, for word suddenly came that the King would see him at once. Bundling into cars, we set off in a cavalcade for the palace, where, instead of being subjected to the usual interminable wait, he, Alan and I were ushered straight into the Royal presence.

King Fahd was thoroughly affable. Flanked by Prince Sultan and other senior members of his family, he greeted the Prime Minister warmly and ushered him to the armchair for the principal guest, at his own right hand. He then launched into a closely reasoned assessment of the present position and how it had come about. Speaking clearly and well, with some emotion, leaving pauses for his interpreter, he summed up his views of the political situation in the Middle East and his personal gratitude at the way the West had come to his aid, as well as his particular indebtedness to Great Britain. He asked especially that his regards should be conveyed to Mrs Thatcher and that she should be invited to call on him if ever she found herself in the Middle East.

After forty minutes or so, a strange event occurred. A door opened and in came a senior member of the royal household, who hurried over to Prince Sultan and whispered in his ear. The Prince, contrary to all precedent, stood up, went across and himself whispered something to the King. Evidently red-hot news had arrived. A few minutes later, Sultan told us in English that frontier radars had detected four helicopters coming in low over the eastern sector of the border with Iraq. Either this was an attack or else some of Saddam's senior officers were defecting.

Sultan hurried from the room and the King continued. The Prime Minister then opened up a useful discussion about the Host Nation Agreement, whereby the Saudis were to pay for the fuel, water, vehicles, food and accommodation which our forces were using in their country. So well did the exchange of views go that the King promised to sign our agreement, but all the time my mind was racing with the possibility that Iraqi generals had begun to abandon ship – something which we had been half expecting for weeks.

After an absence of twenty minutes, Prince Sultan returned to say that there was no further information on the cross-border flight and in due course our audience broke up with the usual exchange of civilities. In spite of repeated inquiries, we never found out the truth about those mysterious heli-copters. They were real enough for the Saudis to send a C-130 Hercules transport plane out to an airfield in the desert to collect whatever passengers had arrived and for many days we too thought that important refugees had come across or that the aircraft had been shot down. It seemed that, with their characteristic caution, the Saudis were keeping quiet about the incident and that, if we had not happened to be talking to the King when it occurred, we would never have heard about it. Later I came to believe that the radar report was inaccurate and that the helicopters were no more than phantoms of some tired operator's imagination, but at the time the story caused a flutter of excitement. When it reached Norman Schwarzkopf, he went ballistic at the idea that any enemy aircraft could have penetrated Saudi airspace at such a critical moment without news of it reaching him instantaneously.

Next morning the Prime Minister and I flew to Jubail together and had another long discussion on board the aircraft. This was the first leg of an immensely full programme of visits to the troops, which we had refined again and again to make sure that he obtained every ounce of benefit from his stay. He went deep into the desert, drove a Challenger, and flew by helicopter to HMS *London* out in the Gulf, where Chris Craig laid on a superb show of strength. The ships of the Task Group had just finished 'Deep Heat', a major work-up exercise which took the form of evacuation of personnel under multi-threat of attack. From the roof of the bridge we watched our ships steam past in line-ahead on either side of us, a rare and thrilling sight. Then a party of Royal Marines came hurtling down a rope from a hovering helicopter and put a dozen men on the deck within ten seconds in the high-speed manoeuvre which they had specially developed for boarding ships suspected of breaking the embargo – another impressive spectacle. Later Major made visits to RAF units and again won an enormous amount of respect through his readiness to mingle with all ranks, sign autographs and exchange banter.

Nothing better epitomized his touch with ordinary servicemen than an incident in the port at Jubail. Because his schedule was so tight, he sent word ahead asking if he could be excused any formal lunch and have a sandwich instead. Martin White made suitable arrangements and in due course one of the cooks produced a large platter, covered by grease-proof paper. Just as the Prime Minister was about to arrive,

Martin's Chief of Staff removed the greaseproof paper and to his horror saw a letter stuffed down among the sandwiches.

'By God!' he said. 'The cook's had the nerve to complain direct to the Prime Minister. What shall we do?'

'Open the envelope,' said Martin, expecting that he would have to destroy the note and reprimand the writer. However, the note turned out not to be a complaint, but a *cri de coeur* from one Chelsea supporter to another, begging John Major, now that he was at Number 10, to sort out the chaos at the team's ground, Stamford Bridge.

'What do we do now?' asked the Chief of Staff.

'Give it to the Prime Minister,' Martin told him. So they did and the Prime Minister, though in the middle of the most hectic tour and beset by new faces on every side, sat down and wrote the cook a full-page answer in his own hand, not only thanking him for his delicious sandwiches, but promising to do what he could to put matters right at the Chelsea ground.

Later I wrote to Bridget:

> This was one of JM's first visits to any military formation and he crammed a year's worth of visits into a day. He spoke very well and sincerely to the servicemen, with no prevarication, and said we go to war if Saddam does not get out. He realized that what they wanted was a straight answer and there's nobody better at giving one. That's what he gave people and it pleased them. Having started the day uncertain of what sort of reception he would get, he soon found he was among friends and gained confidence by the minute. I believe it's been of great value to him, as well as to us.

The passage of time has confirmed that instant verdict. The visit was unique. Here was a Prime Minister, within a few days of taking office, at close quarters with all three Services in the run-up to full-scale war, seeing them stretched to their limits and at their very best, so that he got an indelible impression of their organization, their capabilities and their qualities as people. The effect of the visit was first class, in every way: a potent morale-booster for the troops, but the same also for John Major himself. He soon realized, it seemed to me, that servicemen are quite different from a politician's normal con-

stituents: a disciplined, high-grade group of people, both intel-
lectually and in terms of manners, loyalty and their place in
society. I think he was agreeably surprised by the complete
absence of hostility and by the degree of friendship which he
found, in the desert, at sea and on the air bases.

His own performance was extremely impressive. He came
over as someone totally committed to the servicemen. With
good, plain talk, rather than high rhetoric, he put across the
message that in the United Kingdom fifty million people were
behind them and he fired them up to do the job of evicting
Saddam as best they could. Not many official visitors provoke
the members of a REME workshop to throw their caps in the
air and cheer. John Major did and nobody forgot it.

Unbelievable as it seemed, we could still not obtain clearance for the extra troops which we needed to handle prisoners-of-war and guard our lines of supply, which were going
to become very extended. (London, I later learned, was looking to other nations for contributions for troops who would
not be involved in offensive action, but I did not know this
at the time.) We made it clear that we expected to take very
large numbers of prisoners and we had asked for another
whole infantry battalion to do the essential job of marshalling
and guarding them. Without further reinforcements, we
should have to take front-line men away from the Division,
which was barely up to strength in any case, and clearly
that was not acceptable. In addition, Simon Cooper was still
protesting from London about my failure to insist that Guardsmen attached to other units should wear red-and-blue armbands: his fourth letter on the subject had just arrived, but I
am afraid that in the run-up to war I did not feel inclined to
devote much time to the subject.

Of far greater importance to me was the need to devise a
worthwhile role for our Special Forces. At first Norman
Schwarzkopf had opposed the idea of deploying them behind
enemy lines, on the grounds that there was no task which
could not be carried out by the Allies' overwhelming air power
or, later, by the conventional armoured forces. I myself was not
prepared to recommend special operations unless two conditions were fulfilled: one was that there must be a real, worth-

while role for the SAS to perform, and the other that we must have some means of extricating our men in an emergency.

By the second week in January, however, I had identified what did seem to be a worthwhile role for the SAS in the western desert of Iraq. Their task would be to cut roads and create diversions which would draw Iraqi forces away from the main front and sow fears in the mind of the enemy that some major operation was brewing on his right flank. At the back of my own mind was the idea that the SAS might also be able to take out mobile Scud missile launchers, of which we knew the Iraqis had a considerable number, but at that stage the vital necessity of such a task had not yet become apparent and I regarded it merely as an extra possibility.

We finally persuaded Norman to accept our plans by means of a presentation carried out by the SAS themselves. They had spent many hours working up a clear, concise case for deployment and they presented it so graphically with maps and diagrams that Norman was won over. Feeling that the SAS really had something to offer the Coalition cause, he gave us the go-ahead. I proposed that we should keep him personally briefed on how things were going, in case some operation developed which he might wish to curtail and he accepted this suggestion also.

So the SAS were at last in business and they went off to make final preparations in the few days available to them, for they would have to cross the border right at the beginning of the air war, not when the Allied ground forces went in. Meanwhile, the burning question of Rules of Engagement had still not been settled. Paddy Hine had made some progress in reaching agreement with the Americans, but Whitehall still had not released the full, offensive ROEs which we needed and events suddenly brought the issue to crisis-pitch on 10 January. That day was so fraught and full of incident that I recorded an account of 'A Field Day':

0815   Brief Commander-in-Chief, BAOR, Commander,
       1 Corps, and Air Officer Commanding BAOR, and take
       questions. They are lost for words at the enormity of
       the operation.

0945   Yellow air alert [enemy aircraft approaching].

1000   Talking to Commander, 1 Div [Rupert Smith].
Further yellow air alert. Hostile aircraft (four)
headed down Gulf where *Gloucester* is at about 27'
40" north.

1015   Eight enemy aircraft approaching *Gloucester* in attack
profile. SNOME requests authority to fire weapons
against attacking aircraft at sixty kilometres. I check,
find I have that authority, and delegate it.

1030   Secretary of State's office in panic call from London.
What's going on? Explain. Further panic. Secretary of
State is fuming. Secretary of State is at home and
wants flash explanation, etc., etc. 'Speed of your reply
will lead to his judgment on your competence.' Staff
work up reply. I refuse to hurry, as reply must be
accurate. More abuse from Secretary of State's office.
I confirm I will reply only when I have accurate facts.

1130   Briefing on logistic transport to complete move of
Division. I find that major faults in previous briefing
could lead to critical delay in deployment. I'm very
angry. This was poorly briefed and I was not told of it
earlier.

1200   Senior officer put on official warning, as this is the
second time he has got it wrong. I hope he will now
get it right.

1300   Major leak of key information on British intentions
hits US Press. Sort out our line on it.

1600   Reply to UK on ROE incident.

1800   Fly to Dhahran to host Press supper. Eighty reporters
there. Brief them on our role, then ask for questions.
There are none! Must be unique situation when no
questions asked at Press conference. Have congenial
supper and return home – fifty minutes' flying.

Some of those terse notes need amplification. At 1015 I was
in the middle of a meeting in my headquarters when the
Senior Naval Officer, Captain John Cartwright, burst in with
the news that enemy aircraft were heading for HMS *Gloucester*
and that SNOME urgently needed permission to engage them.

When I asked how long I had got to take a decision, the answer was, 'Thirty seconds'. So I took it instantly, authorizing Chris Craig to defend himself with all the weapons he had. To have delayed at all would have been to invite disaster. In the event, the Iraqi aircraft turned away, but we did not know that they were going to. This could well have been the pre-emptive strike which we had been expecting for some time. As Chris said later, *Gloucester* was 'naked in the arena'. Yet still the Secretary of State kept demanding an explanation.

The leak of information at 1300 by an American blew a dangerous breach in our deception plan. A US Army captain told a group of American reporters that the British Division was about to move from east to west, confirming Press speculation to this effect. As I remarked to Bridget, 'This puts us and the US on a fifteen-all basis in terms of security bloomers', but for the moment there was nothing we could do except remain silent on the issue and hope that the Iraqis would be unable to distinguish solid information from rumours.

The Press conference at 1800 in Dhahran took place at the Intercontinental Hotel. What I knew and the journalists did not, as they collected round me in an informal group near the swimming pool, was that this would be my final briefing to them before war started – although they must have guessed from the tone of my remarks that hostilities were imminent.

I began by saying that we, the military, felt it our duty to protect journalists and we were anxious that as few of them as possible should become casualties. I also made the point that we were all British and that we must all put Britain first: we in the Services were doing it by laying our lives on the line and it was not going to help the cause if reporters started trying to earn a quick buck or two by running stories which put servicemen's security at risk. I said that we would do our best to give journalists safe passage, to look after them in the battlefield once shooting started and to help them send their stories back to the United Kingdom; but in return I asked for their full cooperation. I pointed out that we all had jobs to do. Theirs were quite different from ours and their constant need to find stories to some extent put them in conflict with us. But war was a serious business, involving people's lives, and therefore security must come first.

All this took about fifteen minutes to put over. I then asked for questions and to my amazement there was dead silence. Never before had I known journalists find nothing to say. It seemed that my remarks had brought home to them the unpleasantness of what was about to happen. Already they had been issued with NBC suits, but now they suddenly realized that this was not going to be just another little counter-terrorist punch-up, with a bit of shooting going on over their heads in the street. Instead, they saw that they were going to be in the middle of an all-out war, possibly with weapons of mass-destruction being used, and casualties to match.

Our method of dealing with journalists during the war was to create five Media Reporting Teams (MRTs), consisting in all of one hundred and eighty reporters and technicians – and great was the in-theatre skirmishing when the Ministry of Defence insisted that editors should nominate the men and women to be included, rather than leave us with the invidious job of making the choice. It was symptomatic of the pace at which we were working that, after a packed schedule, I thought nothing of flying to Dhahran and back, some six hundred kilometres each way, to host the Press supper.

Next evening, 11 January, I had a long private meeting with Norman Schwarzkopf, who took me fully into his confidence and unfolded in detail the way he hoped events were going to develop. He was very frank about the conflicting pressures under which he found himself working. On the one hand, he and his generals were well aware of the need to avoid delaying the air war once the political search for peace had been exhausted, and to forestall any chance of Saddam Hussein making further attempts to drive wedges between members of the Coalition. President Bush, he said, was determined to go in early, as was James Baker, and although the Senate was still questioning the need for offensive action, the House of Representatives was all in favour. On the other hand, the US Army was nothing like ready for the land assault and could not be in position to launch an attack for another month at the earliest. This meant that the air war was going to have to run for several weeks and, even if it had to start early for political reasons, it would have to continue until he was ready on the ground. On this point he was adamant: nothing would induce him to start the land war until he was fully prepared. 'Peter,' he said, 'if there's one matter I'll resign on, this is it. If they don't give me the time I need, I'll quit.'

He foresaw four clear phases of the air war. In the first, the primary aim would be to suppress and if possible ground the enemy's air force by bombing runways and knocking out vital air-defence installations such as radars and command centres, so that even if Iraqi planes did take off, they could not be effectively controlled. In this process the RAF would play a key role, since our JP233 bomb had been developed specifically for cratering runways. Another aim of Phase One would be to destroy Scud launching sites. In Phase Two, we would strike at Saddam's capability to produce and launch other weapons of mass destruction, including his nuclear, chemical and biological facilities. In Phase Three we would sever logistic routes, cutting roads and bridges so that the Iraqi forward troops were deprived of essential supplies. In Phase Four, known as 'preparation of the battlefield', we would demoralize and disrupt the forward troops by day and night bombardment, the aim being to reduce the enemy's combat effectiveness by up to fifty per cent. Norman was adamant that the allied air forces should achieve very high attrition before the ground assault went in. The four phases were never designed to be clear cut and distinct from each other and, although one of them would always predominate at any given time, one or two others might run concurrently with it.

The last few days before war broke out were exceedingly tense and many problems remained to be sorted out. One was our Memorandum of Understanding with the Kuwaitis, which, in spite of repeated efforts, we had failed to persuade them to sign. Norman Abbot, my quite excellent civilian Command Secretary, came up with draft after draft, but we could not secure any formal agreement about how the Kuwaitis should recompense us for our efforts to rescue their country.

To my intense relief, the last of our official visitors left for

Presentation of the Legion of Merit by
US President George Bush to the author at
10 Downing Street, London, in the
presence of (*left to right*) Norma Major;
Barbara Bush; John Major, Prime Minister
of the UK; and Bridget de la Billière

Above: HE General Sheikh Jaber Al Khalid Al Sabah, Head of the Kuwait Armed Forces (*left*) together with Sheikh Ali Al Sabah Al Salim Al Sabah, Kuwait Minister of Defence, in discussion with the author

Above: HE General Sheikh Jaber Al Khalid Al Sabah honours the author with a medal after the conclusion of the fighting

Right: Victory in sight: a Kuwait liaison officer celebrates in my headquarters

Left: HE Sheikh Jaber Al Khalid Al Sabah in conversation with the author at the Safwan ceasefire talks

Below: The author with Kuwait liaison officers who worked in his headquarters during the war

Right: HRH Prince Khalid bin Sultan has a quick word with the author during a tense moment at the Safwan talks

Left: The author receives the Order of Abdul Aziz, Second Class, from HE Nasser Al Manqour, the Saudi Ambassador to the UK, at the Royal Saudi Embassy, London

Left: HRH Prince Khalid bin Sultan
with General Norman Schwarzkopf
immediately after the Safwan ceasefire talks

Below: The author with (*left to right*) HE
Nasser Al Manqour, Saudi Arabian
Ambassador to the UK; Major General
Rupert Smith, British Divisional
Commander; and Colonel A. Al Bassam,
Saudi Arabian Defence Attaché; after
receiving the Order of Abdul Aziz

Above: HH Sheikh Zayed bin Sultan Al Nahyan, President of the UAE and Ruler of Abu Dhabi, reviews Gulf defence arrangements with the author

Below: HH Sheikh Mohammed bin Rashid Al Maktoum, UAE Minister of Defence, with the author in Dubai

Above: His Majesty Sultan Qaboos bin Said
Al Said with the author and HE Sir Terence
Clark, British Ambassador to the Sultanate
of Oman

Below: HE Graham Burton, British
Ambassador to the UAE, with the author
and Doctor General Mohammed Saeed Al
Badi, Chief of Staff, UAE Armed Forces

Right: The author discusses the post-war situation with HH Sheikh Isa bin Sulman Al Khalifa, Emir of Bahrein

Left: HH Sheikh Hamad bin Isa Al Khalifa, Crown Prince and Commander-in-Chief of the Bahrein Defence Force, with the author at sundown in Bahrein

Below: HE Graham Boyce, British Ambassador to Qatar (*second from right*), with the author and guests at the British Embassy in Doha

home on 11 and 12 January. Much as we enjoyed seeing them, they were a severe drain on me and my staff, for every one had to be met at the airport by some suitable officer, found accommodation and transport – cars, planes, helicopters – briefed on the latest situation and escorted about. I had established that no outsiders would be allowed into theatre from the twelfth until after the war had ended, whenever that might be, so now we had a welcome respite.

I spent 12 and 13 January visiting Air Force and Army units. The weather turned very cold and heavy rain was falling over the desert: to be soaked and chilled to the bone made me feel that I was back in England. I saw all RAF commanders and Army officers down to lieutenant colonel and found them in very good fettle – confident, determined and very much aware of the dangers of their situation.

There was a fascinating contrast between the maturity of 7th Armoured Brigade, who had been in theatre for three months, and the new-boy look of 4th Armoured Brigade, who had only just arrived. '7 Brigade are fit, brown, lean and confident,' I told Bridget, 'while 4 Brigade are keen, bright-eyed and much less sure of themselves.' As I moved from one unit to another and saw the cream of the British Army preparing for its biggest conflict since the Second World War, I found it increasingly unbelievable that at home the Options for Change defence cuts were going ahead.

At the last minute Tom King had begun trying to make arrangements to talk direct to Rupert Smith, over the chain of command. I took immediate steps to reassert correct procedures. Little did the Secretary of State know that I myself was having serious difficulties keeping in touch with my divisional commander: our equipment, not being designed to work over such great distances, was barely adequate for the task and the last thing we wanted was politicians trying to come in on the net from overseas.

During the morning of Tuesday, 15 January, I wrote in my own hand to the Chief of the Defence Staff thanking him for a note of good wishes which he had sent a few days earlier. 'In general we are well poised, prepared and ready to go,' I reported. Certainly the officers and men are determined and ready: they have no false illusions of glamour or adventure, but there is a dogged professional sense of purpose to do the task and do it well.' I went on to say that I was very conscious of the unstinting support which we had received from home, 'particularly from those commanders who have had to send their cherished and well-trained assets out here, and their unselfish support is something I shall always remember when I look back on the operation'. In conclusion, I wrote that, as we came up to the starting line, 'We as a nation have done our best. Out here we in the Services have all we need and now it is up to us to use it wisely, and to make it work. We shall.'

At 2215 that evening I was in the middle of my routine of telephoning Paddy Hine and having a quick bite of supper, when a call came from my headquarters to say that Norman Schwarzkopf wanted to see me immediately. I had left him only a couple of hours earlier, at his routine component commanders' briefing, known as 'Evening Prayers', and this late-night summons could mean only one thing: that he was going to tell me precisely when the air war would start.

My driver, Sergeant Alan Cain, was living in another house in the same compound, along with my team of bodyguards, so we were on our way within a couple of minutes in two identical, unmarked blue Mercedes, one bodyguard in the front of mine, beside Alan, and two in the second car. As always, I threw a civilian jacket over the top of my wriggly pattern uniform and kept my beret in my hand, so as to look as unobtrusive as possible. Already the city had begun to empty with the threat of attack by Scud missiles and by that time of night the wide dual carriageways were almost deserted. In close formation the cars sped through the night, only slowing down if the lights at intersections were red and then forging across.

At the gates of the MODA building the guard, Ahmed Hussein, recognized my car and me and let us straight through. I found Norman in his upper office, on the second floor, and sat down alone with him, he at his desk, I in a chair at one side. As I thought, he wished to warn me privately that the assault would begin at 0001 hours Zulu, one minute past midnight, Greenwich Mean Time, or one minute past three local time, on Thursday, 17 January. The information was not to be passed on, except to those who needed to have it for operational reasons. He said that he was not really supposed to tell me, but wanted me to know.

He also confirmed the arrangements for formally warning the Saudis that hostilities were imminent: President Bush had already told King Fahd two days before the start and had requested that from that moment the Americans be allowed to launch the air war at two hours' notice. This was done in advance to minimize the chance of top-secret information leaking at the last minute. The British involvement was to be cleared by me with Prince Khalid, unless the Americans had already cleared it with the King on our behalf. I had already established with the Prime Minister and Paddy Hine that Britain could not be committed to war by the Americans, even though we were in such close alliance with them. The only people with the authority to commit us were the Cabinet in Whitehall, who retained control of our forces right to the end. For this reason, I now told Norman I would prefer to clear our involvement unilaterally with Prince Khalid.

He appreciated this and we went on to review our arrangements for deploying the SAS. After his initial hesitation, he had become enthusiastic about offensive operations by Special Forces deep in the western desert of Iraq: attacks on communications and roads were to be their primary activity, with deception and general harassment of the Iraqi forces as secondary objectives, and there was a further possibility of strikes against mobile Scud launchers. Norman confirmed that he had asked Chuck Horner to give our men every support and that if they got into serious trouble, the US Air Force would lift them out.

I went on my way saying a silent prayer of thanks for Norman's superhuman strength and steadfastness. Although under the most colossal pressure, he was showing no signs of exhaustion or impatience. Back in my own headquarters, I instructed Bill Wratten that he should confine his pilots and navigators to barracks on crew rest from 0800 next morning and order all his strike aircraft uploaded. Almost as I did so,

a top-secret signal arrived for me from Paddy Hine, bringing
the coded message 'Zulu 711000'. Here, in prearranged form,
with the date and time backwards, was confirmation of what
Norman had just told me: the war would start at 0001 hours
Zulu on the seventeenth. Soon after that Paddy telephoned,
saying that the signal had come from Washington and had
been endorsed by Number 10 Downing Street.

At 0130 in the morning of 16 January I wrote a note to
Bridget, saying, 'It's going to be a tense night for those of us
in the know. All I would say is that I'm glad I'm not in the
Iraqi forces.' Eventually, about 0200, I went to bed.

By then, after a further review of security, we had decided
that the threat of terrorist attack in Riyadh was high enough
to warrant a state of Red Alert. We had set up a quick-reaction
force capable of deploying instantly to any part of the city in
response to internal emergencies and now we stepped up our
bodyguard regime. The number of men on duty was increased
and I had a twenty-four-hour guard on my house, with a
man either in the garden or sitting downstairs all the time.
Until then bodyguards had tried to keep their weapons out
of sight, but now they went openly armed and I, for the first
time, carried a pistol in the city. Mark Chapman gave Alan
Cain positive instructions to ram any suspicious-looking
vehicle which blocked our passage, whether or not the
obstruction seemed to be intentional and Mark himself abandoned his pistol for an SA80 rifle, which he rammed down
between us in the back of the Mercedes whenever we travelled by car. All movement of military personnel in Riyadh
was brought under strict control and no casual travel was
allowed. Shops were put out of bounds and all ranks had to
make their location known all the time, whether they were
on or off duty.

I found 16 January strangely quiet and difficult to manage.
The normal briefings took place, but my head was full of the
overwhelming information that war would start in the early
hours of next morning and I could not share it with anyone
except Bill and Ian Macfadyen. Neither in my headquarters
nor in Schwarzkopf's was there any buzz of conversation
about the launch: everyone was keeping his secrets tight to

his chest. Everything was done to preserve a show of normality. The screens of our ASMA – air staff management aid, a major computerized source of information, whose data was available to Joint Headquarters at High Wycombe and to the Ministry of Defence, as well as to our units in the field – continued to indicate that a routine flying programme was in progress, when in fact our bombers were being armed up for war.

Outside the headquarters, absolute security was maintained till the last moment, but from the special Notice of the Day, which I sent out to all our forces that morning, it must have been clear that hostilities were not far off. The notice read:

> We are poised for war. After many months of endeavour, each one of you has established a military presence that is the envy of our Allies and is feared by the Iraqis.
>
> We have the best weapons and equipment it is possible for your service to provide and your training is second to none in the theatre. We have the support of our nation, and we have the respect and admiration of our military colleagues at home.
>
> I know you have courage, determination and pride in your Service and your Unit, and these great attributes, together with the support you have been given and the trust that is vested in you, will ensure that what you do will be a credit to Great Britain.
>
> If we fight, it is for the cause of freedom for a small, beleaguered nation: for the right of all those small nations in our world to exist in peace. We have the support of the world for our cause, and our cause will prevail through our success in battle, if that is what is necessary to sustain it.
>
> There will be surprises and setbacks, but we have all that we need to do our duty, and now it is up to each one of us to do it in the manner that our country would expect.

As far as I could tell, we had made every possible preparation. Our aircraft were bombed up, our crews on stand-by. Our ground forces were beginning to move up to their assembly areas in the north-west, from which the ground assault would be launched. At sea our ships were fully worked up, and at 1630 I telephoned Chris Craig, using Brahms and Inmarsat, to inform him, in the prearranged code, of the deadline. (He told me later that he did not pass the information on to any of his commanders. He was confident that they were well prepared and realized that none of them would sleep a wink if they knew that Armageddon was to be let loose in the early hours of the following morning.) In the northern outskirts of Riyadh and Dhahran Patriot anti-missile missile batteries were on one hundred per cent alert against attack by Scuds, and the capital was already known as Scud City, even though no missiles had yet fallen on it. In my house we had lined the downstairs lavatory with sandbags to form a makeshift air-raid shelter, although the precaution was of dubious value, as a direct hit would demolish the entire building.

In the evening I scribbled a note home, knowing that Bridget would not get it for several days, as all civilian flights in and out of Saudi Arabia were about to be stopped for the duration, until the Allies had established air supremacy:

> Provided we get through tonight without him putting in a pre-emptive attack, we shall be first in. We are about to see history made on a grand scale. Let us hope it is not a cataclysmic scale.

At 2200 Alan drove me to the British Embassy, again with two cars and full guard, and I quickly briefed Alan Munro on the imminent air assault. Then we drove swiftly back to the MODA building, where at 2230 I had another short meeting with Norman Schwarzkopf, to make sure that there were no outstanding problems. Finally I went up a floor to see Prince Khalid and to ask him, on behalf of the British Government, for his formal agreement to our participation in the war. He was most appreciative that I had taken the trouble to call and observe the niceties of protocol. Of course we must join the attack on Iraq, he said, but we must also make sure that Israel does not enter the war.

I promised to do what I could. As soon as I reached my own headquarters I rang Paddy Hine, asking him to pass a message to Tom King, saying how anxious everyone was that Israel should not become involved and requesting him to exercise whatever political pressure he could bring to bear. Then, because there was nothing else I could do, I lay down on the bed which I had had made up in a corner of my office and tried to get some sleep, so that I would be fresh when new decisions were needed in the morning. But sleep would not come. As the last hours of peace ran out, my brain was seething with thoughts about our plans. Besides, all Riyadh began to reverberate with the thunder of engines as laden KC-135 tankers laboured off one by one from the military airport close to the north of us and set out to top up the fighter bombers before they crossed the frontier.

I knew that the whole world was on edge, waiting and watching for the spark which would set the Middle East alight, but my own thoughts were focused on the forty-five thousand Britons deployed across the theatre. I thought of our soldiers on sentry in the desert or asleep beside their tanks. I thought of the Navy in the Gulf: our two destroyers up with three American warships in the front line of anti-air defence, in the most exposed position, on constant electronic alert for the Iraqi air attack which they thought must come. I thought of the RAF Tornado and Jaguar crews, already airborne for their thrust into the unknown.

We were all facing a criminal lunatic who cared nothing for his own people and was prepared to sacrifice them by the thousand for his own glorification. He had an army of half a million men and vicious weapons. We fully expected that he would attack with chemicals, possibly with biological warfare agents, and we knew that he was bent on starting a ground war, at whatever cost, for he believed that by doing so he would at least give the Coalition forces a bloody nose and be able to boast afterwards that he had successfully taken on the might of the United States. He was under the impression that we could not sustain an air offensive for more than three or four days and he therefore thought that his army would soon be in action, more or less intact.

As the deadline approached, I thought of the Coalition Tomahawk cruise missiles and aircraft lifting away from the American carriers in the Gulf, but most of all I thought of our Tornados skimming across the border at 800kph and heading north over the sands at ultra low level, with their clumsy, coffin-shaped JP233 bombs slung beneath their bellies. Every crewman carried £800 in gold, to facilitate escape in case of trouble, and also a chit written in Arabic which promised that Her Majesty's Government would pay the sum of £5000 to anyone who returned an airman intact to the Allies.

As I had written to Bridget, I felt 'a long way from the sharp end', and wished I were closer to it. Having many times been at the sharp end myself in earlier conflicts, I knew what the pilots must be feeling. No wonder I lay awake, wondering how things would go and how many of our planes would not return.

CHAPTER 9

WAR IN THE AIR

The air war was an operation of astonishing complexity. Devised by Buster Glosson and his targeting teams, under the overall guidance of Chuck Horner, it was a masterpiece of human planning and computer-controlled aggression, directed with a degree of precision which far surpassed that of any air attack in the past. Each day's ATO, or Air Tasking Order, ran to well over one hundred pages of minutely detailed orders, which coordinated sorties by allied aircraft from all over the theatre in 'force packages' for every period of twenty-four hours. To take one example, for an assault on Balad South-East – an airbase two and a half times the size of Heathrow – no fewer than sixty aircraft took part. The force package was made up of one wave of aircraft to suppress enemy defences (the jammers), the top-cover (fighters), and the bombers (Tornados), as well as reconnaissance planes. The raiders came from all over the kingdom, as well as from carriers in the Gulf and the Red Sea. All sixty had to be coordinated to refuel from airborne tankers on their way to Iraq and all had to hit their targets with a precision timed to one second. Simultaneously, F-117A Stealth fighter-bombers, invisible to enemy radar because of their angular shape and known to the Saudis as *shabahs*, or ghosts, were slipping up one by one from their base in the far south, at Khamish Mushayt, to hit pin-pointed targets, while AWACS early-warning, intelligence-gathering and target-identification aircraft were continuously airborne.

As the air war built up, the allies regularly flew over three thousand sorties in each twenty-four-hour period. No aircraft took off unless it was specified in the daily ATO: with the sky literally full of planes, this was the only way to retain control. The success of the air war was a tribute both to technology, which enabled sorties and aircraft to be deconflicted (or kept apart) in time and space, and to the discipline of the crews, who flew precisely to the profiles given them. In retrospect, it seems astonishing that we did not have a single fatal mid-air collision: several aircraft did touch each other and come back dented, with the crews rather quiet, but that was all. British pilots, used to refuelling from single tanker aircraft, two at a time, now had the extraordinary experience of seeing tankers stacked six-deep, with twelve combat aircraft refuelling simultaneously and a queue of others waiting to come in behind them.

Such was the precision of the whole air operation that one sortie by an aircraft equipped with Alarm missiles, designed to destroy enemy radar, was aborted because its launch time would have had to be one minute early. The aircraft was due to hit its target dead on midnight Zulu, but because British Rules of Engagement freed it for offensive action only at one minute past the hour, Bill Wratten decided that it could not take part in the raid, as to have come on target one minute late would have created an unacceptable delay.

In the air-conditioned comfort of the War Room, two floors underground in Riyadh, the first night of the war felt quite unreal. Although we were all wearing NBC kit, the operations seemed more like a huge exercise than a live war. Norman Schwarzkopf sat in the centre on one side of a long table, flanked by his Deputy, Cal Waller, on his right and Chuck Horner on his left. My seat was next to Horner's, and Tim Sulivan had a place at a desk to my left, against the side wall. In front of us, to right and left, two television sets showed continual up-dates on progress, with pilots' reports and target success rates being flashed up on the screens, while key personnel gave briefings, so that we got an immediate feel for how things were going. At the same time, the CNN television service, coming live from Baghdad, left us in no doubt that our attacks were hitting home.

At first the atmosphere was exceedingly tense. The scene reminded me of the one in the Cabinet Office in May 1981, when I had directed the SAS operation to seize the Iranian Embassy in London. Now, as then, after every possible effort to solve the crisis had been made on the political front, the troops were going in. The operation was under way and, until we knew how things were working out, we held our breath.

Out in the Gulf the ships of the Royal Navy suddenly saw their radar screens come alive with a display such as nobody present had ever witnessed. Just before 0300 radio operators heard the cruiser USS *Bunker Hill* call 'Freeway Zero One – Loose!' and Tomahawk Cruise missiles began to climb away towards targets in the heart of Iraq. In the first twenty-four hours over a hundred missiles and six hundred air sorties were launched by the US Navy alone and, although the British ships were too far away to see the missiles departing, radar operators were astonished by the evidence on their screens. The scale and intensity of the operation were beyond anything they had ever known and, even after thirty-odd years in the Navy, Chris Craig had never seen such a picture as was presented on the command screen aboard HMS *London*.

In Riyadh we knew that, whatever happened on the first night, we had a long way to go and that this was merely the beginning. Nevertheless, as the hours wore on and we saw that things had started well for us, we began to relax. Losses seemed incredibly light; aircraft were returning safely. As target after target was flashed up on the screens, and success followed success, a great sense of excitement and relief flooded through the War Room. By breakfast time on 17 January we had flown 352 sorties against 158 targets, and only one aircraft had failed to come home. By then we thought we had knocked out a great many of Saddam's communications centres and destroyed all the Scuds capable of attacking Israel. In this, of course, we were wrong, but a sense of euphoria spread through the War Room and we were gripped by a premature optimism that the whole thing was going to be easy. At the morning briefing in my own headquarters, Ian Macfadyen was so stirred that he quoted to the assembled company the immortal lines which Shakespeare gave Henry V before the battle of Agincourt:

We few, we happy few, we band of brothers;
For he today that sheds his blood with me
Shall be my brother; be he ne'er so vile,
This day shall gentle his condition;
And gentlemen in England now a-bed
Shall think themselves accurs'd they were not here,
And hold their manhoods cheap whiles any speaks
That fought with us upon St Crispin's day.

During the day the RAF lost its first Tornado. For the time being, its crew – Flight Lieutenants John Peters and Adrian Nichol – were posted missing and the exceptionally hazardous nature of the low-level missions became all too apparent.* To function at optimum efficiency, the JP233s had to be released at an exact height to maximize their chances of cutting a runway. The ideal method of hitting a runway was to fly straight down it; but such was the concentration of Iraqi anti-aircraft fire – known to the RAF as Triple A – that it was extremely distracting, as well as frightening, for the crews and a diagonal approach was considered a better alternative. Oddly enough, very few of our aircraft were being hit: to this day, there is no evidence that any of the Tornados which we lost was shot down by Triple A.† But it was exceedingly difficult to drop weapons accurately in the face of such fierce ground fire.

We soon found how wrong we were about the Scuds. Saddam's response to our first wave of air attacks was swift: during the night of 17/18 January he fired a volley of eight

---

* Peters and Nichol ejected safely and were captured. After being imprisoned, they were released on 4 March.
† In the whole war only one British aircraft, or possibly two, came back with any kind of battle damage. Of the six Tornados lost in combat, two are believed to have flown into the ground, which was hardly surprising when pilots were weaving through total darkness at two hundred feet or less to avoid defences. One aircraft was almost certainly destroyed by a bomb which exploded immediately after release, and two were hit by surface-to-air missiles – one as it pulled up to a higher level some distance from the target and tossed conventional bombs to help suppress the defences, the other as it was completing a level attack from medium altitude. The sixth aircraft was disabled by a surface-to-air missile at medium level.

missiles at Israel. Two landed in Haifa and four in Tel Aviv. In the early hours of the eighteenth the Israelis launched fighter-bombers and it seemed as if our worst fears were about to be realized. 'All now depends on whether Israel will hold off or join in,' I wrote in a note to Bridget scribbled at 0400 on the eighteenth. 'Just heard as I write that Israel has launched F-16s, so it looks as though they are in and will fly over Jordan.'

Had that happened, the results would have been incalculable. Jordan might have come into the war on Iraq's side, perhaps attacking Israel directly. Iran might also have found it hard to remain neutral. The Israelis would have done their best to smash Saddam's mobile Scud launchers, both with commando ground forces and from the air; also, they might well have gone on and tried to take out his nuclear capability while they had the chance. The Coalition would have found itself saddled with an additional dimension which would have been extremely difficult to handle. Either we should have had to allocate the Israeli forces a large area of Iraq, inside which they might operate independently, or we should have had to take them under our own command and that would have split the Coalition wide open. Saddam would have been able to pour scorn and hatred on the Arab nations fighting alongside the Israelis and he would have scored an immense propaganda victory.

Only by a hair's breadth did his scheme to entrap Israel fail on that second night of the war. At one stage we heard that the Israelis had many F-16s airborne and only heavy international pressure prevented them from launching a raid which might have had disastrous consequences. At the hub of operations in Riyadh we were aware that intensive diplomatic negotiations were in progress and Norman himself spoke frequently to a high-level Israeli contact.

Nobody who was in Riyadh on the night of 17 January will ever forget the first Scud attacks on the city. From the moment when sensors detected the heat of a launch, we had about eight minutes before impact if the missile was heading for the Saudi capital. By the time the rocket's trajectory and direction had been established, we had some five minutes left. Then sirens would wail out all over the city. The terse message, 'Scud alert!' would come by every means, television, radio, telephone, and wherever we were, we would struggle into full NBC gear and dive for our safe rooms. Mine, as I have said, was the downstairs lavatory and, if I had a distinguished guest such as Paddy Hine staying, we would argue equally as to who should have precedence to sit on the loo and who would have to make do with the bidet.*

The noise of Patriot anti-missile missiles taking off was prodigious. They went up from a site only six hundred yards from my house with an immense *boom*, followed by a roar like that of an express train, and then another *boom* as each incoming missile was taken out. In Alan's opinion those first few nights' pyrotechnics amounted to the most spectacular and expensive firework display the world had ever seen. On the third night, when six missiles came in and thirty-six Patriots were fired at them, there were tremendous bangs and flashes all over the sky. With each Patriot costing about £800,000, the expenditure certainly ran into tens of millions and next morning in the War Room Norman Schwarzkopf wanted to know why such a volley had been necessary. The colonel commanding the Patriot battery was summoned to explain: he pointed out that the Patriot system was new and had only just been brought into service, and that an error had crept into its programming, which had caused an excessive response. Fine tuning of the programme put things right, but still the Patriots were liable to hit the body of an incoming missile, rather than its nose-cone, so that the explosive warhead would still fall to earth in one piece, albeit not in the target area.

---

* Whereas in conventional warfare air-raid shelters are generally underground in basements, it was sometimes recommended that under the threat of chemical attack safe rooms should be upstairs, since gas falls as it disperses. At the British Embassy Alan Munro and his wife Grania established their own air-raid shelter in their bedroom on the first floor. By a curious fluke of modern communications, their first warning of an attack often came from their daughter in London, who would see on television that Scuds had been launched, and immediately ring up.

At first we thought it highly probable that the Scuds would carry gas and every raid had to be followed by a tiresomely long twenty-minute wait before chemical checks of the environment could be carried out. After the second missile on Night One, we got a scare when our sensor equipment detected the presence of some agent, but soon we realized that it was reacting to chemicals released by high explosive, rather than to poison gas. Later, although we were confident that Iraq was not capable of launching a full-scale nuclear warhead, we thought that in desperation Saddam might order some warheads to be loaded with nuclear material – possibly spent fuel rods from a reactor – in the hope of creating panic and we therefore ordered special equipment to monitor radioactive contamination in Riyadh and Dhahran.

The early Scud attacks had a miraculous effect on Riyadh's traffic problem. Suddenly the streets, and indeed the whole city, became empty and road journeys took half their normal time. Then, as people saw that Patriot worked and could deal with most of the attacks, confidence gradually returned. Soon it was being cynically remarked that there was one infallible way of distinguishing between journalists and the military, when all were wearing uniform: if, when a Scud warning came, you saw a man heading rapidly for the cellar, you could be sure he was a serviceman obeying orders; but if you saw someone running up the fire-escape towards the roof, you knew he was a reporter or a cameraman, bent on getting a grandstand view of the proceedings. Nevertheless, the Scuds remained a threat and were an infernal nuisance, as they constantly disrupted sleep, got one up at all hours of the night and contributed to exhaustion which was already serious enough.

They also led to a ridiculous incident. Late one night I wanted to ask Bill Wratten something and, rather than cross the compound to the house which he shared with Ian Macfadyen, I tried to ring him on the telephone. The number was engaged and continued to be so; in fact it had been engaged whenever I had tried it during the past few days. With mounting irritation I rang it again and again, more and more certain that one of them was having some prolonged conversation.

In the end, unable to stand it any longer, I stormed across, burst in and demanded, 'What's going on? Your telephone's permanently engaged.' Bill and Ian were rather startled, but protested their innocence. They had not been on the telephone at all.

'Then the line must be out of order,' I snapped. 'You ought to have it repaired.'

'Wait a minute,' said Bill in his usual calm, analytical fashion. 'What were you dialling?'

When I told him, my anger suddenly evaporated and we all collapsed with laughter. For the past hour, and for days, I had been dialling my own number.

Late on the evening of 18 January a personal telephone call came through for me from John Major in London. He rang on an open, insecure line, so we could not discuss anything secret or classified, but that did not matter, for the Prime Minister had called as a friendly gesture, to pass on encouragement and to obtain for himself a feel for the way things were going. I warned him that although we had made a good start, there were bound to be setbacks and he particularly asked me to thank the RAF for their outstanding work. After our talk, I felt that his call was entirely in character: straightforward, sincere and demonstrating his close interest in the fate of British citizens everywhere.

Within the first two days of war it became clear that the US Air Force's laser-guided bombs could be dropped with astonishing accuracy. Before the war began, many British service people, myself included, without direct experience of these weapons, had been faintly sceptical about the claims which the Americans made for them. Now we saw that everything they had said was justified. I wrote to Bridget:

> I've seen delivery-aircraft pictures of a bombing run and it is incredible. They put 2000lb bombs into air vents on the roof and, in the case of a ten-storey building, the bomb went to the bottom of the lift-shaft before exploding and the whole building imploded. Pictures of Saddam's new palace show it to be a roofless shell of rubble. The strikes have been extraordinarily accurate and there has been minimum damage to civilian targets. We've struck chemical and biological sites with

the same success – but there are a lot of them and so plenty
yet to go.

Attacks on airfields were a different matter. One problem was
the sheer number and size of Iraqi airbases. With runways
and taxiways covering several acres, it was impossible to close
them all at once, even given the weight of effort available.
The plan instead was first to disrupt operations as widely as
possible and then to follow up by destroying aircraft in their
shelters on the ground, as well as other airfield facilities.
Much was hoped for from the RAF's JP233, a weapon specifically developed for counter-airfield operations in the Warsaw
Pact countries. The bomb consists of a series of cratering
devices, like rockets, which float down on parachutes and
detonate just above the ground: shaped charges drive down
into the runway and explode underneath it, heaving up the
surface and excavating the ground beneath, which should
make the damage difficult to repair. At the same time, the
weapon releases a large number of minelets, which lie about
unexploded, inhibiting repair work.

In Iraq, given the size of the airfields, RAF crews concentrated on trying to sever the access tracks and taxiways leading from hardened aircraft shelters (HASes) to runways,
to trap Iraqi planes in their lairs. Intelligence reports later
showed that these attacks were extremely accurate, but also
that the bombs were causing a disappointing amount of damage, and that areas that had been hit were often back in action
within a few hours. Analysis suggested that the sand, on
which most of the airfields were built, tended to absorb blast
and minimize the heave factor. If deep concrete is broken up
into lumps and slabs, it is very difficult to smooth down again,
but on the Iraqi airfields it seemed that only a thin layer of
concrete or tarmac had been laid and this was relatively
simple to bulldoze flat after a raid. This took some time to
emerge, but the fact remained that of all the weapons available to the Allies for putting enemy airfields out of action,
JP233 was the only one which could achieve disruption over
a significant area, and this was very important at the outset
of the air campaign.

As the air war built up, we in Riyadh quickly settled in to a new routine. This began with a briefing in my headquarters at 0715, followed by a briefing from Norman Schwarzkopf in the War Room at 0800. After an RAF briefing at 0915, I would discuss the night's sorties with Bill Wratten and then conduct other business for the rest of the morning until the Command Group briefing at midday. At 1630 there was another briefing in my headquarters, followed by Schwarzkopf's Evening Prayers at 1900, and then numerous telephone calls to the United Kingdom. As I remarked in a letter home, 'You are not your own master when it comes to the day.' The same applied to the nights, which were repeatedly broken up by Scud attacks. After several nights on the bed in my office, I took to sleeping at home unless some immediate crisis was threatening, because I got a better night's rest there and I knew it was important to conserve energy and avoid over-stretch. The War Room functioned twenty-four hours a day. I always had a seat at Norman's table there and Tim Sulivan was on duty all day, every day, handing over to a senior staff officer from my headquarters, Lieutenant Colonel Mike Davidson of the Parachute Regiment, for night duty. I divided any spare time I had between there, my own headquarters and essential outside visits.

One of these, on the first full night of the war, was to welcome 205 Field Hospital, formed from Territorial Army reservists, when they arrived at King Khalid International Airport, fresh from civilian life in England. Their introduction to the theatre could hardly have been more dramatic. Here were some of the country's finest surgeons, nurses and technicians, making the most commendable personal sacrifices. Many were losing salary – some up to £700 a month – yet they were full of enthusiasm as they plunged into this strange new environment. Just as they were coming down the steps of the TriStar, sirens wailed out a Scud alert. Within seconds they found themselves being bundled into the basement of the unfinished building where they were to set up their hospital and struggling to don unfamiliar NBC suits. As soon as the all-clear had sounded, I spoke to the assembled company in the basement, giving a quick outline of what was happening and saying how glad we were to see them. When I finished, they broke into loud applause. Not being used to receiving spontaneous ovations, I felt pleased but rather stunned. Then, as if to put me in my place, another gas warning sounded and we all had to dress and mask up again.

I also received members of the International Red Cross, who wanted to talk through the arrangements which British forces had made for handling prisoners of war. Under the terms of the Geneva Convention, the nation which captures prisoners is responsible for their welfare, even if they are passed on into the care of some other country. The aim of British forces was to hand over prisoners as soon as possible to the Saudis: neither we nor the Americans wished to keep Iraqi prisoners on our hands. All the same, our engineers were building large tented camps inside wire cages for receiving them and holding them until transfers could be arranged. The IRC representatives had inspected the cages and were making a few recommendations, to which we reacted. I said they were welcome to visit the camps whenever they wanted, but I also challenged them on what they were doing about our prisoners in Iraqi hands. The answer was that although the IRC had kept representatives in Iraq throughout the eight-year war with Iran, it now had very limited access and was pressing for more.

Within three days it had become clear that the most immediate menace to the Coalition was that of the Scuds, especially those on mobile launchers in the western desert, not so much for the physical harm they might do as for the political upheaval which they might create. The Iraqi air force had shown little will to fight: at first it seemed that the enemy were holding their aircraft back in the hopes that they could preserve them for use in the ground war; then, when they did start to fly, they were promptly shot down and in only a few days the Allies had established air superiority. The Scuds, however, were another matter. We began to realize that we had seriously underestimated the number of missiles in Saddam Hussein's armoury and that, with typical low cunning, he had ordered the construction of many dummy rockets.

From the air these looked perfectly realistic and often contained substantial quantities of fuel, so that they exploded
satisfactorily when hit by a bomb and caused the pilot of the
attacking aircraft to chalk up another kill. Thus, although
many genuine launchers and rockets were knocked out, an
alarming number remained untouched, and none caused us
greater concern than those within range of Israel. By the third
day of the war we were putting forty per cent of all our air
sorties into our effort to destroy the launchers widely spread
out in the desert round two airfields known as H2 and H3.
'The Israelis nearly came into the war today,' I wrote to
Bridget on 19 January. 'We may have the greatest difficulty
keeping them out tomorrow and it will be impossible if there
is another Scud attack on them.'

In Riyadh the Scuds had so far proved more of a psychological than a physical menace and enforced nocturnal vigils
proved good for letter writing, as extracts from a despatch
composed at intervals in the middle of the night of 20 January
show:

> 0105   Just stood-to for an air-raid warning. Several bangs,
> Patriot scrambled. Incoming Scuds. We are dressed,
> having a cup of tea, in the drawing room, in gas kit.
> It sounds as if Patriot may have intercepted them.
> We wait for news. Masking up, so must stop reading
> the *Gazette*, as I can't see without spectacles in mask.
> 0200   Unmasked, but all-clear for gas not yet sounded. We
> are told there were six incomers, all taken out by
> Patriot. Bad for sleep.
> 0240   Just had another warning, so we're waiting for the
> bang . . . No Scud arrived yet, so it must have failed or
> fallen short. We've now been offered *another*
> vaccination. It's being kept very low profile, and the
> cover-name is Cutter!*

Our anxieties over Israel were further increased when bad
weather closed in and severely hampered air operations for

*   Simon Cutter is my farming partner.

the next three days. Low cloud and rain over the desert made precision bombing difficult, if not impossible, and the strategic air assault fell behind schedule. Norman Schwarzkopf therefore made an early start on round-the-clock attritional bombing of the Iraqi army, particularly of the Republican Guard, who had better tanks, were better trained and motivated than any of Saddam's other forces, and were being held in reserve, behind the front-line troops, so that they could roar down on the Allies when they were already bogged down in battle. In theory this preparation of the battlefield belonged to a later phase of the air war, but the Coalition had such a wealth of aircraft that in practice several phases could be run concurrently. Since attritional bombing could be carried out by giant B52s from high level and could go on in any weather, there was an obvious advantage in starting it early. Its aim was to destroy as much armour and equipment as possible, but also to demoralize and exhaust the Iraqi soldiers by denying them proper sleep for days on end. The attacks were therefore made irregular and unpredictable, concentrating on one unit for several days before suddenly switching elsewhere, so that nobody could tell what the next target would be.

At the same time, psyops, or psychological warfare, at last came into its own. On the British side there had been much discussion about whether or not such tactics were ethically desirable and the team which we assigned to the subject was miserably small (at first we had only one man, later reinforced by a team of twelve whom I had brought out from England). The Americans, however, had waded in with their usual lack of inhibition and had a whole battalion working on it. When Allied air raids knocked out the Baghdad television and radio broadcasting systems and left Iraqis with nothing to watch or listen to, the time seemed ripe to launch strategic broadcasts. This the Americans proceeded to do, but only after due consultation with the Saudis, who were very nervous about what went out over the airwaves from the kingdom.

Early in the war we also began tactical psyops, bombarding the Iraqi troops verbally as well as with high explosive, both from powerful loudspeakers set up on poles along the border and by radio from aircraft and local transmitters. At the same time, we began to drop leaflets inciting soldiers to desert. The scheme was ridiculously simple. One day the Iraqis were showered with leaflets in Arabic saying, 'Tomorrow we are going to bomb you, so we suggest you give yourselves up to the friendly Allied forces across the border.' Next day we would bomb them, as promised, and the day after we would follow up with more leaflets, this time saying, 'You see what happened. We said we would bomb you, and we did. Once more we recommend that you surrender, in which case, you'll be well looked after, fed, housed in camps and generally befriended. If you stay where you are, we'll come and bomb you again.'

These tactics, crude as they were, in time proved very effective: Iraqi prisoners told us that they caused much unrest and a fair amount of desertion. Clearly the bombing by B52s was deeply demoralizing and preyed on people's nerves, as it was designed to. It was physically difficult for soldiers to surrender, since they were trapped between wire and mines in front of them and execution squads behind, but some did escape, including one junior officer who, when asked why he had given himself up, said it was because of the high-level bombing. Told that in fact his own position had never been attacked by B52s, he replied, 'I know, but I visited one which had been!'

With the war barely a week old, my headquarters eventually moved into its new building. It may seem an extraordinary time to have chosen – and it was – but it was also the best that could be managed. After prolonged haggling about the rent and endless arguments with contractors, we had gained possession on 8 January and Ian Macfadyen had supervised the conversion of the building with exemplary efficiency. Now at last, after months of ever-increasing congestion and over-crowding, we had more space than we needed, in a basement and three upper floors. Some adaptation of internal walls and partitions was needed, but by far the most complex task was the installation of our communications, including microwave and satellite equipment, a job brilliantly carried out by the Royal Corps of Signals, under Lieutenant Colonel

Neil Donaldson. Not only did the equipment in the new head-quarters have to function perfectly from the moment we moved in, but the old headquarters also had to continue to operate until that moment, without any break. The result was that, while new equipment was being installed and some old equipment moved across, vital hardware had to remain where it was until the very end. The climax of the transfer came when the Land Rover fitted with the guts of the satellite receiving system, which until then had been parked in the grounds of the British Embassy, was driven up the steps and into the new building, where it was immediately connected to the dish on the roof and immured for the duration. After a break of no more than ten minutes, the system was up and running – a tribute to the skill of the signallers and the effectiveness of Ian's organization.

The new building was an immense improvement on the old. For the first time in five months everyone had plenty of room, with a command cell on the second floor and a joint operations room on the floor above. In the basement, origin-ally designed as a garage, we set up a restaurant for all head-quarters personnel, an excellent establishment, which served really good food and soon was known as the Scud Dodgers' Bistro.

With the war under way, Press briefings became the bane of our lives. The system of media reporting teams, out in the field, was working well, but in Riyadh we had to give a central Press conference every evening in the Hyatt Hotel, which had been taken over by the media to such a degree that its outside walls were festooned with huge, spaghetti-like loops of tele-vision cable. Needless to say, the man whom British reporters wanted to see and hear every night was the British Com-mander; but I was wary of appearing too often and sought to vary the bowling by getting Bill Wratten and Ian Macfadyen to hold the fort in turn. Soon people began to snipe at me for not being available more. The American CinC was always in front of the cameras and microphones, they said. Why did the British Commander not bother to turn up? But in fact I was right to ration my appearances. Norman Schwarzkopf made so many in the early days that people began to snipe at *him* for being too keen to take the stage, whereupon he backed off for the time being.

At that stage he had not yet won his reputation with the British public and many people in the United Kingdom still regarded him as a typically gung-ho and autocratic American general. I knew better and I thought it would be useful to make some public show of the close harmony which existed between British and American forces. I therefore suggested to Norman that he and I should hold a joint Press conference. He was prepared to do it, but after further discussion with Paddy Hine we all agreed that such a stunt could go wrong and look like a Mutt and Jeff act, so we dropped it.

Such was the pressure of media interest and such the thirst for information, that I had asked Paddy Hine to send out a man who could handle it as a full-time job. The result was the arrival, on 19 January, of Group Captain Niall Irving, who had been running the RAF's Presentation Team, which tours the United Kingdom explaining the role of the Royal Air Force. He proved ideal for the job, having exactly the right approach and intellect, and an instinctive understanding of how much to say or not to say. He was also excellent at answering questions and had the indispensable knack of being able to feed the Press enough to keep them happy, while steering clear of areas which were sensitive.

Management of the Press at local level, however, was only part of my public-relations problem. The other part lay in London and Washington, where media coverage of the air war seemed to obsess the politicians. I wrote home on 22 January:

> The Press remains a major issue, driven by Tom King. I had the CDS on the phone for forty minutes. Both of us would have liked to discuss military matters, but most of our talk was perforce about the Press. Then TK came on for an hour and I could only persuade him to talk about the war for five minutes. They're obsessed with it, and Washington is the same, worse, and gives Norman Schwarzkopf a very hard time.

While the world's attention was focused on the air war, I was faced by another pressing problem, that of Special Forces.

Having steam-rollered Norman Schwarzkopf into agreeing
that they should be sent in, I now found myself repeatedly
wondering whether they would find a worthwhile role in the
western desert. Their first plan was to send in four groups by
vehicle, but at the last moment they were asked also to provide three observation posts, to keep watch on the main supply routes, and a debate broke out within the SAS about how
these three patrols should deploy: some people thought it
best to move around on foot, after being dropped by helicopter, and some wanted to take vehicles. There were good
arguments in favour of both alternatives. Vehicles would give
mobility, the means of carrying heavier weapons and the
chance of escape if a patrol were bumped by enemy forces;
on the other hand, Land Rovers would take some time to
drive in, they would be hard to conceal and might easily
betray the presence of Special Forces, thereby attracting more
Iraqi troops into the area. Men on their feet, in contrast, could
be deployed quickly by helicopter at night and could hide
themselves effectively, but would have less mobility and no
means of escape if they were bounced.

Fortunately, much of the area in which they were going to
operate was far less flat and open than the desert across which
the mainland assault was due to be launched. Known as the
Jordanian lava plateau, the land was high, hilly and seamed
by deep, rocky wadis, which flash-flooded after storms. Loose
rock lay everywhere and there was very little sand. As the
desert fell away towards the Euphrates in the east it became
progressively flatter, but in the central area of operations it
offered plenty of cover.

When war broke out on 17 January, our Special Forces
were still at their training base in the Arabian peninsular,
and had to move fast to get all their men, vehicles and equipment up to a forward holding base nine hundred kilometres
north-west of Riyadh and over fifteen hundred kilometres
from the base. With the Allied air forces by then flying several
thousand offensive sorties a day, it was no easy task for the
Hercules aircraft transporting them to pick their way across
the flight paths of warplanes heading for Iraq and they flew
at low level, under American control every inch of the way,

in windows designated by the US Tactical Aircraft Control Centre (TACC) in Riyadh.

The SAS reached a compromise about their tactics in characteristic fashion. As is traditional in the Service, the decision about how to deploy was largely left to the patrol commanders and reached by democratic discussion. In the end two of the observation patrols decided to go in on foot. The leader of one of these groups took a quick look round the area in which the helicopter landed him, saw that it was lethally flat and insisted, with no mean courage, on immediately being flown out again. One other patrol was lifted in to operate on foot and others drove in aboard specially stripped-down Land Rovers and motorcycles.

We took every possible precaution to keep their deployment secret. No matter how empty the desert may seem to a casual visitor, there are always Arabs about and we did not want local tribesmen or frontier guards to start talking about strange little formations setting off into Iraq. I therefore asked Prince Khalid to brief the local Saudi military commander and swear him to secrecy, and the senior SAS officer on the spot did the same.

Hardly had the Special Forces crossed the border on 20 January, however, when the whole deployment was threatened by the likelihood of Israel's intervention in the war. On 22 January, when we heard that another Scud had penetrated the defences in Tel Aviv and caused seventy-odd casualties, I feared that we could no longer keep the Israelis out and began to devise a plan whereby we would allocate their ground forces a sector of Iraq in which to operate exclusively. If this had happened, it would have meant the end of the SAS operation: we should have had to pull our own men out, to prevent any chance of one patrol inadvertently fighting another, and the task of recovering them became more difficult with every kilometre that they penetrated into enemy territory.

I was still wondering whether I was right to have committed our people and whether they could achieve anything which our aircraft could not when, on 23 January, Special Forces brought off their first success, blowing up a substantial stretch of the communications network between Baghdad

and forward areas. This was a high-risk operation, separate
from the SAS deployment, carried out by the Special Boat
Service with great skill, determination and courage in a most
hostile environment. The raiding party flew in at night in two
Chinooks to a site less than sixty kilometres from Baghdad:
in the distance to the north, the sky was lit up by the flames
of the capital under bombardment. While men ran in to attack
the cables, their helicopters, which had landed a short distance from the main road to Basra, had to keep their engines
running – although with rotors disengaged, to cut down the
noise – so that they could be sure of taking off swiftly in an
emergency. The men then dug down, exposed the cables,
removed a length for analysis, placed charges and withdrew,
blowing out a considerable section. They also took with them
one of the above-ground markers which had designated the
cable route and next day they gave it as a souvenir to Norman
Schwarzkopf, who was so delighted and impressed by the
success of the mission that he immediately reported it to Colin
Powell in Washington. Powell in turn passed the good news
back to London, so that this first raid made a major contribution towards establishing the reputation and capability not
only of our Special Forces, but of those of America as well.

Just at that moment, in typical fashion, luck seemed to turn
against us. One of the SAS patrols which had gone in on foot
was bounced and scattered: eight men were missing, though
whether they were at large or had been killed or captured we
could not for the moment discover. This in itself presented us
with a difficult decision. If any of them had been captured,
there was a risk that the Iraqis might parade them on television, as they had already paraded the shot-down Tornado
pilot John Peters, and the news would come as a severe shock
to their relations, who did not even know that they had gone
into enemy territory. If, on the other hand, we informed
next-of-kin that the men were missing, word of the SAS's
involvement, hitherto top secret, might leak out and the Iraqis
might realize that Special Forces were operating inside their
territory, putting further lives at risk. After an intense debate
with Whitehall, my own view – that we should inform next
of kin, but swear them to secrecy – prevailed.

The area into which the SAS had deployed was a vast rectangle, covering several thousand square kilometres, which soon became known as Scud Alley, or the Southern Scud Box. Within the first few days, events obliged us to turn priorities right round. We had quickly found that the Coalition air forces could not deal with mobile Scuds as easily as they had supposed: bad weather was one factor in the enemy's favour, but it also became apparent that the Iraqis were most skilful at concealing launchers. To a pilot flying at ten thousand feet, a missile in its horizontal, travelling attitude looked just like an oil tanker and, if it was parked under a motorway bridge, a favourite hiding place, it could not be seen at all by satellites or surveillance aircraft; yet it could be run out, set up and launched in only twenty minutes. Then, even if surveillance satellites pin-pointed its position from the heat of a launch, its erector-trailer would have disappeared again by the time an aircraft could be directed on to the spot.

So, from information-gathering, deception and offensive action in general, we hastily switched the SAS's aim, as Norman put it, to 'Scuds, Scuds and Scuds again', so vitally important did it seem to close down the attacks on Israel. Yet when I sent out orders to this effect, little immediate improvement was discernible. Missiles were still being fired out of the western desert and the political situation remained extremely volatile.

In fact the SAS had gone to work in typically vigorous and effective fashion. At first their communications were erratic, but in spite of this handicap they began to call down air strikes on mobile launchers with deadly effect. When they found a target and reported it to headquarters in Riyadh, the message was relayed to the US Tactical Aircraft Control Centre, thence to an AWACS aircraft and thence to one of the fighter-bombers – usually A-10s by day and F-15Es at night – on combat air patrol. The trouble was that, even with all the sophisticated equipment available, it often took fifty minutes or more for an aircraft to arrive on target and often that was too late. Increasingly, therefore, patrols took matters into their own hands and, rather than see a Scud escape, engaged it with their own Milan anti-tank missiles. They also destroyed many microwave relay towers and communications bunkers, blowing them up with plastic explosive. One of their most valuable single successes was the capture of an Iraqi artillery lieutenant, with all his battle maps, which at last gave the Allies some valuable intelligence about enemy dispositions.

Conditions on the plateau were exceptionally harsh. Like the enemy, the weather was actively hostile. The SAS had underestimated the cold: in spite of their heavily padded jerkins and cloaks, they still suffered from sleet, snow, hail and frost so bitter that they had to light fires beneath their Land Rovers to stop the diesel fuel freezing. Fog and sandstorms added to their problems. Nevertheless, after a week or so the mobile patrols became bolder, driving by day as well as by night, and testing the enemy in a number of clashes: one fire-fight lasted four and a half hours, with American aircraft repeatedly coming in to hammer the Iraqis before they were eventually driven off.

In Riyadh our immediate problem was that news of all this good work did not emerge immediately. With Scuds still flying, the Americans became insistent that they too should deploy Special Forces in an attempt to stamp out the menace. 'Of course they want the same job and the same area as we have,' I told the SAS commander. On 29 January General Wayne Downing, who was to command the US Special Operations Forces deployed in Iraq, flew into Riyadh and listened with great care to a recital of our experiences, reverses and all. We told him what the country was like, how bad the weather had been, how active the enemy was and we gave an indication of how we thought the Americans might best operate. Downing was quick to learn from our successes and failures: he applied the lessons we had learnt to the deployment of his own troops and the result was a first-class example of cooperation between British and American forces. The obvious demarcation line between our territories was the northernmost of the three main supply routes running north-east/south-west from Baghdad to Amman: if the Americans operated mostly to the north of it, in an area they christened Scud Boulevard, or the northern Scud Box, and we kept to Scud Alley, south of the main road, there would be no danger of one side fighting the other. With that decided, we set up close liaison arrangements, with British officers and NCOs on the American Special Forces staff, and vice versa, so that each of us knew exactly what the other was doing, and when, and we could each offer assistance when necessary.

We also received outstanding cooperation from Chuck Horner, Buster Glosson and their air force planners. Through their expertise we were able to achieve an extraordinary level of flexibility and control. Chuck was quite happy that our men were at large in the desert, but he asked us to give him notice, every day, of the five-kilometre square in which they would be operating during the next twenty-four hours. They themselves could tell exactly where they were from their ground-position indicators − satellite-driven navigation equipment − which gave them their position on the face of the Earth to within about fifteen metres. Their signals and situation reports all went straight into the US air headquarters, so that their precise locations were on the computers and map boards in the operations room. The American planners then kept aircraft out of that square for the duration, unless they were specially called in, to minimize the risk of an accidental, blue-on-blue attack. So versatile was the control system that if plans had to be changed in the desert and it turned out that a patrol was in a different area from the one expected, the new information could be fed into the USAF computers at the last moment to ensure that there was no clash. (In spite of all these precautions, an American aircraft did once bomb an SAS patrol, but fortunately missed, causing no casualties.)

On the whole the mobile Scuds travelled along roads and tracks, generally known as MSRs (Main Supply Routes), and once the SAS had begun their surveillance, they soon were able to identify a missile on the move, along with its support vehicles. They could then follow it and destroy it themselves or call in an air strike. By these means, and by continuously refining their own tactics, they turned their campaign into one of outstanding success. Not only did they take out launchers with ruthless precision, but also the suddenness of their own attacks and the uncanny speed with which enemy aircraft arrived overhead so inhibited the remaining launch teams that after a while the Iraqis scarcely dared to bring their weapons into the open. The result was that attacks on Israel were effectively suppressed. With the help of the Americans operating north of the road, the SAS drove the Scuds further and further into the Iraqi hinterland, until they were all but out of range. Even though fireable rockets still existed, and were found after the war, no effective launches at Israel were made after 26 January, and the next five weeks remained clear. Between them, Special Forces managed to give the Iraqis the impression that the Allied formations at large in the western desert were about ten times the size of the units actually deployed there and so drew a useful number of troops away from the main theatre of operations.

It took some days for the full extent of this success to start filtering back to headquarters in Riyadh. In general, Special Forces try to maintain radio silence and do not make calls unless there is a real need to. Gradually, however, we realized that no more Scuds were reaching their targets in the west and that the danger of Israel entering the war had receded. It became apparent that the SAS had done the Coalition proud, as I had always felt they would, provided they were given a definite task.

As the war went on, and we realized as never before what a vast arsenal of weapons and equipment Saddam Hussein had built up for his armed takeover of the Middle East, my remarks about him in letters home became less and less charitable. On 26 January, after reporting 'a bad night, having had further injections, sore and aching all over, felt ill and faint', I went on to say:

> We are dealing with a truly evil man, and I do fear for the prisoners of war, as he may misuse them out of spite when he sees he is losing. It's amazing that he is prepared to let his country be destroyed for the sake of Kuwait, which he is doing his best to wreck anyway [by this point, the Iraqis had begun releasing torrents of crude oil into the Gulf]. It's clear that we did the right thing going in, as he has set up a military infrastructure to annexe the whole of the Arabian peninsula.

On 11 January – as mentioned in the preface – I had found time to write to the editors of London newspapers and express heartfelt thanks, on behalf of all the servicemen and women in the Gulf, to the readers who had responded so generously to various Christmas appeals and bombarded us with gifts. All the newspapers published my letter; but one, the *Daily Star*, which had already 'adopted' HMS *Gloucester* as its own warship, went further and on 21 January, under the heading 'CHEER UP OUR BOYS WITH A TASTE OF HOME', published a short article inciting readers to bake cakes and forward them to me. The paper printed a simple recipe for a fruit cake devised by its chef, Patrick Anthony, with instructions to wrap cakes in greaseproof paper and a double thickness of foil to keep them fresh, and gave my address – BFPO 646 – at the bottom.

The result of that one article, and a brief follow-up next morning, was astonishing. Within a few days cakes began to arrive by the hundred and, whenever I visited units in the field, I took sackfuls of them with me. Yet it was not merely for their food value that we welcomed them. What thrilled everybody was the thought behind them, the love and care which had gone into their preparation and the evidence which they brought that people at home had not by any means forgotten us. The only sad feature of this avalanche was that a special cake, ordered for me by Bridget from Marks & Spencer, went under in the flood and never arrived.

The torrent of mail from England had reached extraordinary proportions. I was receiving thirty or forty letters a day, almost all of them from people whom I had never met. Some came from cranks or manifest lunatics, but the vast majority were from ordinary citizens who wished us well and wanted us to know that we were in their thoughts. I tried to answer them all, either personally or through my staff. Schoolmasters, schoolchildren, doctors, vicars, nurses, old age pensioners, people of every age and station put pen to paper. Some found it difficult to express the strength of their emotions in ordinary terms: for instance, one woman on 22 January made out a cheque on her account at the Yorkshire Bank in Brighouse: 'PAY SADDAM HUSSEIN AND HIS HENCHMEN IN KIND, ONE MILLION TIMES, FOR ATROCITIES COMMITTED'. And who could remain unmoved by this postcard from an eleven-year-old boy in Shrewsbury:

to General Billiere

I cannot make you a cake because I am not allowed to use my Mums cooker. But on Saturday when I get my Pound pocket money I will send you some sweets. OK I think you are very brave and I like your tanks and aeroplanes. I wanted to join the army but I have fits so I cant. Good luck to all the men and ladies in the nasty war. Love, M.E.

The men who needed most luck and support were the crews of the RAF Tornados. In the first week of the war we lost five aircraft and our rate of attrition was far higher, proportionately, than that of the Americans. Within three days of the start of the war I noted:

> The RAF are having a bad time, with heavy losses in percentage terms compared with the Allies. It could be they've got the wrong philosophy – ultra-low approach – for this sort of campaign. Very understandable, and of course the US spend far more on their aircraft. We approach at 900kph, down to a hundred feet, while the US come in at 10,000 feet plus and are above the Triple A and flying easy.

It is worth explaining why the RAF adopted these particular tactics. The Tornado and JP233 had been developed for operations in Europe, where a combination of factors such as the need to minimize exposure to Warsaw Pact air-defence radars and fighters, and variable weather which for most of the time would preclude accurate bombing from medium altitude, had led the RAF and most other NATO airforces to adopt techniques of low-level penetration and attack. Operational analysis, trials and exercises had all shown that in Europe attrition could be minimized in this way. But in Iraq, with enemy fighters and surface-to-air missiles neutralized in the first few days of the war, it was the Tornado crews flying at low altitude who came under the most intense fire, from Triple A deployed on and around enemy airfields. These low-level sorties, flown at night, proved both demanding and hazardous; yet we had to keep them going until we were sure that the Iraqi pilots were either not going to show at all, or were husbanding their resources until the start of the ground campaign.

For the courage and skill of our Tornado crews, I had

nothing but admiration. I saw that their bravery was of a quite exceptional order. The first of our people to go into action, they were also the first to break through the barrier of enemy resistance, ground-fire and missiles. Their aircraft had never been tested in war, and most of the crews had themselves never flown in anger. Now they were required to fly to the limits of survival not once or twice, but night after night – and to do that required sustained courage of a special kind. I admired particularly the leadership and fortitude shown by senior officers – the wing commanders and squadron leaders – who flew extra sorties and led from the front to set an example. Anyone who did that, taking on more missions than the call of duty demanded, deserved the highest commendation.

Their gallantry emerges shining from the citations for medals awarded after the war – and I hope that it will not seem invidious if I quote the example of Squadron Leader Nigel Risdale, of 15 Squadron, who was in the forefront of the early Tornado raids. His citation for a Distinguished Flying Cross records that he 'displayed exceptional fearlessness in making low-level attacks at night against heavily defended enemy airfields':

> Despite the extreme danger to himself and the other aircrews in his formation, he displayed great courage and coolness in leading and pressing home attacks to deliver JP233 bombs with outstanding accuracy . . . (His) bravery and calmness have been an inspiration to all when other aircrew were lost in action . . . By rising instantly to all the demands made of him, and through the exceptional results he achieved in confronting the enemy in the heart of his territory, he has shown himself to be a magnificent leader under fire.

Squadron Leader Risdale was only one of many RAF heroes. And yet . . . I soon began to wonder whether such very great courage was not being misused, when weighed against the limited success which we were achieving. Chuck Horner, himself a professional airman of immense experience, was sceptical about our low-level delivery system from the start. One day in the War Room he turned to me and said, 'Gee,

Peter, I sure admire the courage of your pilots, but I'm a little bit concerned they ain't achieving much in relation to the risks they're taking and the effort they're putting in.' I made some cautious reply, but from this and other comments I could tell that Chuck considered our method of operation a pretty crazy one in this environment. Everyone in the headquarters was well aware that over the past few years the Americans had considered, and rejected, the low-level option which we were pursuing, and gone for medium-level, laser-assisted bombing instead. (The Americans did also fly low-level sorties during the first days and nights of the war, but they soon went up to medium level.)

It was therefore an immense relief to me when, on 23 January, after four aircraft had been lost, Paddy Hine and Bill Wratten decided that low-level attacks should be abandoned for the moment. I had made my own views on the subject clear – and indeed, as Commander of British Forces, I could have taken the decision myself, but because I had two very experienced airmen above and below me in the command chain, it seemed appropriate that they should be the arbiters. The fact was that after seven days the Iraqis had almost ceased to fly. The odd fighter which did take off was soon shot down, but most aircraft never left the ground: the enemy were husbanding their assets and keeping them inside their hardened shelters. This being so, there was no point in, as Paddy put it, 'going on putting holes in the runways, which they would fill in within forty-eight hours, and running the risk of losing more aircraft.' It seemed far more sensible to go up to medium level, to give our crews a rest from the extremely demanding, low-level night sorties, and let them have a chance to recover their morale, which had been shaken by the initial losses.

For the next week or so the Tornado crews were tasked – still at night – against a variety of targets, including radar sites, petroleum refineries, storage tanks and ammunition depots, all from medium altitude (around 20,000 feet), using radar techniques to deliver free-fall 1,000lb bombs. The crews adapted readily to attack procedures for which they had had very little training, and the post-mission reports were generally encouraging; however, it was not possible for several days to obtain accurate battle damage assessments (BDA) because extensive cloud-cover prevented satellites from contributing their photographic imagery. When BDA did become available, we could see that the radar bombing had been largely ineffective. This was not surprising, because the Tornado weapons system had been designed primarily for low-level delivery. Moreover, the Americans also found that their aircraft, when not using precision-guided (so-called 'smart') bombs, were having no better success.

Once these disappointing results became known in London, proposals were put to Paddy Hine for making more effective use of the Tornados and JP233. Considerable work had been done, both by senior staff officers in the Ministry of Defence and in industry, to evaluate the effectiveness of the weapon against targets other than airfield surfaces, and as a result recommendations were made that low-level attacks should be resumed against certain key targets which were less heavily defended than the airbases.

On 29 January, concerned that our pilots and navigators had had a tougher time than anyone else, and wanting to see for myself how they were standing up to it, I flew down to Dhahran to talk to them. They seemed in excellent form, very mature and realistic about the position, and proud of their achievements, despite their losses; but they told hair-raising stories of how, as they approached a target, the horizon ahead would suddenly erupt in streaks, flares, whole curtains of white, yellow and red light as Triple A and surface-to-air missiles hurtled up to meet them. Chatting with them in the crew-room, I talked through their problems, and found them surprisingly relaxed, but at the same time quite clear that it was not worth risking aircraft and lives on low-level missions when the enemy had ceased to fly.

The proposals from London for new JP233 attacks therefore caused us some consternation. While Bill and his commanders were considering them, I happened to see an informal letter from a high-ranking RAF officer (who, I must stress, was not in the chain of command) suggesting that the whole future of the Tornado and JP233 would be called into question after the war if the combination was not seen to be more effective. The implication was that, by failing to take this important consideration fully into account, Bill Wratten was not acting in the best interests of his Service.

This made me extremely angry. Bill was the man directly responsible for RAF operations, and, in line with my own policy, he considered that his paramount duty lay in hitting the right balance between achieving maximum operational effectiveness and not exposing his aircrews to undue risk. Besides, he did not believe that the JP233 had failed. In his view, the weapon had done exactly what it was supposed to: his crews had flown brilliantly, with immense courage and dedication, and had achieved extremely accurate results. Yet his conclusion, based on advice from all the station and squadron commanders involved, was that JP233 could not be used against the alternative targets suggested without exposing the attackers to considerable risks, and that this was not justified, given the successful overall progress of the air campaign. Paddy supported this view, and so did I. But a heated exchange continued for a week or more and caused Bill considerable anxiety, before the attempts to make the RAF return to low level gradually faded out.

By 27 January, in any case, we had declared air supremacy. With enemy planes grounded, destroyed or dispersed, we could fly tankers or other non-combat aircraft into Iraq airspace with impunity, and new bombing tactics were called for. The trouble was that the RAF did not have an effective alternative immediately available. What we urgently needed were aircraft with laser-designation capability, to give us the pin-point accuracy which the Americans were achieving.

In November, when Paddy suggested bringing out Buccaneers, he had been told by Chuck Horner that there were plenty of American designator aircraft which could fly with ours, if necessary, but now, when we wanted them, we found there were none available, since every spare plane had been diverted on to the hunt for Scud launchers. Rapid approval was given for twelve Buccaneers to come out as fast as possible. As it happened, both squadrons nominated were away from home on detachment, 12 Squadron in Gibraltar and 208

Squadron in Cornwall. But they responded with remarkable alacrity, flew back to Lossiemouth in Scotland, repainted their aircraft in desert pink, did some extra training and completed the nine-hour flight to Bahrein, all within five days.

The Buccaneer was twenty-one years old and known as 'the flying banana' on account of the slightly undulating shape of its fuselage, but in spite of its antiquity, its crews loved it and swore that as a weapons platform it was second to none. Now it proved its worth in short order: on its first live sortie – two Buccaneers escorting four Tornado GR1s, with a third Buccaneer as a back-up – it achieved complete success, punching clean through an important bridge over the Euphrates with laser-guided bombs.

Elsewhere, too, the RAF learnt swiftly. In the western desert, for instance, where Tornado GR1A reconnaissance aircraft were making low-level sweeps with their infra-red sensors to gather intelligence at night, we soon realized that it was safer for the planes to fly singly than in pairs. An aircraft travelling at 900kph and two hundred feet is gone before a man on the ground can react, but if another is following a few seconds behind, he may well have time to aim and fire a weapon at that. Similarly, it had become standard RAF practice to go in against big targets with four- or eight-ship formations: now it became clear that in the face of concentrated low-level defences, such tactics were asking for trouble and that greater unpredictability was called for.

Throughout the war our Jaguars, based at Muharraq, flew day and night against enemy installations in the KTO, attacking artillery ammunition dumps and other tactical targets. On one occasion, when the Iraqi navy made its short-lived attempt to mount operations down the Kuwaiti seaboard, they sank an enemy landing craft. Throughout the campaign their pilots flew every sortie like clockwork, attacking from high level with tactics quite different from those which they had practised during their NATO training.

CHAPTER 10

NORTH-WEST PASSAGE

In due course it became clear that the SAS had achieved a major success in the western desert; but all I knew about their fortunes at the end of January was that soon after their deployment one of the foot patrols had been bounced and scattered. Eight men were missing and that, in comparison with the very light overall casualties suffered so far, seemed an enormous loss. Knowing the SAS as I did, I felt certain that they would not have given in without a damn good fight, against both the elements and the enemy. Thinking back to other occasions on which patrols had run into trouble, I reckoned that they had a good chance of survival; escape and evasion were their special skills. But the mere fact that we did not know what had happened to them left an unpleasant feeling in the pit of my stomach. My instincts were right: heroic deeds were being done, but only later did the details surface. The superhuman courage and endurance displayed by one soldier, whom I will call Corporal Chris X, who had been separated from his patrol and forced to undertake a phenomenal cross-country march through the desert, make an amazing story and one which perfectly exemplifies the spirit and traditions of the SAS.

For two days the patrol, of which Chris was a member, lay up near the head of a dry, dead-end wadi, about five metres deep, watching for movement of Scud launchers along a Main Supply Route (MSR). The desert all round them was flat rock, but some two hundred metres to the north, beyond the road, the ground rose and on the ridge they could see two S60 anti-aircraft gun positions. The weather was bitterly cold, with temperatures well below freezing at night and scarcely rising to zero during the day.

On the first day they heard goat-herds calling and judged from the voices that the men were only a hundred metres away; then, on the second afternoon, one of the Arabs came so close that he spotted them. When he shouted something and ran off, it was obvious that the patrol had been compromised, so they started trying to make radio contact with base, but before they got any acknowledgement, they heard a tracked vehicle drive into the bottom of the wadi.

Thinking it was a tank or an armoured vehicle, they pulled on all their kit and cocked their 66 rocket launchers, but the intruder turned out to be a bulldozer with its blade raised – a local coming on armoured reconnaissance. The patrol leader decided that there was nothing for it but to move out. As he led out of the wadi, to his left he saw two Arabs watching. The servicemen had put on *shamags* (veils) to hide their faces and tried waving at the strangers to see if they could bluff their way past, but the Arabs started moving on a parallel course.

No sooner was the patrol in the open than a big dumper truck came bowling down towards them: as it scorched to a halt, armed Iraqis leapt from it and opened fire. Moments later an armoured Land Rover-type vehicle arrived, with a mounted ·50 machine gun and that started firing too.

The patrol returned fire, with bullets flying all round them. Then the S60s opened up on them as well. They tried to run, but their Bergens (packs) were so heavy – up to sixty kilogrammes apiece – that it proved impossible. (They were also wearing belt-kits loaded with ammunition, grenades and so on, and these alone weighed some twenty kilos.) The patrol leader shouted to his men to abandon their packs.

Just as Corporal Chris X went to dump his, a bullet tore through it and exploded one of the clips, right beside his hand. From the force of the impact, he guessed that the round had come from the machine gun. Grabbing his rocket-launcher, he ran up the slope. Suddenly he remembered that in his Bergen was the hip flask which his wife had given him for Christmas as a good luck charm. With everyone else yelling at him, he ran back and grabbed the flask. By some miracle all eight men reached the top of the slope unscathed. As Chris later recalled, 'The rounds were literally passing between our legs, tracer over the guys' shoulders. We honestly thought somebody would have gone down, so when we all got into cover we could hardly believe it and had a good laugh.'

They began to walk for their lives. Their aim was to head for the nearest frontier, which they reckoned was a hundred and twenty kilometres from their lying-up position, but to throw their pursuers off the scent they first put in a feint to the south, suggesting that they were on their way back to the Saudi border. As dark fell, they could see the headlights of several vehicles following them. So, steering by compass, and with the help of their Satnav global positioning system, they walked southwards for twenty kilometres before turning west for ten kilometres, and then on to a northerly heading.

By the time they came back to the MSR, it was midnight. Already they had walked for seven hours and covered sixty kilometres. One of the team was showing signs of exhaustion, so the rest took his kit and weapons off him and put him behind Chris, who was leading. At that point the MSR itself was two or three kilometres wide – a dangerously flat, open stretch, with dozens of sets of tracks side by side, spread out across the desert. Chris warned everyone that they would have to make a good push to cross it, to avoid getting caught in the open by a passing vehicle.

He led off at a fast pace, but when he reached the high ground beyond the road, he turned to find that five of the patrol had disappeared. Later, he learnt that they had heard an aircraft and stopped to see if they could contact it with their radios, which contained rescue beacons, but the man who was failing never heard the order to get down, nor passed it up the column, so that he, Chris and Mick (who by then was second in line) had kept walking.

Sitting on the high ground, Chris looked down through the night-sight mounted on his rifle. Scanning the flat plains, he could see for at least ten kilometres, but there was no sign of the missing men. He switched on his radio and tried to raise them on the hour and half hour, but no answer came. In the end he decided that he and his survivors must move on, away from the MSR.

So they continued, for four more hours, on a north-easterly bearing, over flat rock. By 0500, just as Chris was starting to worry that they would be caught in the open when dawn broke, they came across a small tank berm, horse-shoe shaped with walls of soil two metres high, and knee-deep tank tracks leading away from it. In one of these ditches they lay down, head to toe, but when the light came up Chris realized that there was some sort of enemy position – a hut or a box vehicle with aerials sprouting from it – only six hundred metres away and this pinned them down.

Afterwards, he remembered that day as the longest of his life. Although a mountain guide, he had never felt so cold. Hardly had dawn broken when snow began to fall. As the blizzard continued, the ditch filled with water and the three men lay there unable to move, soaked and frozen, wearing only desert-combat overalls and thin, Second World War smocks. They had very little water left in their bottles and almost no food. In his belt Chris had two packets of biscuits. Everything else – all their excellent kit, rations and spare, heavy-duty clothes – had gone with the Bergens.

About 1830, as dark was falling, he told his companions to crawl back into the tank berm and walk about to start their circulations going. By then, after twelve hours prostrate in icy water, they were so chilled that they had no feeling in hands or feet, and the cold had gone into their joints, knees and backs. They were so crippled that they could not pick up their weapons, but had to put heads down through the slings, straighten up and let the guns dangle.

Mick had perked up, but the third man could hardly move and when they set off again he kept falling behind. At one point he called Chris back and said that his hands had gone black. Chris realized his companion was delirious when he saw the man was wearing black leather gloves and he reassured him that the colour would come back into his hands if he put them in his pockets. Trying to provoke some reaction, he asked questions about his children, but the man began to shout, clearly out of control. Chris himself could feel hypothermia setting in and feared that none of them would last the night. He found it hard to concentrate on navigation and had to do everything in slow motion. The Satnav had gone with the rest of the patrol and he was steering by compass, his map being too small scale to be much use.

By now they were on very high ground, crossing patches of snow, with bare rock between. At some point he turned round and found that his third man had disappeared. Leaving Mick, he back-tracked, starting across snow, retracing his own footsteps. But then on bare rock he lost the trail. A painstaking search produced no clue. As he said, 'The guy could have walked off left, right or straight back.' So he had to make the agonizing decision to leave him. (He died of hypothermia and his body was later returned to the Allies by the Iraqis.)

Down to two, the survivors walked all that night until about 0530, when they came off the high ground down a slight gradient and ended up in a very shallow wadi, only a metre deep, in which they lay cuddled into each other for warmth. Mercifully, the weather cleared and the sun rose in a clear, blue sky – never hot, but warm enough to begin drying their sodden clothes.

By then Chris's feet were badly blistered and he tried to bandage them, without much success. At about 1230 a man appeared at the bottom of the wadi with a big herd of goats. The fugitives lay and watched him, discussing in whispers what they should do if he spotted them. As he was a civilian, it went against the grain to shoot him. Besides, if he was a Bedu, he might help them – the Bedouin were said to be friendly to the Allies' cause. Perhaps they should tie him up and restrain him. Even then, he might die of exposure, if no one found him. And if someone did find him, dead or alive, it would put the enemy on their trail.

The Iraqi was wearing an ancient overcoat of dark tweed. Chris kept thinking how warm it looked and how good one of the goats would be to eat. The herdsman sat with his flock for some time, then he began to wander about . . . and walked straight on top of them. Mick stood up, shook his hand and started a conversation in sign language. The stranger offered them food, for which they would have to follow him in a certain direction. The two soldiers fell into an argument. Mick trusted the man and wanted to go with him. Chris was against any fraternization. In the end Mick went off, taking his weapon but leaving his belt-kit in the wadi.

He never returned. Chris had agreed that he would wait until 1830 that evening, and then, if Mick had not come back, he would move out, leaving the belt-kit and some extra ammunition. Now he kept to the plan and not a minute too soon. He walked on a prearranged bearing, due north, aiming for a big river: it was thirty-six hours since he had drunk and he badly needed water, but after only fifteen minutes he saw the lights of a vehicle behind him, heading for the spot where he had lain up and he began to run back, thinking that Mick had commandeered help. Then suddenly he saw the lights of a second vehicle and inferred, correctly, that Mick had been captured (in fact the goat-herd had led him straight to an enemy position). He was badly beaten in captivity, but was returned to the Allies after the war and made a full recovery.

Alone now, Chris walked for the rest of the night, his third on the run. The sky was clear, the ambient light good. After nine hours on the go, at about 0430, through his night-sight he saw the broad silver band of the river in a flat plain below him, with palm trees and houses scattered along its banks, irrigated fields and a small village to his right. Dogs were barking from the houses, but he made his way cautiously down to the river's edge. As he stepped into the water he instantly sank to his waist in soft mud and had to drag himself out. Then, lying on his face, he filled his water bottles. Soaked again, he lay up for the day in a dry wadi system, some five hundred metres from the village, with his morale at a low ebb. The water was drinkable, though filthy, and it helped quench his thirst, but his feet were in a bad way: he had lost all his toenails and his blisters had turned to cuts along the sides of his soles, weeping pus. With his adrenalin still running strongly, he did not feel particularly tired and, although he tried to sleep, the air was so cold that after every ten minutes or so he woke up shuddering violently.

As dark fell he moved off again. By this time, unknown to him, three of the other group had just been captured and two had died after tremendous night marches and a final shoot-out within ten kilometres of the border: the Iraqis had deployed 1600 troops that day and night, and alerted civilians along the river bank to look for the rest of the patrol. The result was that Chris constantly encountered troops on the move or civilians walking about and in the whole night, from 1830 to 0500, he advanced only ten kilometres, scanning through his night-sight, stopping, back-tracking, watching and waiting.

In the early hours he found another lying-up place, this time on a cliff face, two hundred metres high, from which he could look straight out over the river. Having climbed down part of the face and into a crack, he could see across into a village on the other bank. The people there were walking about peacefully, the women in black veils, and life seemed to be normal. For hour after hour he watched two men fishing in the river, pulling out a good catch, and kept thinking that he wouldn't mind a couple of the fish.

That night, his fifth on the move, he found himself between the river on his right and a highway on his left, in a corridor which varied in width from two to ten kilometres. To save energy, he tried to keep out of the wadi systems coming down towards the river from his left, since they demanded continual descents and climbs. As he walked parallel with the road, he heard the drone of a large vehicle coming up behind and presently through his night-sight he saw a black dot on the motorway, slowly growing. It proved to be a Scud convoy on the move, the missile on the back of a very noisy vehicle, with its tarpaulin flapping. True to his training, he made a note of the time and place.

In the distance a civilian vehicle illuminated a motorway sign, and when he warily approached the board, his spirits fell: he was fifty kilometres further from the border than he had thought, and he realized that he had at least two more nights to go.

He kept on for one more hour, but could find nowhere to basha down except in a culvert, two metres high and three wide, which passed under the motorway embankment. At 0700, soon after daybreak, he heard the inevitable jingle of goat bells: a herd was coming through the tunnel on its way to pasture. In a flash he was out of the culvert and lying flat in a ditch which ran up the side of the embankment. Out beneath him walked a man, a donkey, six dogs and a mass of goats. It seemed inevitable that the dogs would scent him. Ideas raced through his mind. Should he shoot the man, or just run for it? In the event he lay still and the whole lot went past without detecting him, less than six feet below, the dogs' noses apparently baffled by the stink of the goats.

Even so, Chris realized that at some point before nightfall the goat-herd would return. Therefore he had to move on, for the first time, in daylight. He began crawling along a wadi, going to ground whenever a car came down the road. After ten kilometres or so of this staccato progress, he found a hole in the ground and lay there for the rest of the day. By then the terrain consisted of small hills covered with scrubby thorn bushes and complex wadi systems, so that walking across it was like scrambling up and down through endless quarries.

Dehydration had become a serious problem, but he had decided to keep away from the river because every house along the bank had a dog and the chances of being compromised there were so high, and he thought he could survive without water until he reached the border. By now heading due west, he walked again all that night until he stumbled on some heavily guarded facility. Suddenly an air-raid siren went off, and when he searched the darkness ahead with his night-sight, he made out a number of anti-aircraft positions and patrols walking about, with tall towers which looked like radio masts on high ground behind. Assuming he had walked into a signals command post, he tried to pull out on a back-bearing and, by what seemed a miracle, came on a small stream of clear liquid flowing over a white rock bottom. Quickly he filled his water bottles and went on.

He spent most of that night trying to extricate himself from the complex and in the end found himself stuck between a three-man vehicle-control point on a junction and an anti-aircraft gun-site. Unable to move forward any further and determined not to go back, he crawled into a culvert full of rubbish beneath the road.

His feet had become extremely painful and he was starting to be tormented by hunger. At least, he thought, he could have a drink. But when he took a swig from his bottle, he spat the liquid out violently, for it tasted disgustingly bitter and acid, and was obviously contaminated by chemical effluents from some industrial process. Even that one taste left his mouth scorched and burnt. (Later he discovered that the installation was a plant processing uranium ore.)

That was another heavy blow to his morale. He knew he was on his last legs and that he had very little time left. He was feeling desperately weak and, although his feet were his worst worry, cuts on his hands had also gone septic and were stinking. Again he lay up all day and when at 1830 he stuck his head out of the culvert, he was glad to see that the sky was black with clouds. That meant the night would be dark and when he reached the vehicle control-point, he simply walked past it unseen in dead ground. An hour later a big flash lit up the sky behind him. Thinking he had triggered an alarm, he hurled himself to the ground, but then, looking back, realized that an air-raid was going in on the facility which he had found.

He knew from the map that there should be an Iraqi town with a big tower somewhere to his right and then, beyond the frontier, another town without a tower. Suddenly, in the dark night, he came on what seemed to be the border itself: barbed wire piled in three coils. But the only town he could see, lit up, was in the distance beyond it. Was that the Iraqi town with the tower? And was this wire some form of false or outer frontier?

Having waited for a motorized patrol to pass, he climbed the wire at a point where three stakes had been driven through the coils, cutting his arms and legs. By now he was easily confused and had to sit down to try and work things out. The town he could see seemed to be in the wrong place. All the same, the only thing to do was to press ahead on the same bearing. By his own account he felt 'absolutely knackered', and did not know how he kept walking. His mouth was cracked. He had no saliva. He could not speak.

Then, as he took the night-sight off his weapon, his head suddenly filled with a crackling roar like static electricity. He saw a big white flash, as if he was 'looking at things through a negative'. He seemed to have fallen asleep. Waking up, he paid no attention to these unpleasant phenomena and started walking once more, but as he turned round, the static fired off in his head again. There was another flash and everything went white a second time. Coming round, he found himself on the ground and thought, 'Get a grip! That was a stupid place to fall asleep.' The next time it happened, he evidently kept on walking, for he woke up face-down on the ground with a broken nose. With the mirror built into his compass, he saw that his nose was pouring blood.

He realized that he was in serious trouble, that if he did not find water, he would soon collapse. At 0600 in the morning, with dawn just breaking, as he sat with his back against the wall of a wadi, he suddenly heard one of his mates in the squadron call out to him that the rest of them were waiting for him round the corner. The voice was so real that he stood up and hobbled along, as if walking on bed of nails, fully expecting to see the squadron lined up. There was nobody in the stream bed, and he said to himself, 'Steady on, you're starting to hallucinate.'

What he *could* see, about two hundred metres away, was a goat-herd's house, and he decided to go there, even if he was still in Iraq. 'I've got to have water,' he told himself. 'If necessary, I'll shoot them. It's them or me, and that's the bottom line.'

So he walked over to the shack. Outside it a woman was kneeling over a fire, cooking nan bread on a pan like an upside-down wok. Near her, children were playing and in the distance a man was herding goats. As Chris approached the barn, a lad of about twenty came out and greeted him with friendly gestures, then shook hands and said something in Arabic. Chris croaked, 'Where is this?' but for a few moments the youth did not understand. Then at last he pointed back and said, 'Iraq! Iraq!' Now, belatedly, Chris saw in the distance the Iraqi border town with its tower, which had been blacked out when he passed it in the dark, and the second town as well, which also had a tower.

'Thank God,' he thought. 'I've made it.'

The youth beckoned him inside and brought a big metal bowl, like a dog's bowl, full of water. He drank it straight down, and another immediately afterwards. Inside the house an old woman with tattoos on her face was feeding a child; there were rolls of bedding, and straw in the part where the animals slept. In the middle was a paraffin heater and Chris sat by it, grateful for the warmth. After the drink, he could speak and he began to talk to the children, who had been drawing pictures on paper – aircraft on fire, tanks blazing.

The cook came in with some of the new bread, still hot, and he ate a piece, but immediately felt full, so much had his stomach shrunk. Then the youth gave him a glass of hot, sweet tea and as soon as he had drunk that, he felt much more in command of his senses.

Trying to explain to the boy that he must see a policeman, he took off his jacket and webbing, stripped his rifle down, wrapped it in the jacket and stowed everything in a polythene sack so that he would present a less aggressive appearance. Then they set off for the distant town, the boy carrying the bag, Chris hobbling beside him. After an hour or so a Land-Cruiser appeared and the driver, who spoke some English, offered them a lift into town.

On the outskirts he stopped and shouted something into a shack. Out came an Arab dressed entirely in black. The driver exchanged a few words, then ordered the goat-herd out of the car. The boy got out, looking very worried. Instinctively Chris trusted him, but not the driver, who then set off again, making provocative remarks. 'You shouldn't be here,' he said. 'This isn't our war. Why not go back to Iraq?'

Chris produced his indemnity slip, which said in Arabic that anyone taking this soldier to a British Embassy or to the Allied forces would receive the equivalent of £5000. Thinking it was money, the driver took it and put it in his pocket, so Chris demanded it back and said sharply, 'No, you have to take me with you or you won't get paid.'

Further into town, the driver stopped at a garage and called. A man came to the passenger door, took one look, then ran back inside. Thinking that he was about to have his throat cut for his weapon, Chris grabbed his bag and started to pull it out. The driver seized his arm, so he punched him a couple of times and struggled out. By the time he had his feet on the ground, the driver was sprawled across the front seat with his head sticking out through the passenger door, so Chris gave the door a good kick, jamming his head in it.

Running as best he could, he went down the street and round a corner, where he came on a man standing guard beside a pill-box, armed with an AK-47 and wearing webbing pouches.

'Police?' he shouted.

'Yes.'

'British airman!'

The sentry grabbed his arm and dragged him into a bunga-low, the police station. Men in leather jackets were sitting about, one behind a big desk. Then the driver of the Land-Cruiser burst in and they all started arguing in Arabic.

When Chris showed them his rescue chit, they laughed at it and hit the driver and threw him out. Then they searched the bag of kit and sent Chris into the office belonging to the chief. He spoke no English, but motioned their captive to write down his name and details. He gave his own name, but a false unit, pretending that he was an air medical orderly whose helicopter had been shot down.

The police chief made a couple of telephone calls, spelling out the details which he had taken down. Then Chris was told to put on Arab dress, including a face-veil, and was frog-marched out to a waiting vehicle by two men with AK-47 rifles. He could not make out what was happening and no one explained. Was he a prisoner about to be sent back to Iraq or merely being treated as a prisoner to fool any locals who might be watching?

His uncertainty persisted through most of the day. After an hour's drive they pulled up behind two Mercedes on a motorway in the middle of the desert. Half a dozen men were standing about, one with a pistol in his hand. Chris was blindfolded and made to kneel in the road. His head was pushed forward. 'This is it,' he thought. 'After all this, I'm going to be topped.' He was not so much frightened as annoyed with himself for walking into a trap.

But then, after an exchange of words, he was bundled into the back of one of the Mercedes, which drove off. After two hours they came to a big sign with an arrow saying 'Baghdad'. As they drove on, his escorts began making heavy jokes: 'Yes, we going Baghdad. You our prisoner. We Iraqis.'

When evening came on, Chris was so exhausted and confused that he could not remember whether the sun set in the east or in the west. To decide, he had to think back to his boyhood on Tyneside and the sun coming up over the coast, in the east. That clinched it: they were heading west, towards safety.

By 2300 they were in the outskirts of a big city. His escorts put out their cigarettes and straightened their ties. As they pulled up behind another car, a smartly dressed, middle-aged man climbed into the passenger seat and asked in good English, 'Are you all right?' When Chris answered 'Yes', he said, 'It won't be long now.'

The two other men were in awe and fear of this newcomer. When the car finally drove into a compound, they leapt out to open his door. Chris, tottering out, found he could hardly stand. The man snapped his fingers and the other two carried him into a building, the headquarters of the secret police.

In a large office-cum-apartment, he was greeted by a man in a blue blazer, striped shirt and tie, who shook his hand and, through an interpreter, said, 'Welcome!'

The Chief of the Secret Police had all the trappings of office: a gold-plated AK-47 on the wall, pictures of his leader, expensive furniture. Seeing the state Chris was in, he offered him a bath and led him through his own bedroom fitted with gym equipment into a large bathroom, where he put a new blade into his razor and set out soap and shampoo.

As Chris was stripping off, in came a young man with a tape measure who proceeded to size him up. The circumstances were so bizarre that his reaction was only to hope that they were not measuring him 'for a wooden box'.

He had two baths: the first was soon filthy, so he straight-away ran another. As he wallowed, someone brought him a cup of coffee. Then the interpreter came back and asked a few questions, though not aggressively. Chris repeated his story of flying in to pick up a downed pilot and the helicopter crashing. He had the impression that they did not believe him, but they seemed happy to leave it at that.

Only when he saw himself stripped off did he realize how much weight he had lost. His muscles had burnt away until his biceps were no thicker than his wrists. Out of the bath, he found a set of clean underwear, a white shirt and tie, socks, shoes and a brand-new suit of dark pin-striped cotton, run up by some tailor within the past half hour, in the middle of the night. When the trousers turned out to be too big round the waist, the police chief ripped into the boy who had taken the measurements – and by the time a doctor had been to dress Chris's feet, the trousers were back, fitting.

The police chief then offered food. A banquet of steaks, kebabs, vegetables, fruit and bread had appeared. Chris drank pints of water and ate half a steak, but it seemed to stop half-way down to his stomach and he could not manage any more. His host then offered to show him some local night life out on the town.

Apologizing for his lack of enthusiasm, Chris said, 'I'm sorry, but I must ask you to take me to the British Embassy as soon as possible.' The police chief seemed disappointed, but telephoned the Embassy and reported that a car was on its way. Before bidding his guest goodbye, he asked him to check all his kit, which had been laid out on a table: every-thing was in order and it was all handed back. When the driver came in, he bowed to the chief and carried the kit out to the car. Then Chris shook hands, said thank you for everything and left.

At the Embassy he was received with some excitement. Messages went straight to Joint Headquarters at High Wycombe and to Riyadh, and arrangements were made for him to fly out the next evening. Yet, as he said, he could never relax fully until he was reunited with his squadron. Then at last he felt 'back in the family, and safe'.

As far as he could tell, he had walked some three hundred kilometres. He had eaten nothing except his two packets of biscuits, and had gone without water for most of the eight nights and seven days. He attributed his survival to the fact that he had built up a lot of muscle by intensive weight-training during his months in the Gulf. When he went out there, he had weighed thirteen stone. Now he was down to just over ten stone. In his time on the run he had lost nearly forty pounds. As he said, he had lived on his own meat.

It was two weeks before he could walk properly and six weeks before feeling returned to his fingers and toes. He had a blood disorder, enzymes in his liver from drinking river water, and a viral infection, but all these problems were cured and he finally emerged unscathed from one of the most remarkable feats of physical endurance ever recorded.

CHAPTER 11

COMBAT ON ALL FRONTS

Just after midnight on 30/31 January, under a full moon, an Iraqi force of T-55 tanks, armoured personnel carriers and some four thousand troops stormed across the border close to the sea and bore down on the abandoned coastal town of Khafji, a few kilometres inside Saudi Arabia. Contrary to what CNN and other television stations reported, this was not, for the Coalition, a serious breakthrough. It was exactly what we had expected and hoped for, as it brought enemy vehicles, weapons and men out of their prepared positions and into the open, where our pilots were able to see them and pick them off. The screen of Allied troops near the front executed a well-planned manoeuvre and let the invaders through so that the next line of Coalition forces, who were mobile, could cut them off from their supporting weapons and deal with them piecemeal.

That said, the invaders came further than they were meant to. There was an element of duplicity in their advance, in that the gun barrels of their tanks were pointing to the rear, which indicated that they did not mean to fight and our second-line forces were slow to come to grips with them. The result was that the Iraqis managed to occupy one sector of the town and the fierce engagement which followed lasted thirty-six hours, but the Saudis and Qataris acquitted themselves well and our tactics, as I reported to Bridget, 'worked a charm. A Saudi brigade has defeated a much larger Iraqi force, causing the enemy at least eight hundred casualties. To remind everyone of the type of people they are, the Iraqis put up a white flag and then shot at the Saudis who came out to take their surrender.'

This minor invasion was a great shock to King Fahd, who felt that his kingdom had been defiled. No matter that Khafji was by then more or less a ghost town: the fact that it had been entered by the enemy was an outrage. It so happened that Prince Khalid was in the Khafji area, visiting his forward troops, when the Iraqi attack began. Taking personal charge of local Arab forces, he got his first taste of battle and emerged with his reputation enhanced. Immediately afterwards I sent him a note of congratulation and Khalid wrote back saying, 'We demonstrated the folly of the enemy's policies and, by the Grace of God, gave ourselves a victory . . . Together we will prevail, to liberate Kuwait and rid the world of a tyrant.' Later he told me that he showed my letter to his father, Prince Sultan, confiding to me that the Defence Minister was delighted to know that the Saudi and Qatari troops and their commander were so highly regarded by one of their major allies.

Almost more than anything else, Khafji was a battle by television and it perfectly illustrated the dangers of using live television as a reliable source of information. Because CNN reported a major attack and build-up, the US Marines started to deploy in response, only to discover that the reports had no solid foundation. Hardly was the battle over before I had Tom King on the telephone because some local Press pundits thought that it should have been managed differently. 'It really is war by TV,' I wrote home, 'and goodness knows what is going to happen when the ground war starts in earnest.' Partly as a result of Khafji, I had all the television sets removed from my own operations room and installed elsewhere. Before I did that, people would not only sit transfixed, failing to do the work which they were supposed to be doing; they would also take what they saw on screen as gospel truth, which it easily might not be. Even if a news report was basically accurate, it could only be a small snapshot of one part of the big picture, so that any decision based on it was liable to be a bad one.

The attack on Khafji and a follow-up border incursion the

same night at Al Wafra put the Coalition very much on its guard. A week earlier, on 23 January, Intelligence reports had revealed a large-scale movement among the Iraqi troops on the border just north of Hafar al Batin, where many of the Allied ground forces were forming up, together with their vulnerable logistic units. We did not know whether the enemy was merely reorganizing his forward troops or whether he was deploying for an attack: in any case, our own troops hastily dug in to meet the threat. This was a tricky period for us, since our Division was spread out over a distance of several hundred kilometres as it moved up to its assembly area, and a major assault by the Iraqis at that moment would have been a nightmare. Looking back, I do not think that they were up to it, militarily, but we did not know that at the time. In the end, nothing came of their shifting around, but Khafji, following close on the scare at Hafar al Batin, suggested to us that Saddam was keen to provoke a major battle on the ground. He was taking heavy punishment from the air and believed that the desert, where he reportedly outnumbered us two-to-one, was the only place in which he had a chance of scoring off us. Another reason for the cross-border raids was that the Iraqis badly wanted intelligence about the forces ranged against them and hoped to discover who their opponents were by capturing prisoners.

The other phenomenon of this time was the flight, in ones and twos, of almost a hundred and fifty Iraqi aircraft to Iran, nearly a quarter of Saddam's entire air force. Was this a mass defection by his pilots or a conservation measure? For the time being we could not be sure. At first we thought that individual rats were beginning to desert the sinking ship, but later we changed our minds. Bill Wratten's view, shared by Chuck Horner and his Intelligence staff, was that Saddam was trying to save his assets for another day, probably for the ground war. Once Allied bombers had started to take out his hardened aircraft shelters with precision attacks, the Iraqis evidently realized that they could not protect their planes on the ground and that the only way to preserve them was to move them out of harm's way.

The fugitive aircraft included many of Iraq's most modern

types and the exodus seemed too well organized to be simply casual desertion. By then the Allies had combat air patrols flying over the middle of Iraq, but time and again Iraqi jets would slip away across the northern end of the Gulf just as the CAP was changing over or at a time when none was flying in that particular area, which showed that enemy electronic intelligence was still operative. Nevertheless, the fact that several of the fleeing pilots ran out of fuel or became disorientated and crashed *en route* to Iran confirmed the low standard of flying competence that prevailed among them: some of them could not even take off, navigate and land safely, let alone tackle any more complicated task, such as vectoring on to an enemy aircraft. We had already surmised that their level of ability was low from the small number of training sorties which our surveillance systems had recorded before hostilities began and now this piecemeal exodus confirmed it.

The status of the escaping aircraft was of high interest to Chris Craig and his Task Group in the Gulf. From the moment the air war started, he had at the front of his mind the possibility that Iraq might try to draw Iran into the conflict or to use her territory as a springboard, so that there was always a chance of an air attack from the east. When these warplanes began arriving in Iran, the threat seemed all the greater and the need for vigilance correspondingly strong.

After the phenomenal activity in the first seventy-two hours of the war, US naval air operations dropped away to a mere four hundred carrier-launched sorties a day, but from three days before H-hour until the end of the ground war on 28 February, the Royal Navy never changed its high anti-air defence profile. As Chris put it, 'We were constantly expecting the Iraqis to try to slip down under cover of the returning Allied aircraft and see if they could give us a bloody nose. And of course they tried.'

We had a clear picture of the kind of raid which the Navy could expect. The enemy would look for the cover of a big Allied force package returning home and make a high-level feint with Mig 23s or similar aircraft, which would be obvious on radar. Once Allied attention had been drawn by that, the real raiders – Exocet-carrying Mirages – would come in ultra-low on the same axis, aiming to hit a ship. Sure enough, almost exactly this happened on January 24.

The raid was called initially by an Allied AWACS aircraft overland, which detected the genuine element of the attack first, two Mirages coming down the coast at medium level. A minute or two later the AWACS picked up the high-level decoys as well, Mig 23s. At sea, the raid was well called by the USS *Bunker Hill*. There followed a few moments of confusion as other ships came on the air with requests for information, but all the vessels in the forward air-defence line, including the two British destroyers, were at missiles-ready by the time the attackers broke away from the coast. Then came an unexpected but welcome intervention. A thirty-year-old Saudi pilot, Captain Ayedh al-Shamrani, was airborne over the coast in his F-15: the AWACS vectored him on to the attackers and, although he was perilously low in fuel, he shot both of them down with air-to-air missiles in a single pass, returning to base a national hero, with justification.

After that, Iraqi aircraft never attacked the fleet again, but at no stage until the war had finished did our naval crews relax. For weeks on end they remained at defence watches, expecting a raid at any minute, and the cumulative strain became colossal. I was glad to know from Chris Craig that, on the air-defence side, cooperation between British and Americans was first-class: the two navies melded together and worked up common techniques of fighter control and missile defence.

With the threat from the air now under control, the Navy's next main aim was to eliminate the enemy surface threat all the way up to the Shatt al Arab at the head of the Gulf; and, while the land battle for Khafji was in progress, the Task Group had a lively engagement of its own, the large-scale mêlée which became known as the Bubiyan Channel battle. (During this the BBC World News service proudly announced that we had recaptured an island called Qaruh. At first this sounded a major achievement, but on closer inspection the place turned out to be only two feet high and sixty feet long.)

For day after day Iraqi fast patrol boats tried to break out of their hideouts between Bubiyan Island and the mainland, to go to the aid of their land-based colleagues attacking Khafji. The most dangerous craft were the TNC 45s, with Exocets on board, which had been captured from the Kuwaitis, but the Iraqis also had Russian-built Osas, armed with Styx missiles, which were very effective against surface targets, and vessels with lower capability known as Zhuks. For day after day Royal Navy Lynx helicopters flew low-level, long-range sorties in poor visibility against these elusive targets, supported by fixed-wing aircraft from the American carriers and shore-based squadrons. The battle reached its climax on 29 and 30 January, when helicopters from *Gloucester*, *Cardiff*, *Manchester*, *London* and *Brazen* used our two forward destroyers as stepping stones, landing on them to refuel and bouncing off again for their continued attacks. The final tally of kills was slightly uncertain, after helicopters had been wheeling and diving in repeated assaults, but we reckoned that eighteen of the twenty-five Sea Skua missiles fired by Lynxes hit their targets, that seven vessels were sunk by them, that hits were registered on a number of smaller ships and that, in all, twenty-five per cent of the Iraqi navy was destroyed. The extended action was extremely taxing for the Lynx crews, who maintained flying rates about three times their normal, but their success was outstanding.

The battle left the Allied navies facing one last major surface threat: mines. We knew the Iraqis had sown the northern waters of the Gulf with three types of mines – some tethered to the sea bed, some *on* the sea bed and some floating free – but we never gained any definitive intelligence on dispositions. The free-floaters were a constant menace, as they came drifting southwards towards our ships with the set of the current: to avoid them, the captains on station would move north during daylight hours, their lookouts spotting by eye with the help of electronic surveillance sights, and then drift back with the tidal current during the night, so that floating mines could not bear down on them. A number were found and destroyed, but they remained a severe constraint on ship movements. It seemed ironic that in an ultra-modern ship, packed with high technology, the only defence against this threat was a single sailor posted in the bows, concentrating intently for half an hour at a time, in radio contact with the bridge. An enormous responsibility fell on this one man and his job, often in bitter weather, was an exceedingly tough one.

Phase Three of the Allied naval operations was to move to the north of the Gulf and take the American battleships in through the minefields so that they could bombard Faylaka Island, some twenty kilometres out from Kuwait City, and the coast of the mainland, to help persuade the Iraqis that an amphibious assault from the sea was imminent. The island had been abandoned by the Kuwaitis – except for one old man, who dug himself in and remained there throughout the war – and had become an Iraqi defensive stronghold.

This was the most contentious phase of the naval campaign and the one which gave me most cause for concern. It was clear from the start that the Royal Navy would have to take the lead, for our five Hunt Class MCMVs (Mine Counter-Measure Vessels) were in a league of their own and far more effective than the helicopters which the Americans favoured.

From frequent discussions with Chris Craig, I knew that liaison between the US fleet in the Gulf and Norman Schwarzkopf was by no means as close as it might have been, and Norman himself several times grumbled to me that, when it came to surface operations, his admirals never told him what they were doing. The reason for this weakness, I felt sure, was that the US naval forces were never welded into the CinC's headquarters in the way that the Royal Navy was welded into ours. Moreover, the lack of understanding between them was exacerbated by a fundamental ambiguity about the role of the US Marines.

To the end of the war, I was never certain what role Norman meant the Marines to play. They, of course, desperately wanted to carry out a full-scale amphibious landing on the coast and attack Kuwait from the sea, but he was reluctant to give them the go-ahead, as he feared, rightly, in my view, that such an operation could result in enormous and unjustified casualties. With the main land attack coming in from the west, there was no point in risking lives simply to give the Marines a part in the action and the option which he preferred by far was to use them as a feint. In the end, I understand, he told them this, but I also believe that, with his characteristic tactic of postponing difficult decisions while he gathered more and more information, he kept them waiting for an answer to the very end. Thus whenever Chris Craig asked the American naval commanders what the plans for the Marines were, they could not tell him – and I myself was far from clear.

This lack of certainty was a considerable handicap to both of us, for it directly affected our approach to the problem of mine clearance. If an amphibious landing had been critical to the success of Operation Desert Storm, because it would have failed without one, we should have felt justified in taking substantial risks if thereby we could obtain a good chance of clearing the approaches to the Kuwaiti coast; but if the role of the seaborne Marines was distinctly peripheral, as I believed it was going to be, I did not feel like risking ships unnecessarily, especially as we were winning the war from the air anyway.

Pressure to commit our minesweepers came on us heavily from all sides. The Marines' commanders implied that if in the end they could not land it would be our fault for not going into action quickly enough, and rumours began filtering out from the United Kingdom that the Royal Navy was not making sufficient effort. Norman Schwarzkopf, however, did not seem particularly anxious that our minesweepers should go in and fortunately his position and mine were much the same, although for different reasons.

I determined that we should use our MCMVs, but sensibly. In discussions before Christmas I had told Chris Craig that although I wanted him to help win the war as quickly and emphatically as he could, I did *not* want him to take risks out of proportion to the likely rewards. He had therefore stipulated to Vice Admiral Stanley Arthur, the US Naval Commander, that he would commit his MCMVs and their support arm and escorts right forward, to penetrate the minefields, *provided* he was brought in on the planning for the operation. On 26 January he was thus unpleasantly surprised when, summoned to a conference on board the USS *Tripoli*, the mine counter-measure command ship, he heard a senior American naval officer expound a totally unworkable plan which, Chris considered, could not be approved without further debate, and of which, until then, neither he nor I had heard a word.

The basic idea was that the Royal Navy mine-hunters should proceed through the most dangerous area high up the Gulf, at a fair speed, to a position only five kilometres off the enemy coast and there begin clearance operations, working day and night, from inshore outwards, until they had swept a box or rectangle big enough to admit the battleships, which would then suppress the shore defences with their sixteen-inch guns, while further mine-clearance proceeded.

To Craig, this was tantamount to suicide. He knew that the Iraqis had eighty thousand troops on the coast, with artillery and mobile Silkworm missile launchers, which had a range of ninety kilometres. His 'little coracles', as he called his mine-hunters, would be easy meat for the defenders as they went pottering about their business at three knots, and at point-blank range. It seemed that the American architects of the plan had no idea of how counter-measures should be under-taken in that environment.

When asked for his views, Chris gave them in robust terms and many senior American officers cried, 'Hear! Hear!' At the end of the main briefing he emphasized that he must know the United States' overall strategic aim: were they going for a full amphibious assault on the coast or was the whole bom-bardment going to be merely a feint? The plan which they had proposed would lead to massive casualties and he could not countenance taking such a risk unless it was absolutely imperative.

The upshot was a series of conferences held in Bahrein, at which plans for the clearing of a battleship box were pro-gressively refined. With my approval, Chris made two basic stipulations. One was that all possible air power should be concentrated to suppress the coastal defences when the mine-sweepers went in, and the other that the operation should be conducted from the outside inwards, rather than vice versa. Much depended on the degree of clearance which the

American commanders wanted. For a full amphibious landing, they needed eighty per cent clearance, but a detailed study showed that this would take much longer than anyone had anticipated. As planning went on, the original figure of twenty-eight days was extended to thirty-five.

On land, with the Allied air forces still hammering the Iraqis day and night, we had to steel ourselves increasingly against outside criticism, particularly in America where public opinion was extremely volatile, that we were slaughtering innocent civilians unnecessarily. In fact we were taking every possible precaution to avoid causing civilian deaths and to concentrate on military targets. At each Morning Prayers Norman Schwarzkopf listed the achievements of the air campaign to date. We had severely degraded Saddam's airfields and disrupted his command and control structure. We had broken his communications links to the front, particularly in 3 Corps area. Ninety per cent of Iraqi internal communications had been knocked out, and the distribution of fuel severely disrupted. Damage to ammunition storage dumps so far was light, but a key factory manufacturing Scud fuses had been bombed, so that the long-term supply of missiles had been interrupted, and the production of chemical warfare stocks had been hard hit. The national electricity grid had been shut down. A strike on an ammunition dump west of Basra had caused a colossal explosion: the initial blast and secondary detonations had released as much power as a small volcano, or three launches of the American Space Shuttle . . .

Throughout this intense campaign, Saddam Hussein himself was not a designated Coalition target but, as Commander-in-Chief of the enemy forces and the man running the war against us, he inevitably became a military target from time to time. Since the war I have many times been asked why we did not eliminate the dictator while we had the chance. The answer is that we would have taken him out, had it been possible, but he was crafty and well protected, and also had the luck of the devil. Nevertheless, on at least two occasions he was thought to be in a military environment which had been targeted for attack. Once, when we heard that he was moving from one location to another, American aircraft found the convoy and attacked it, destroying most of the vehicles, but either Saddam was in one of the few cars which escaped, or he had never been present at all. On the other occasion, we received intelligence that he planned to spend the night in a mobile caravan headquarters which he used from time to time. Again, the target was destroyed, but again, Saddam was not at home. Prince Khalid believed, then and later, that if we had succeeded in killing him, we should only have turned him into a martyr, that someone equally ruthless would have taken over control of Iraq and that we should have made things even more difficult for ourselves.

Even as our bombers concentrated on strategic targets, Saddam himself was ruthlessly putting his civilians in the line of fire and so earning odium in the eyes of the world. It was entirely in character that he should be prepared to sacrifice his own people and invite the destruction of his country's holy places, simply to score points in world opinion charts. Thus he moved headquarters into schools and office buildings, and sited guns and military vehicles in schools and hospitals, hoping that the Allies would not attack them there, or that, if they did, they would undermine their own cause in the eyes of the world. He also began to strip the wings off military aircraft, tow them down village streets and park them next to mosques or among ordinary houses, in the hope that we would bomb them there. In fact we took pains to leave them alone: spread about as they were, unable to take off, they posed no threat to us.

In any case, both the British and Americans had a very clear targeting directive and all holy shrines were strictly off-limits. Any target which might give rise to collateral damage had to be rated essential – that is, the planners had to decide that its destruction would shorten the war or protect Coalition lives – before we flew against it. Inevitably, even laser-guided bombs went astray from time to time and, when they did, it was disappointing for the aircrews that the Western media gave the accidents such prominence. The final decision on whether or not a target should be attacked was always left to the pilots, and many aborted their missions on their own initiative when they saw that the risk of causing civilian casualties was too high. Never in the history of warfare has such care been taken in the planning and execution of a campaign to avoid causing casualties among the civilian community.

In deliberately mixing military and civilian matters and seeking to cloud the difference between the two, Saddam descended to his nadir, and nowhere more grotesquely than in his use of the Amiriya bunker in Baghdad. When two Stealth fighter-bombers demolished the building on the night of 13 February, and more than three hundred civilians were killed, there was naturally uproar in the world's media. But this was exactly what Saddam wanted. He was using part of the building as a headquarters, and he was well aware that civilians were taking refuge in other parts of the building during air raids (the Coalition did not know this). Whether he put those people there on purpose, or whether he merely failed to have them turned out, he without doubt deliberately risked sacrificing them, in the knowledge that, if the building were hit, he would gain favourable publicity in the eyes of the world. Again, we were witnessing the actions of a psychopath bent solely on his own survival, no matter what the cost in human life. (At the time we felt certain that the bunker-basement of the hotel occupied by CNN housed an important command headquarters, but we could not hit the building without destroying the television station and its journalists in the process.)

As the air assault pounded on, our land forces were building up towards full readiness for war. Norman Schwarzkopf had asked me to have the British Division up and running by 31 January and, in meeting this target, Rupert Smith achieved an astonishing feat. Back in November, he himself had been appointed to command a division only two weeks before being nominated for the job in the Gulf. Then, in barely six weeks after coming out, with the help of his Chief of Staff, Colonel John Reith of the Parachute Regiment, he had welded together a diverse mass of servicemen, many of whom had never met before. He had made them ready for war in an environment strange to most of them and one for which they were neither trained nor equipped. He had transported his entire Division, with all its armour and artillery, more than three hundred kilometres to the north-west and then had brought it alongside the Americans, and had coordinated procedures and techniques for operating with them. Altogether, it was an outstanding feat. I was particularly pleased that he had met the deadline, because it meant that I had fulfilled the second of two important promises which I had made to Norman: the first was that the SAS would achieve something worthwhile, and the second that our Division would be ready on time, without calling on the Americans for logistic support.

One reason for this success was the outstandingly high level of our own logistic back-up, which, under Martin White's able direction, had continuously expanded and adapted to meet every new demand. In the early days of the deployment, with 7th Armoured Brigade sitting in a defensive position on the long, low spur known as Cement Ridge, only twenty kilometres north of the Al Fadhili training area, Martin had planned for a fourteen-day defensive battle. Next, as the Coalition prepared to move on to the offensive, he had to think in terms of a fairly rapid advance due northwards and began planning to set up a Forward Force Maintenance Area (FFMA) at Al Mish'ab, a town on the coast. Then, with the resubordination of our Division to VII Corps, he had to change his plans comprehensively and establish his FFMA on the edge of the American Log Base Alpha, just south of the Tapline road some three hundred kilometres from Jubail. Log Base Alpha was nothing but a rectangle of desert defended by berms and wire fences, and on the side of it the British constructed their own forward logistic depot.

By now the scale of the supply operation was colossal. Our ammunition site alone occupied an area ten kilometres by seven, with munitions piled in the open in two-hundred-ton stacks, each a safe distance from the next. By the end of January nearly twenty-four thousand tons of ammunition had been moved forward, as well as three million litres of fuel. The force bakery had also deployed forward to Log Base

Alpha and the Division continued to enjoy fresh rations right into the middle of February (the BBC television reporter Kate Adie used to call in to the bakery for fresh rolls and a shower). Our lines of supply, though not yet at full stretch, were already immensely long: the round trip from Jubail to the FFMA and back was more than seven hundred kilometres and our drivers lost count of the number of times they went up and down, stopping for food, sleep, fuel and repairs at the half-way halt known as the Happy Eater. If we had not obtained air supremacy, we could never have used the Tap-line road as we did: had the Iraqis been flying, we should have had to travel at night only and the resulting delay would have been enormous. As it was, everything flowed with amazing ease.

When I visited the Division on 6 February in the Keyes concentration area north of Qaysumah, I found them quietly confident, having just conducted a demanding work-up exercise with the American division destined to make the initial breach through the Iraqi minefield. Rupert had brought off a major night move, put the British Division into the right position and then taken them through a simulated minefield breach. I came away well pleased with the rapport which had swiftly grown up between us and the Americans.

Like Rupert, Brigadier Chris Hammerbeck, commanding 4th Armoured Brigade, had done a remarkable job in training his men for a new environment and welding them together. An exceptional military thinker, with a sound background knowledge of warfare – and armoured warfare in particular – Chris seized this opportunity of putting theory into practice. For someone fairly new in command, it was a daunting experience to arrive in such an alien environment, with so little time left before hostilities were likely to begin, but he quickly proved himself excellent at talking to his servicemen, putting the right message over to them and enthusing them for the task in hand. Being an old friend of Rupert Smith – they had both been parachutists – he was immediately at one with his divisional commander, and anyway had a similarly unconventional turn of mind. By his own account, he regarded himself as 'the tick on the camel's back', and revelled in constructive argument.

Even at this late stage I was still concerned about the unreliability of our armoured vehicles. Rupert assured me that it was coming right and would be right on the day. Phenomenal improvements had indeed been made, partly by the sheer effort of crews, who looked after their Challengers and Warriors better than they would have cared for their own cars: the fighting vehicles were, after all, their passports to battle, their mobile homes and their armoured protection, all rolled into one. As Martin White remarked, 'In that situation, if the manual tells you to clean the filters daily, you bloody well clean them.' The other ingredient of success was that all the vehicles had been brought up to a high state of maintenance. In this, as in most things, the key was money. Whereas in peacetime maintenance tends to be skimped because of shortages of cash and manpower, now on the eve of war we had everything we wanted, with close REME support and abundant spare parts. If a vehicle broke down, it was repaired immediately: the power packs of tanks, which were the engine and gearbox combined and weighed six tons, were replaced in the field within a matter of hours. The Division as a whole achieved a remarkable standard of mobility. No praise is too high for the efforts of the REME, whose technicians made a major contribution to the British military effort through their expertise and dedication. The same is true of the teams from civilian firms such as Vickers, General Electric and Land Rover, who not only supported their products in the relative safety of Jubail, but also went through the breach into Iraq once the ground war had started.

Rupert's records showed that in the early days of January, if he drove his whole fleet at once, one Challenger I power pack gave out on average every 2·8 kilometres. This had made him rather pessimistic, because he had only a limited number of spare power packs and he could predict, within about fifty kilometres, the spot at which he was going to start leaving tank hulls stranded in the desert because he had no engines to put in them. By now, however, the mean distance between failures had almost tripled, to 6·8 kilometres, and he was altogether more sanguine.

Morale was not nearly so high in the camp for battle casualty replacements (BCRs) at Jubail. To act as a BCR is a depressing business at any time, as I myself know full well, having been one in Japan as an eighteen-year-old subaltern before I fought in Korea. One's role is no more and no less than to wait for somebody to be killed or seriously injured and then step into the casualty's shoes. Because replacements may be needed for men in a wide variety of skilled posts, the reservists are picked individually from different units and separated from their regiments and friends, but while they are hanging around, they cannot practise their skills and so are liable to become demoralized. We had radio operators with no radios to operate, tank drivers with no tanks to drive, REME mechanics with no vehicles to work on, RAF fitters with no aircraft to maintain, medical staff with no hospital facilities, and many others similarly frustrated, all uprooted from their normal backgrounds.

I was so struck by the need to pull them all together that I had them collected for a personal briefing and stood on a box with a hand-held loud-hailer to tell them how closely I identified with their difficulties as a result of my own experience. I reminded them that they would have a vital role to play in sustaining the momentum of battle when we started to take casualties and I told the junior officers, particularly, that this period of waiting would be a major test of their individual qualities of leadership. I should judge them, I said, by their ability to manage what I acknowledged was a difficult and challenging problem. They must use their drive and imagination to create interesting, worthwhile tasks to keep their men in good heart.

News of the SAS, in contrast, was good. Some of the men from the bounced patrol were still missing in the western desert, but the Scud strikes on Israel had been suppressed and stories of astonishing heroism and endurance, in the best traditions of the unit, had begun to filter back. Of these sagas, none was more striking than the great escape recounted in the last chapter, which reminded people of the trek by the legendary Jack Sillito through the Western Desert of Africa in 1942. But there were numerous other Special Forces men who displayed outstanding bravery and resource in their battle against the Scuds, a fact reflected by the very high number of awards for gallantry won by the SAS during the war.

There was a bad moment early in February when it transpired that Iraqi radio transmitters sited in Jordan were deliberately jamming the distress frequency on which downed pilots or stranded members of the Special Forces sent out Mayday calls. I immediately asked for this to be taken up at the highest political level. Alan Munro raised the matter in Whitehall and Norman Schwarzkopf in Washington, and the jamming very soon ceased. My impression was that the Iraqis had set it up without the knowledge of the Jordanians but that, as soon as the Jordanians received a diplomatic complaint, they had it stopped.

Later it transpired that, in all, four members of the SAS lost their lives behind enemy lines. I was naturally much distressed by these deaths, but I derived no mean satisfaction from the fact that in the fiftieth year of their existence the SAS had travelled right back to their origins during the Second World War, when they were established to attack Rommel's airbases deep behind German lines in the North African desert. In recent times the need to maintain a desert capability had often been questioned by pundits in the United Kingdom, but the Regiment had always insisted that it was essential – and now their claim had been thoroughly vindicated.*

The American Special Forces, deployed into their Scud Boulevard in western Iraq by long-distance helicopter on 8

---

* Colonel Sir David Stirling, founder of the SAS, had died in November 1990 at the age of eighty-five. Bridget represented me at his memorial service in the Guards' Chapel on 7 February 1991. In 1989 he and I had been guests at a lunch given in London by the German Ambassador, Baron Rüdiger von Wechmar, who had fought in Rommel's army in 1941. As the meal progressed, David and his old adversary swapped stories of the Western Desert with increasing relish and the conversation became absolutely fascinating. But then as we left David turned to me and said, 'By the way, I'm expecting you to take over from me as President of the SAS Association when I die.' It was a bequest which there was no escaping.

February, also did excellent work. Because their helicopters could fly at night almost regardless of the state of the moon and were so heavily armed that they could blast their way out of trouble, the Americans operated much more openly than we did.

Our helicopters needed a certain amount of ambient light to fly at night, with the result that nocturnal air sorties were limited to about twelve nights a month and our special operations remained comparatively furtive. Even so, the SAS became ever bolder, harassing the Iraqis by day as well as by night, and creating widespread alarm. Their problems of re-supply were solved most satisfactorily when an armed convoy of vehicles drove deep into Iraq in broad daylight. The Special Forces were of course much helped by the fact that the Iraqi air force had been grounded: had enemy helicopters been flying, their existence behind the lines would have been far more threatened. But such was the confidence of the patrols that on 16 February, in the shelter of a dry wadi strewn with innumerable rocks, deep inside Iraq, they held a full meeting of the Warrant Officers' and Sergeants' Mess. After business had been conducted with suitable decorum, minutes were written up and the occasion was recorded in an official photograph, later signed by senior commanders, including Normal Schwarzkopf and myself.

Of course, I did not know of all these exploits when, on 9 February, Norman Schwarzkopf made time for me to meet the American Defence Secretary Dick Cheney, who was visiting the theatre with Colin Powell. Yet I already knew enough to demonstrate that our Special Forces had made a major strategic contribution to the war. The American visitors had a hectic schedule, but Norman found me a quarter of an hour in which to give them an overview on the British contribution, with particular reference to what the SAS had done. They showed keen interest and I felt that this was an exceptionally valuable meeting, since it underlined the harmony between Britain and the United States and showed how closely our forces could work and fight together in the field.

In March, a few days after the war had ended, Norman

wrote a most generous letter to Paddy Hine, commending the SAS for their 'totally outstanding performance', and describing them as 'the only force deemed qualified' for the critical task of suppressing the Scud threat to Israel. 'From the first day they were assigned their mission until the last day of the conflict,' he wrote, the performance of the SAS 'was courageous and highly professional'. In spite of the hazards posed by weather, terrain and enemy forces, the SAS succeeded 'in totally denying the central corridor of western Iraq to Scud units. The result was that the principal areas used by the Iraqis to fire Scuds on Tel Aviv were no longer available to them.' When the United States Special Operations Forces were introduced, the SAS 'provided invaluable assistance . . . They took every possible measure to ensure that US forces were thoroughly briefed and were able to profit from the valuable lessons that had been learned by earlier SAS deployments.' So well did British and Americans combine that 'the synergistic effect of these fine units ultimately caused the enemy to be convinced that they were facing forces in western Iraq that were more than tenfold the size of those they were actually facing. As a result, large numbers of enemy forces that might otherwise have been deployed in the eastern theatre were tied down in western Iraq.' In conclusion, Norman declared:

> The performance of the 22nd Special Air Service Regiment during Operation Desert Storm was in the highest traditions of the professional military service, and in keeping with the proud history and tradition that has been established by that Regiment.

As preparations for G-Day went ahead, my own thoughts were reaching out beyond the war. It was clear that as the Middle East settled down again the Arabs would need substantial help from the West in restoring the region, and that there would be numerous opportunities for Western industry and business, most obviously in Kuwait, which was going to need major reconstruction work, but also in Saudi Arabia and the Gulf as a whole. Already I had tasked the Special Boat Service, who had so far had a rather quiet war, with the job of reoccupying the British Embassy in Kuwait at the earliest possible moment and instructed them to make plans under the cover name Operation Trebor. (We assumed that the building and grounds might well be booby-trapped and even that a detachment of Iraqi kamikaze troops might have been left behind to thwart any attempt at repossession.) Norman Schwarzkopf was anxious that the Western Allies' return to Kuwait and the recovery of the embassies should be carried out in dignified fashion and not turn into a race between nations; all the same, I wanted to be sure that it was the British who were first into our own property.

I also sent an officer home with my first ideas on the postwar reconstruction, but from the reception which he received I gathered that people in the United Kingdom had not done much to address the problem and were surprised by my initiative. I was therefore glad when the Foreign Secretary, Douglas Hurd, arrived for a short visit on 10 February: he took a lively interest in everything and I seized the opportunity to discuss my concerns about the future, immediate and more distant. A few days later, Paddy Hine came out with two senior advisers from the Foreign Office, one of whom, Andrew Palmer, was an old friend and had been acting as political adviser in the Joint Headquarters at High Wycombe. We had a most useful day discussing postwar arrangements and as a result my visitors agreed that a paper should be put to Ministers within a week.

One of my chief short-term preoccupations was prisoners of war. Having seen pictures from Iraqi television of John Peters looking severely bruised about the face and having heard that two captured American pilots had been stripped and beaten, I was pleased that the British government was making the treatment of prisoners a major issue. It was particularly important that the world Press should keep up the pressure for all the prisoners of war to be treated properly, in accordance with the Geneva Convention. I was determined that, as soon as the Iraqis had been expelled from Kuwait, I would do what I could to exact the release not only of all prisoners taken during the conflict, but also of three British civilians whom Saddam had been holding in gaol.

At first we had imagined, somewhat naively, that we would be able to use Iraqi prisoners for bargaining: later we realized that the Geneva Convention would not permit any such trading. In any case, even before the ground war started it became apparent that our captives were worthless to us. Their great leader did not want them back and many of them refused to go. This was hardly surprising, for as the final showdown approached, Saddam's methods grew increasingly drastic. Wounded men were forbidden to return to their own villages and forced into hospitals where no relatives or friends would see them, so that the truth about what was happening at the front might not become apparent. Families who lost a member were forbidden to mourn, and on 16 February we heard of a new edict on the treatment of deserters from the Iraqi III Corps: one man from each battalion was to be hung and left hanging for five hours in view of his former colleagues, and the remainder who had tried to run away were to be shot.

On our side, we were building camps for holding prisoners on an enormous scale. Our main prisoner-handling force was three infantry battalions, one each from the Coldstream Guards, the Royal Highland Fusiliers and the King's Own Scottish Borderers. The Coldstream Guards were glad to have escaped from ceremonial public duties in England and, after a short period of acclimatization and training, went forward to the combat zone for their critical and dangerous role of dealing with newly taken prisoners, before handing them to the Americans, who in turn would hand them on to the Saudis. Separate accommodation was needed for prisoners of senior rank, particularly general officers, who would have to be segregated so that they did not mix with the *gundi*, or other ranks.

Out at sea, the British and American navies moved north on 14 February, proceeding up the east side of the Gulf until they were level with Kuwait, before turning westwards and heading straight for the coast, with our MCMVs in the lead. Now Chris Craig's little coracles really came into their own. They are the most sophisticated mine-hunters in the world and are themselves protected by a variety of subtle devices. With their non-magnetic hulls and engines specially damped so that the only noise emanating from the ship radiates at a harmless frequency, they are the maritime equivalent of the Stealth bomber, with the difference that they aim not merely to evade radar, but also to kill mines.

They have several modes of operation, but all are are slow and time-consuming, and, as Chris put it, 'do not fit the mind-set of people who want to go in and storm the beaches.'

The mine-hunting force came in from the east in two columns, with the MCMVs leading. There was much uncertainty about the disposition of the minefields and, after long debate with the Americans about where the ships should start sweeping, they began well out. They were feeling in the dark and the risks were high, but by then Chris was convinced that they had to be taken.

They began by clearing a channel, but after two days and nights, at 0430 in the morning of 18 February, the USS *Tripoli* detonated a mine which blew a hole six metres by ten in her side just forward of starboard beam. At the sound of the explosion, which carried far over the sea, the crews of every other ship froze. The Americans wanted to withdraw at once, but they refused to move without British MCMVs to lead them away. Five hours later, as the little coracles led the big ships out of trouble one by one, there was a second explosion when a bottom-mine went up aft of the USS *Princeton*: the hundred-and-fifty-metre ship's whiplash flung one stern lookout into the air and he fell twenty-five metres into the sea, but was recovered not much the worse. The *Tripoli*, meanwhile, had had a miraculous escape. The next section aft from the point of impact was the ship's main mess deck: seventy men had been asleep there when the mine struck and most of them would have been killed if it had gone off a few seconds later. As it was, only three men were injured and within a few minutes they were air-lifted to our hospital ship *Argus*, which was up with us in close support against just such an emergency. The *Tripoli*'s Captain said later that if the sea had been two states higher during the night, his ship would have gone to the bottom. As it was, his own crew made an excellent job of temporary repairs and later that day diving teams from our repair ship *Diligence* helped make safe the hold.

After these setbacks, the force regrouped itself and went back in to start again. It was highly demanding work, in easy range of Silkworm missiles on shore, and called for courage and stamina of the highest order, but after five days a large enough envelope had been cleared for the American battleships to come in and start shelling the shore. Led by the *Missouri*, they opened up from a range of thirty kilometres, but later moved in to only twenty kilometres, at which distance they were immensely effective. Guided by Pioneer remote-controlled drones, with video links back to the mother ship, gunners brought down devastatingly accurate fire on Iraqi defensive positions and undoubtedly fostered the enemy's belief that the Allies were planning to come ashore in strength.

It so happened that I visited the mine-hunters on 13 February, my twenty-sixth wedding anniversary. I had arranged for a shop near home to deliver flowers to Bridget and, in due course, I was delighted to hear that they had arrived on time. Romantic anniversaries were very much in the air and by St Valentine's Day, on the fourteenth, the flood of cards, letters and parcels from home had reached such proportions – sixteen tons a day – that I had to fly in thirty-seven extra postal workers to help deal with it and put fifty-five BCRs on to sorting mail. I myself was still receiving over thirty letters a day, almost all from strangers who wanted to send British servicemen their good wishes, prayers and love. Mayors, nuns, farmers, old soldiers, schoolgirls, firemen, widows, clerks . . . the variety of correspondents was extraordinary, as was the variety of ways in which people expressed their message. One woman in Northamptonshire sent a postcard bearing an aerial view of the town of Raunds, with the legend, 'X marks the factory which has designed and is manufacturing the new desert boots.' A publican near Sheffield, who had raised funds for a Gulf parcel appeal, wished me to know that 'We have named our giant bear after you – it is sat facing the bar at the moment, and it will go to its new home next week when the raffle is drawn.' An eleven-year-old boy from Bromsgrove was anxious about my personal wellbeing: 'What do you live in? When the bombing starts, how worried do you get?' A girl of twelve, with wisdom far beyond her years, remarked, 'People think it's all right for the generals, as they don't really have to fight, but you must have the hardest job of all, to make all the decisions, because if anything goes wrong you have got it on your conscience.' Some people wrote anonymously, some on behalf of organizations, some with tears falling on the paper. Every message that came was tremendously welcome and every one was answered, to the best ability of my over-stretched outer office.

All this time the air war was continuing unabated, with the emphasis switched now to attacks on the Iraqi forward troops in Kuwait itself. It was impossible to tell how many casualties we were inflicting, but we were confident that enemy morale was being severely eroded. At last the destruction of strategic communications was forcing the Iraqis to use their radio networks, with the result that we were belatedly starting to pick up useful intelligence. Snippets of discontent began to surface, among them the following exchange:

Callsign 13: When are we getting our next issue of rations?
Callsign 16: In three days' time.
Callsign 13: What are we supposed to eat in the meantime?
Rocks?

It may sound callous to say so, but in Schwarzkopf's headquarters the air war had become routine, as Chuck Horner and his planners worked methodically through their endless lists of targets. Every day at Morning Prayers the CinC would reel off a list of the damage done to the enemy: sixty-five per cent of his ability to control and run the military has gone; twenty-eight per cent of his NBC storage capacity has gone; sixty per cent of his power production has gone; thirty-eight per cent of his command and control signals are degraded; the capacity of road and rail bridges is sixty per cent reduced . . . None of us derived any pleasure from the deaths of hapless Iraqi soldiers, still less of civilians, but it was a fact of war that the more demoralized the army became, the fewer

Coalition lives would be lost when the ground war began. Also, if Saddam Hussein had agreed to meet the terms set by the United Nations, the bombardment would have stopped. Many times in my letters home I returned to the fact that all this suffering was being caused by one man: 'I am increasingly convinced that we need to get rid of him if there is to be any lasting peace in the Middle East . . . The key is to get rid of Saddam Hussein.'

I made a note that the RAF, who had only 3·25 per cent of air assets in theatre, had flown 4·8 per cent of all operational sorties, a figure that revealed the dedication with which our crews were working, a contribution out of all proportion to their numbers. Medium-level bombing was certainly less dangerous than low-level work, but still extremely exacting, and much highly courageous flying was done. For instance, Wing Commander Jeremy Witts, a Tornado pilot from 31 Squadron, was awarded a DSO for his exceptional flying skills and his outstanding leadership both in the air and on the ground. On 8 February he led an eight-ship formation in a daylight raid on the petrol refinery at Al Kut and, while the rest of the formation made a level bombing run at medium altitude, he himself dive-bombed the target and achieved direct hits, in spite of heavy defensive fire.

Such deeds stirred the blood of everyone in headquarters and under their cover the Allied ground forces were moving up into position. The British were ready and waiting, but until the last moment American reinforcements continued to pour up the Tapline road in an unending stream. Helicopters and fixed-wing aircraft were constantly shuttling up and down between Jubail and Ray, the assembly area north of Qaysumah, while on the ground vehicles were on the road almost twenty-four hours a day, with brief halts for refuelling and servicing, and crews changing over in rotation (the crews of armoured vehicles were flown up by Hercules or helicopter, while their tanks and Warriors travelled on low-loaders). During all this movement to the west, tape recordings of British units exercising were being broadcast every day from a truck on 7th Armoured Brigade's original location in the east, to cover the fact that our Division had gone elsewhere.

For as long as it was possible I continued to visit units in the desert and at sea. On 13 February, as mentioned above, I flew out to HMS *London* as she was about to move north with the mine-hunting pack. Her crew were in good fettle, in spite of the fact that they were at defence watches night and day, in full operational kit. On my way back I called on the Crown Prince of Bahrein, Sheikh Hamad bin Isa, who had been asking to see me for some time and wanted to be kept closely briefed on what was happening: as ever, the Bahreinis' support was enthusiastic and unwavering.

Because I had committed the Navy to a high-threat environment and knew that they were under great strain, I was anxious to receive assurance from some outside authority, competent to judge, that I was not asking too much of Chris Craig and his men. I therefore asked Joint Headquarters to send out a senior naval officer who could visit the Task Group and make an independent assessment of the Navy's role, as Paddy Hine had for the RAF and I was able to do for the Army. At first they seemed curiously reluctant to support this request, so to back up my case I pointed out that although many senior Army and Air Force officers had come out to see their units in action, no comparable naval officer had visited the theatre since September. I thought it important that such visits should be made, not just in this campaign, but in all overseas deployments, so that single-service chiefs in the United Kingdom could be briefed accurately and personally by their own Services on how their people were functioning, and not have to rely on reports coming down the chain of command. Eventually, on the eve of the land war, Rear Admiral Peter Woodhead, Flag Officer Flotilla One, made exactly the kind of tour I had hoped for, calling on many ships. The crews were delighted to see him and his visit was an immense success: apart from its value as a morale raiser, it confirmed the opinion I had already formed, that all was well on our eastern flank.

On 14 February I escaped from work for a few hours, something I had not managed since before Christmas. 'Had a marvellous day, took it off,' I told Bridget. 'Had to go to briefings until 1100, then came home, slept till lunch, bowl of soup, slept till tea, then cleared papers which had been dumped in my house. Then back into briefings, followed by one and a half hours of Press interviews.' If that does not sound much of a holiday, my pleasure at the break gives some idea of the pressure under which we were living, far removed though we were from the front line.

On 14 February, under cover of Exercise Dibdibah Charge, the Division began to move up to the assembly area code-named Ray, due south of the point at which the Iraqi defences were to be breached. For the past three weeks the British fighting units had maintained radio silence, while in the far east, where they had come from, signallers continued to broadcast tape-recordings of radio traffic made during training on the Devil Dog Dragoon range up the coast from Jubail. During Dibdibah Charge the Division came on the air again – it was essential to practise radio drills – but again their signals were recorded and this time played back from vehicles slowly retreating south-eastwards to give the Iraqis the impression that the British were withdrawing in that direction.

On the seventeenth I went to 22 and 33 Field Hospitals, out in the desert, not many kilometres south of the border. 'I have to admire the doctors and nurses, and the way they keep their morale up, without patients for weeks on end,' I told Bridget. 'I *hope* most of their casualties will be Iraqis, as they must have hundreds of wounded, many of whom have little hope of getting treatment from their own side.' On the twenty-first, I paid my last call before the ground war on our divisional headquarters and the two brigade commanders. Rupert Smith was at last getting some of the intelligence about the disposition of the enemy forces opposite him which he had long been seeking: unmanned drones equipped with cameras had been filming the Iraqi positions and sound-ranging equipment had pin-pointed the sites of artillery and mortars. GR1A Tornados had also been flying reconnaissance sorties over his sector of the front.

Our officers and men all seemed in excellent form, though they were finding the wait difficult. The more I saw of Rupert, the more he filled me with confidence: I felt certain that in battle he would handle the Division with skill and panache, and that our forces could manage the task which they had been allotted, of guarding the right flank of the main Allied thrust against the Iraqi Republican Guard. 'We're now in the countdown period,' I told Bridget, 'and by the time you receive this, the battle will be well under way.' I added a rider which turned out to be all-too prescient:

> The only matter requiring attention is the deconfliction of close air support from the ground troops. In a fast-moving battle of armour, where everyone is mixing it, it is very difficult to avoid blue-on-blue, or fratricide, as the Americans call it. The only way to do it is to use procedural means, i.e. to keep a line ahead of the battle behind which air is not permitted to attack. There is a conference tomorrow to discuss the whole business.

Norman and I had repeatedly talked about this difficult subject over the past few weeks and we had done everything we could to resolve the problems. Little did I know that within four days my anxiety would be vindicated in tragic detail. For the moment, though, I continued my tour of our units with a final quick visit to Tabuk, the airfield in the north-west from which an immense number of sorties had now been flown, not least by the Tornados. Then, with the start of the ground offensive only thirty-six hours off, I returned to base in Riyadh, knowing that I would not see the Division again until it had broken through the Iraqi defences and was well into the battle.

In spite of all our elaborate preparations, we still hoped that a ground war might in the end prove unnecessary. On the one hand, we were expecting a major battle, with heavy casualties and the probability of chemicals being used. On the other, we wanted to avoid it if we could. There might be less glory around, but there would also be many more people alive, which was what mattered most. 'I cannot help feeling privately optimistic that the Iraqi army will collapse before the land campaign goes in,' I told Bridget. 'There is information from prisoners of war that the troops are in a poor state, starving, with lice and sores, and not defending their own country.' Yet in the middle of February I was surprised to hear from Norman that Washington, far from pressing him to delay, as they had in the past, now wanted him to launch into the land battle before Saddam Hussein could withdraw of his own accord and thereby keep his enormous army intact. The ground forces themselves, of course, were eager to press on with their job, since they saw battle as a sure route to repatriation and home. Thus we were under conflicting pressures from many different directions, the normal lot of senior commanders.

One subject which caused persistent disagreement was battle damage assessment, or BDA. To everyone in theatre, it was evident that the Allied air forces were dealing Saddam heavy punishment, but analysts in Washington were reluctant to agree with local estimates of the degree of damage caused to the Iraqi war machine. One problem was that at least thirty-six hours elapsed between the moment at which a surveillance aircraft took photographs and that at which the pictures were seen by the analysts in America, so that all their information was out of date by the time they received it. A more serious obstacle was their demand for incontrovertible evidence of destruction. To accept that a tank, for instance, was out of action, they needed to see that it had physically been blown to pieces or at least was upside-down, whereas in fact, even if it still presented an intact image to airborne cameras, it might well have been disabled by a bomb or missile. Equally, even if Iraqi units were still occupying their foxholes in the desert, they might have been so severely deprived of water, food and communication as to have become practically useless, but this was something which no aircraft could see.

The result was that no consensus could be reached on the extent to which the fighting potential of the Iraqi army had been downgraded. Nevertheless, as February progressed, we felt confident that we were advancing steadily towards the figure of fifty per cent which Norman had set as the mark before which he would not be willing to commit his ground forces.

As the start of the land campaign drew close, we felt – with a mixture of anger and incredulity – that in Britain and the United States sympathy was shifting away from the Coalition and towards the Iraqi people. It was the poor Iraqis who were getting the caning, and we were coming to be regarded as big bullies. (After the war, at a seminar, one alleged military specialist seriously asked Bill Wratten why the RAF had not confined its bombing of bridges to daylight hours, so that the Iraqis could use them safely at night.) Such an attitude, though entirely misconceived, took some fighting-off, and I was very glad to hear at one stage that the Saudi Crown Prince had told the American Ambassador in Riyadh that his Government was strongly in favour of the air war. This may sound obvious, but, with mutters of opposition increasing all the time, it was good to know how we stood with the host nation. 'I detect a fearful questioning coming up in the UK as to whether we should go on being nasty to the Iraqis,' I wrote home. 'My answer is that if we stop early, we pay in British lives, and this is not a deal I wish to do.'

Right to the end, we took elaborate steps to keep an escape route open. At Morning Prayers on 22 February, for instance, Norman opened the proceedings by saying that the information which he was about to divulge was for in-theatre use only and must not be passed up or down the chain of command. His news was that at the eleventh-hour of the Russian peace initiative President Gorbachev was still trying to negotiate an Iraqi withdrawal. The United States' proposal was that the Iraqis should pull out of Kuwait completely within ninety-six hours. They could take their soft-skinned vehicles, but would have to leave all their armour and artillery behind, so that their army would be emasculated. The Iraqis said that it would be impossible to leave in that time, because so much damage had been done to roads and bridges: it would take them six weeks to pull out. They also demanded that, once they had withdrawn two-thirds of their forces, United Nations sanctions should be lifted, and that as soon as the withdrawal was complete, all UN resolutions against Iraq should be cancelled.

At a meeting in the White House the night before, Norman reported, Colin Powell had said that if a rapid withdrawal was still possible, we should take that option and avoid a ground war, but the Iraqis were to understand that there could be no bargaining. Moreover, if the enemy were in earnest, they must start to pull out on a massive scale by midday, 23 February. The question then arose as to how we would signify our intention of letting them go without an attack. The answer was that we would call a temporary halt to the air war, a two-hour suspension of raids, to give the Iraqis a chance to start moving. This meant that we would need to devise some means of recalling every aircraft in mid sortie, even those almost at their targets. Chuck Horner, consulted as to whether this would be possible, replied with his usual methodical calm that he could fix it, but that it would take him a couple of hours to work out details.

When Norman asked for comments, several Arab nations made it clear that any such settlement would be highly unwelcome to them. By now they were determined to go through with the ground operation, to break the back of the Iraqi army and to smash Saddam's nuclear and chemical capability. As Norman closed the meeting, he repeated that everything must be kept under the closest security and not be discussed outside the room.

In spite of all this secrecy, I do not think any of us seriously believed that Saddam had the slightest intention of withdrawing. His negotiations with Gorbachev were no more than a device for gaining time and his past record was such that it was impossible to believe anything he said. All the same, it was clear that we needed to have a fall-back plan in case he changed his mind. The last thing we wanted was to breach the minefields and start the war, only to have to stop because he had indeed begun to pull out, or was saying he would.

On 23 February John Major rang again, once more a personal call on an insecure line, to wish our Division luck in battle. As I reported to Bridget, he was 'embarrassingly complimentary about me, congratulating me on how things had gone: ". . . handled with extraordinary skill" and so on. I had to point out that it was not much to do with me, but with the excellent people I had working for me. Looking back, I seem to have kept myself extraordinarily busy, but I can't see that I personally have achieved much of significance.'

The Prime Minister told me that he had been receiving large numbers of blueys from servicemen and their wives. The letters, he said, taught him much about the quality of the people in the Services: some had demanded higher pay, and one author had had the nerve to say that he did not join the Army in order to fight a war, but most correspondents were constructive and enthusiastic about what they were doing. As before, the call from Number 10 left me with the comfortable feeling that we had an exceptionally human and sympathetic champion in Whitehall.

Aggressive patrolling and a steadily increasing flow of deserters daily strengthened our impression that the air war had done more damage to the enemy than the Pentagon officially estimated. We sensed that the will to fight was fast evaporating and that many troops were being kept in position only by the threat of the execution squads. This led me to hope that the battle would be brief. But meanwhile dire news was coming out of Kuwait, and not only about the five-hundred-odd oil wells on fire. 'Awful horrors too bad to put in a letter are being perpetrated,' I told Bridget. 'The only way we shall find out the facts is when we meet the Iraqis on the battlefield. Now the real test is about to come. If the Division's operation goes wrong, I shall of course be held responsible: my fault for redeploying them up there instead of leaving them with the Marines.'

There was one small positive action which I could take on the eve of battle. I rang the wives of my senior Army commanders and told them that their husbands were in good fettle. The men, being out in the desert, could not make contact in this way, but from Riyadh it was easy enough. I knew that the wives of all ranks were having a difficult time at home, in the United Kingdom or in Germany, sitting and waiting while they wondered what would happen, and I was glad to make a small gesture to help a few of them.

I heard later that my calls had a powerful effect on morale. Maggie Denaro said she felt as if she had 'a shot of heroin in the backside', and I think Susie Smith was equally pleased, in spite of her typically domestic reaction. Expecting to hear news of her family, I asked if she had any message for Rupert and was taken aback when she said, 'Well, thank you so much for calling. I'm glad to hear he's OK. But you can tell him from me that once he gets home this time, I'm not letting him go off to any more wars!'

When G-Day came at last, I found it odd to reflect that although our air and naval crews were already veterans, with five weeks of war behind them, our soldiers were still waiting for their first sight of the enemy. From my own experience, I knew how they were feeling. 'I see it as similar to a parachute jump,' I wrote home. 'They're now standing in the door of the aircraft with the red light on, waiting for the green.'

CHAPTER 12

DESERT SABRE

The ground war began at 0400 on G-Day, Sunday, 24 February, when two major invasion forces crossed the border simultaneously. In the east, elements of the 1st and 2nd (US) Marine Divisions broke through the minefields into Kuwait with a classically executed operation and began to fight their way due north towards Kuwait City, as the enemy had been led to expect the Coalition would. At the same moment, in the far west, elements of the American XVIII Corps, with French reinforcements, began a wide sweep across the desert. The aim of the Americans was to sever Highway 8, which runs from Basra to Baghdad, and so trap the divisions of the Republican Guard, while the French secured the western flank of the advance.

The third and most dramatic part of the invasion was the airborne attack by the 101st Assault Division (the Screaming Eagles), whose mission was to establish a forward operating base, known as Cobra, eighty kilometres inside Iraq. Delayed by fog until 0740, the mass deployment was made by three hundred transport and assault helicopters. Within four hours two thousand men had been ferried into Cobra, together with their artillery, stores and fuel, and were striking at Highway 8. While all this was in progress, the Coalition air forces carried out surge operations to support the ground formations and keep up pressure on strategic targets. Meanwhile, in the east, deception continued on a grand scale, with the US Navy shelling the coast as if in preparation for an amphibious landing and the 1st US Cavalry Division continuing artillery raids and reconnaissance patrols in the area of Wadi al Batin.

So well did the initial operations progress that Norman Schwarzkopf took a characteristically bold decision and brought forward the deployment of VII Corps (of which the British Division formed part) by fifteen hours. In consequence, the massive artillery barrage planned to precede the breaching of the minefield at their entry point into Iraq had to be reduced from more than two hours to only thirty minutes. Even so, the breaching proved much easier than expected. Just before noon armoured bulldozers of the 1st Mechanized Infantry Division (the Big Red One) began ploughing through the minefield and within eighty minutes they had opened up sixteen lanes, enabling US cavalry units to push through, brush past poorly defended Iraqi positions and establish a semicircular screen some fifteen kilometres to the north.

From the War Room in Riyadh, we monitored the launch of the ground offensive with satisfaction, almost with incredulity, as we saw the speed at which the Coalition forces were advancing. The one determined counter-attack of the day, against a Marine division, was soon beaten off, with the loss of three American tanks. Norman had imposed a total news blackout while the invasion was being launched, but on Sunday evening, with everything going so well, he called a Press conference, at which he was in ebullient form. Ten hours into the offensive, he said, more than five thousand prisoners had been captured and hundreds more men were waving white surrender flags. Resistance as a whole had been feeble and Allied casualties were very light. Having adroitly declined to reveal any detail of the plan or of particular progress, Norman gave a memorable description of the Allies' strategy for defeating the forces of Saddam Hussein: 'We're going to go around, over, through, on top, underneath, and any other way it takes to beat 'em.'

On G+1, Monday, 25 February, the British Division at last seized its chance to join in the land battle. It was a lowering, grey afternoon, with a strong wind blowing across the desert. In training the plan had always been that 4th Armoured Brigade would lead the British advance: Rupert Smith expected that the Division would have to fight its way out into Iraq through heavily defended positions and 4th Brigade, with its high infantry content, was best suited to this role. The idea was that it would open the door and let 7th Brigade use its speed to strike out across the desert. On 23 February, preparing his men for battle, Chris Hammerbeck had issued a Special Order of the Day:

> Be firm with those who resist, and humane and caring for those who surrender and are injured. Respect human life for what it is and do not allow yourself to sink, no matter what we may see in the days ahead.

In the event, the roles were reversed and it was 7th Brigade who led, spearheaded by the Queen's Royal Irish Hussars under the command of Arthur Denaro. By 1400 their tanks were grinding forward up the lanes cleared by the 1st Mechanized Infantry Division: the job had been brilliantly executed and the lanes were marked with tape and huge coloured boards, red and blue, the size of barn doors, bearing enormous capital letters, so that there was no chance of getting lost, and also the legend 'WELCOME TO IRAQ, COURTESY OF THE BIG RED ONE'. Excited American soldiers waved the Challengers on their way.

Inside the turrets, the tension was electric. For the young soldiers in the leading squadrons, some of them only seventeen or eighteen, it was by far the most frightening day of their lives. After months of training and weeks of waiting, they were about to go into action. Now, as they saw their first Iraqi prisoners coming back under American escort, they faced their biggest test. If the enemy was going to use gas, the most likely place for him to use it was on troops in the breach-head, where he knew the Allied armour would be bunched in a small area. Yet Arthur had taken the calculated risk of instructing his men to leave off their gas masks, because they could see and fight much better without them, and they were anyway protected by their vehicles' filter systems.

As they paused on the start line, codenamed New Jersey, where American servicemen were digging in, a scraggy old dog fox jumped up ahead of the leading tanks and loped away

across the desert, causing Arthur, a keen hunting man, to call
out over the radio not only 'Move now!' but also 'Tally-ho!'
So 7th Armoured Brigade led the way into Iraq. With helicopters overhead to give warning of targets in the distance,
the Challengers rolled forward and charged towards the
north-east at 40kph, three hundred yards apart, in arrowhead
formation. Their first objective, codenamed Copper North,
was thought to be a brigade position and their aim, now as
all through the battle, was to press ahead as fast as possible,
destroying enemy armour and artillery, but bypassing infantry positions which could not influence the main battle or do
them harm. Their objectives, all named after metals – Copper,
Brass, Steel, Zinc, Platinum, Tungsten – were simply rings
drawn on the map round enemy positions. As Rupert Smith,
the divisional commander, had several times reiterated, the
circles did not indicate any particular features of terrain,
merely concentrations of Iraqi forces. The aim of the British
was not to capture patches of desert, but to clear them of
enemy armour and keep moving.

For the first hour the Hussars had the luxury of knowing
that everything in front of them, man or machine, must be
enemy, but then, as the Staffords and Scots Dragoon Guards
went on ahead of them, everyone had to take the greatest
care to distinguish friend from foe. Patrick Cordingley had
hoped that his brigade would fight its first battle in daylight,
but in fact darkness came down before it made contact with
the enemy and heavy rain began to fall.

Very soon it became apparent that two particular pieces of
Allied equipment were potential war winners. One was the
global positioning system (GPS) driven by satellites, similar to
that used by yachtsmen, which gave tank commanders their
position to a ten-figure grid reference, or to within about
fifteen metres on the face of the earth. The other invaluable
device was the TOGS (Thermal & Optical Gunsight), which
enabled crews to see in the dark. By picking up heat emissions, the sight gave tank commanders the ability to detect
enemy vehicles at least two thousand five hundred metres
away and fire accurately at them long before the Iraqi gunners
could even see the opposition. So sensitive were the sights

that the commanders' video-display units were constantly alive with small, moving blobs of light – jerboas scurrying about the desert floor.

At about 1830 the Hussars paused for forty minutes while the navigation satellites were below the horizon and out of contact. Then, with their grid references accurately reestablished, they went on again, more slowly, until at 2100 they came within reach of the first main Iraqi position. Settling down to wait while the Scots Dragoon Guards and the Staffords closed up on him, Arthur pushed his young tank commanders forward to reconnoitre and find out what was going on. For them, it was an unnerving assignment, as they peered through the dark and rain into the unknown. When they reported that they had discovered a considerable enemy position, Arthur pulled his whole group back and called down heavy artillery fire from the British 155mm guns and the American Multiple Rocket Launch System regiment placed under Rupert Smith's command by General Fred Franks.

Then, at midnight, on orders from Brigade Headquarters, his Regiment went forward again and continued advancing until 0300, by which time he reckoned that his tanks had gone 'about as far as our nerves would let us on that first night'. Yet that was by no means the end of the night's action. Sitting quietly in the dark, the Challenger crews began to pick up hot-spots on their TOGS screens. First there were a dozen, then twenty-five, then nearly fifty. Clearly the Iraqis were about to try one of their favourite ploys – a counter-attack immediately after a retreat. The Hussars, with the overwhelming advantage of being able to see without being seen, kept still and let them come on until they were two thousand five hundred metres away, then opened up. The ensuing battle, in which the Staffords played a distinguished part, lasted ninety minutes, and the young commanders from both regiments showed great coolness and leadership. Our tanks scored many hits on Iraqi vehicles, but the enemy could never see the Challengers, except momentarily when they were lit up by explosions, and never hit one with a main armament. In the end, they turned and ran.

First light on Tuesday, 26 February, revealed that ten

enemy armoured vehicles had been knocked out, but that the position which the Hussars had overrun was only a subsidiary one. The main stronghold, designated Zinc, lay a short distance to the east, where large numbers of tanks and infantry were established in berms. With a sandstorm limiting visibility, the Hussars attacked from the west, firing their main armament from only four hundred metres, the furthest they could see, while the Staffords came down from the north and drove the Iraqis out. The tank gunners' main difficulty was that enemy infantry began giving themselves up by the hundred in the ground between the Challengers and their armoured targets, and they had to avoid firing at soldiers on their feet. Early in the afternoon the Regiment advanced still further to the east and attacked another brigade position, Platinum, overrunning it quickly and taking large numbers of prisoners. So the headlong advance went on.

Rapid progress was being made on every sector of the Coalition front. In the north-west the Americans had successfully cut the highway to Baghdad and in the east the Arab forces had stormed northwards towards Kuwait, with the Egyptians giving an admirable lead and taking large numbers of prisoners. Allied casualties were miraculously light, and even the US Marines, whom I had expected to sustain heavy losses, surged forward almost unscathed against rapidly crumbling opposition. Extraordinary as it seemed, the Iraqis still had not appreciated what was happening: their attention was firmly focused on their southern front and they had not realized that VII Corps's big left hook was gathering momentum, about to deal them a hammer-blow from the west.

The task of the British Divisional commander, Rupert Smith, was to protect the right flank of VIII Corps as it advanced towards the divisions of the Republican Guard in the far north-east. His plan, in brief, was to fight his two brigades as if he were a boxer, punching first with one, then, while that brigade replenished, punching with the other. His own artillery had been powerfully reinforced by a United States National Guard artillery brigade comprising MRLS and guns, and he planned to use it not as a third brigade, but in direct support of the other two, switching it from one to the other as the situation demanded. In spite of last-minute improvements, Rupert's intelligence about the disposition of enemy forces was by no means good and he was afraid in any case that, once the Allied attack began, the Iraqis might all rise up like an ants' nest and start moving about. Should this happen, his aim would be to attack any formations which looked like threatening the main Corps advance.

In the event, it soon became apparent that the Iraqis' will to fight had been severely eroded by the air war. Weeks of bombardment, lack of sleep and proper food had reduced their efficiency so much that their morale was at rock bottom even before the Coalition launched its ground offensive. Then, under the speed and ferocity of the Allied assault, they collapsed, unit by unit. Far from rising up like a swarm of ants, they had no idea or intention of moving about. Their entire strategy was based on defence: indeed, most of their tanks and guns were so well dug in that they could not even be turned round to face the Allied attack when it came at them from an unexpected direction. This made them easy meat for the Coalition armour and robbed them of the mobility which their tanks should have given them. The Republican Guard on the Division's northern flank, however, remained a threat which could not be ignored.

The British Division was not only extremely mobile but thoroughly well found: it had everything it wanted in terms of equipment and logistic support and, as it drove forward, the Sappers were constantly at work behind it, extending a road forward from the breach-head. The road had a dual role: it gave the supply drivers a track so that they would not become lost or bogged down, and also, if the enemy had counter-attacked, the British fighting units would have known where to locate and protect their own logistic tail. In fact the desert was so flat and hard that the big fuel bowsers were able to drive straight across it to designated exchange points. One or two did become bogged, but they were towed out, and their general mobility laid to rest our worries that the desert surface would consist of a thin crust over sand or mud, and would not bear loads.

The logistic tail, meticulously planned by Martin White, met the Division's every requirement and in fact the war ended so quickly that he never had to implement several of his plans. For example, he had been proposing to establish an ammunition dump inside Iraq, but as things turned out, this was never needed. Similarly, 22 Field Hospital, which had been standing by with all its equipment packed in containers north of Qaysumah expecting to hurry north through the breach to a new site inside Iraq, never had to move.

As the Coalition forces surged forward on land, the Royal Navy's mine-hunters were still at their deadly dangerous work in the Gulf, in easy range of Silkworm missiles on the coast. The Americans claimed to have eliminated all the missile sites, but Chris Craig and his commanders did not believe them: the ships were constantly picking up radar emissions from Iraqi fire-control units and expected an attack by missile or rocket at all hours of the day and night.

On the night of 25 February HMS *Gloucester* detected the attack which had so long seemed inevitable. Two Silkworm missiles were fired from the coast immediately opposite. Their flight time would be well under two minutes. *Gloucester* instantly called the attack and obtained command approval to retaliate. One Silkworm splashed not far offshore, but the other kept coming. The ships opened up with everything they had and a Sea Dart blew the missile up almost directly overhead, so that pieces came scattering down close astern of the flagship, HMS *London*. In the excitement one of the rapid-fire Phalanx anti-missile guns sprayed a couple of rounds into the USS *Missouri*, fortunately without causing casualties. The mine-hunting force then made a tactical withdrawal, to take stock and see if any more missiles were coming their way; but none did, so the ships went back in and carried on their delicate task until the end of the war. By then they had cleared enough space for one of the battleships to shell Iraqi shore positions from a range of only twenty kilometres – point-blank for the sixteen-inch guns.

During the night of 25–26 February 4th Armoured Brigade had also been heavily involved, particularly in a confused battle for Copper South, where the Iraqis had about twenty tanks and fired back vigorously at the invaders. Like Patrick Cordingley, Chris Hammerbeck had elected to command his brigade from a tank, the place in which he felt most secure and comfortable. His own Challenger was nicknamed Nomad and decorated around the commander's position with scurrilous cartoons drawn by a gunner. Afterwards he reckoned that for the first eighteen hours of the battle he scarcely looked up from his TOGS sight, and he wrote a vivid account of the action:

> A tank battle at night is a curious affair, since the action is fought entirely on thermal sights and therefore in green, white and black, which removes much of the drama. You cannot see the enemy firing at your own tank, but you are aware that it is happening as a supersonic bang is heard as each round passes close by. A hit on the enemy is simply a black or white spot on the target, followed by a wisp of thermal smoke. In reality, this hides the catastrophic explosion of a tank, with the consequent loss of its crew.
>
> For my crew, the battle was a confused jumble of target acquisition followed by engagement sequences: 'Fin [ammunition] . . . Tank . . . On . . . Fire!' Small groups of enemy who had baled out were sheltering in the blackness, which must have been broken by the flash of our gun . . . Inside the tank, pandemonium reigned as targets were spotted and engaged. The mix of smells ranged from the smoke of the main armament to that curiously acrid smell that humans give off when they are charged with adrenalin and, to be frank, scared.

Until the afternoon of G+2, 26 February, everything went splendidly for the British forces. For me, in Riyadh, it was immensely satisfying to witness our Division operating as I had always intended it should: manoeuvring fast and freely in the open desert, covering ground at an extraordinary rate, and maintaining the flexibility which I had hoped would be its hallmark. American air support proved highly effective and our two brigades leap-frogged from one objective to the next at impressive speed, destroying large numbers of Iraqi armoured vehicles and guns. But then our luck ran out.

Objective Brass had proved to be a large enemy position, containing most of an armoured brigade. At about 1400, in a phased assault led by Challengers, a 4th Brigade battle group approached it from the north-east. So little were the enemy expecting an attack from that quarter that they were caught facing the wrong way. Soon more than thirty of their tanks and nearly fifty armoured personnel carriers were destroyed, and Allied infantry – the 1st battalion of the Royal Scots and the 3rd battalion of the Royal Regiment of Fusiliers – dismounted from their Warrior armoured vehicles to clear the trenches.

The terrain at that point was a flat and featureless gravel plain, with little except wrecked Iraqi vehicles dotted about to act as landmarks. Soon after 1500 the Fusiliers were clear of Brass and on their next objective, Steel. After the short, sharp sandstorm during the morning, the weather had cleared and visibility was good. All the British vehicles were displaying their standard fluorescent recognition panels on their upper surfaces, as well as inverted black Vs on the sides of their bodies and turrets.

Along with the rest of 4th Brigade, the Fusiliers paused for reorganization on the eastern edge of Steel and some of the infantrymen came out of their Warriors while they had the chance. During the wait, orders went out for the Royal Engineer troop attached to C Company to blow up a number of enemy guns and, when the Sappers had their charges in place, they told the company commander that they were ready. He then instructed his platoon commanders to close down their Warriors and move away from the gun emplacements.

By then 8 Platoon of C Company had been stationary for a few minutes, but as the men started to re-board vehicle Callsign 22, it suddenly blew up and caught fire. The commander of Warrior Callsign 23 at once ordered his vehicle to a position in front of the burning wreck and ordered three of his men to help him recover the wounded. But they had hardly begun carrying casualties to the nearest first-aid post when Callsign 23 itself blew up in a ball of fire. In all, nine soldiers were killed and eleven injured.

The explosions were so violent and unexpected that some of those present at first thought they had been caused by

Above: It could be said the Coalition air forces won the war. Laser-guidence was so precise that Coalition aircraft were able to deliver two bombs into the same crater – a level of accuracy unprecedented in warfare

Right: Bombing-up with JP233, our runway assault weapon, critical to crippling Iraqi air capability during the early phase of the air assault

Left: For the courage and skill of the Tornado crews I had nothing but admiration. They were the first to break through into the unknown and find out what lay beyond in terms of enemy resistance, ground fire and missiles

The War Room. Here we planned and ran the war. At the table, with our communications to Washington, London and our commanders in the field before us, sat *(left to right)* Lieutenant General John Yeosock, Army Commander; Lieutenant General Calvin Waller, Deputy CinC; General Schwarzkopf, the CinC; Lieutenant General Chuck Horner, Commander of the Coalition air forces; myself; Major General Bob Johnson, US Chief of Staff. Over the latter's right shoulder is Brigadier Tim Sulivan, my permanent representative in the War Room

Air Commodore (now Air Vice-Marshal) Ian Macfadyen, my Chief of Staff, a man of drive and energy who masterminded the staff planning of all the British forces in theatre

Lieutenant Colonel (now Brigadier) Arthur Denaro, Commanding Officer of the Queen's Royal Irish Hussars, shouted, 'Move now!' and then, 'Tally-ho!' as his Regiment's tanks stormed through the breach into Iraq

Right: At a Press conference in Dhahran on the eve of war, I made the point that we in the Services were laying our lives on the line. We would do our best to give journalists safe passage and to look after them once the shooting started, but that security must come first. At the end was dead silence – first time I had ever journalists find to say

The Royal Marines SBS brought off Special Forces' first success of the war when they blew up a substantial stretch of the fibre-optic communications network between Baghdad and the forward Iraqi areas. They showed great skill and courage in a most hostile environment

Attacks on communications and roads were the primary activity of Special Forces, but once behind the lines it became clear they possessed a unique opportunity to destroy Scuds laid against Israel

Schwarzkopf was kept personally briefed on a daily basis about the activities of Special Forces patrols

Milan anti-tank missiles, used by SAS patrols on the ground, provided an effective means of destroying Iraqi Scud missiles. Together with American Special Forces, the SAS drove the launchers further and further into the Iraqi hinterland

SAS motorcycle patrols deep inside Iraq: much of the desert was as level and featureless as a calm sea

Time for a family snap – somewhere in the desert behind enemy lines

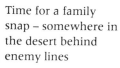

Islamic troops rumbl[ed]
through Kuwait City
immediately after its
liberation. Coalition
leaders were carefu[l]
to ensure that the
honour of recaptu[r]
ing Kuwait fell to
Arab forces

Left: The Safwan peace talks, 3 March 1991. At the remote air field just inside Iraq, General Schwarzkopf and Prince Khalid face Iraqi Lieutenant Generals Sultan Hashim Ahmed and Salah Abud Mahmoud to arrange the cessation of hostilities as a preliminary to full cease-fire negotiations. After the merest flicker of greeting, the leaders of each side confronted each other. I, seated at General Schwarzkopf's right shoulder, took an instant dislike to the Iraqis: I distrusted them and sensed in them all the evil that exists in Saddam Hussein and his regime

Below: A safe conduct pass. Hundreds of thousands were dropped over Iraqi positions, guaranteeing fair treatment on surrender to Coalition forces

Iraqis troops surrender to the British. Terrified by their own propaganda, they believed the Allies would torture them if they gave themselves up

Postwar reunion at Heathrow. I escorted
Schwarzkopf on his valedictory visit to the
United Kingdom, in which he was received
by the Prime Minister and visited some of
the troops that served with the Coalition

mines. Then the Divisional and 4th Brigade Air Liaison Officers (ALOs) realized that an attack position reported by American A-10 Thunderbolt aircraft coincided with the position of British forces, and it looked as though the fighter-bombers were implicated. News of the disaster reached my headquarters within minutes. Like everyone else concerned, I was shocked and saddened by the waste of life, because all through our elaborate planning for the land campaign I had done everything I could to make sure that British casualties were kept to a minimum. Yet I was not surprised, because I knew all too well that such setbacks are an inevitable part of modern war. As a young officer in Korea I had lost a quarter of my platoon in battle accidents and now, in the Gulf campaign, this was by no means the first such tragedy. Already more than twenty Americans had been killed in fratricidal incidents and I knew that errors of this kind were very difficult to prevent, especially in a fluid and fast-moving armoured battle such as we were fighting. But I also knew that without the magnificent American air support which our ground forces were receiving, our own losses would be much higher: hundreds of similar missions had been flown without mishap. I further knew that the CinC had done everything possible to develop means of avoiding such accidents, by establishing procedures to ensure adequate separation. Over the past months he and I had discussed the problem repeatedly and we had recently introduced the new recognition panels and inverted V markers to make it easier for pilots to recognize friendly vehicles from the air.

When a terrible event like that occurs, it is all too easy to react emotionally, especially if one is tense and tired from the strain of war. An horrific mistake had been made, traumatic for the comrades and families of the men who had been killed or wounded. It would have been all too easy for me, as Commander of the British forces, to make an emotional outburst to the media, to stick up for our soldiers and blame the American pilots. But that, in my judgment, would have achieved nothing. It would not have brought the dead back to life, or given solace to their next of kin. On the contrary, it would have been positively dangerous, as it could well have opened up cracks in the Coalition, which in turn could have led to military setbacks and further loss of life. If the Americans, for example, had withdrawn air support from the British Division, our casualty rate could have risen disastrously. Furthermore, it was important that we should not allow the setback to destroy the confidence with which British and American forces were operating together, and the momentum which their combined drive into Iraq had built up.

Besides, it was not yet at all clear what had happened, or how the disaster had occurred. Obviously an error had been made, but, no less obviously, it *had* been an error and not a deliberate attack. Pilots and ground controllers had been working at immense pressure and the Allied advance had gone much faster that anyone had predicted. The desert at that point was criss-crossed by dozens of tracks leading in all directions and, although the American aircraft carried inertial navigation systems, there were no landmarks such as hills, valleys, rivers or towns to allow a pilot to confirm his bearings.

I therefore took a carefully considered and important command decision, and resolved to play the incident down as much as possible. It seemed to me that two actions needed to be taken immediately. The first was to assemble all available data, so I gave instructions that the wrecked vehicles were to be located, examined and photographed. The second was that we should follow up an initial Press announcement in the United Kingdom with one of our own, in line with our policy of being open about the causes of such incidents. We had no wish to hide the reasons for the disaster, and I knew that any attempt at a cover-up would be both futile and damaging, as the Services had found out to their cost in the Falklands and elsewhere. I therefore instructed my Press liaison officer, Lieutenant Colonel Nick Southward, to prepare a suitable statement.

By the evening we had more information. This showed that shortly before the incident the Americans had carried out two air strikes against Iraqi armour on Objective Tungsten, some twenty kilometres to the east of Steel, with parties of A-10 and F-16 aircraft. An assistant Divisional Air Liaison Officer

(DALO) attached to the British Division had then tasked a further mission of two A-10s, armed with Maverick missiles, to attack the same armour again. It appeared to have been this strike which caused the disaster.

I knew that until a formal investigation had been held, we would not get a full picture of what had happened; in the meantime, there was no point in trying to apportion blame and I said as much when I saw Norman Schwarzkopf next day. The war had to go on. I also said I thought there was nothing to be gained by holding an immediate inquiry, but that we should collect all the evidence, so that it could be examined in detail later.

Norman went along with me. On this issue, as on most others, he and I were at one. In retrospect, I believe our decision was the right one: the most important thing at the time was that we should press ahead with the war and not risk rupturing Anglo–American relations, which had been most close and cordial, with a hasty and ill-considered review of events.

This did not in any way mean that I had no sympathy for the families of the dead. On the contrary, my heart went out to them and, as soon as I could, I wrote personal letters of condolence to them all. But if one is fighting a war, one has to expect casualties and at the time I saw it as my paramount duty to prosecute the campaign against Iraq with all possible despatch. I was heartened by the arrival of a brave signal from the Fusiliers' home base in Germany, which echoed my own thoughts exactly:

> Whilst we are much saddened by the tragic accident, we real-
> ize that such unwanted events are an unavoidable conse-
> quence of operations. Rather than dwell on this loss, we prefer
> to spotlight the many other casualties which would un-
> doubtedly have occurred had not the tactical air support been
> of such outstanding quality, despite severely adverse con-
> ditions. Please inform crew concerned that our own thoughts
> are with them as well as with the bereaved, and no hard
> feelings exist here, only a sense of comradeship.

The one man who seemed unable to accept this courageous offer was Chuck Horner. Normally laconic and laid-back, he now became deeply emotional, and could not agree that the issue needed to be left open until a formal investigation had been carried out. I immensely respected his professionalism and he had been particularly helpful to me over the deployment of the SAS. Now, though, in the War Room, he made it clear that in his view no blame could attach to his pilots. At first he claimed that the accident had been caused by mines – an echo of the initial, shocked response of the men on the spot – and then proceeded to defend his Service with aggression. This took me aback, because if anyone had cause to be aggressive, it was I, and yet I was going out of my way to calm things down. As I tried to explain to him why we had thought it essential to release news of the incident, he walked backwards out of the room, barely able to speak.

I did not go after him. I had more important tasks in hand. Having spent the past five months doing all I could to make the Coalition work, I was not going to risk splitting it now, in the middle of the battle. But as I wrote in a note to Bridget, the USAF were 'not in line with our interpretation of events', and we were left knowing that we would have to investigate the matter in more detail if we were to have any chance of establishing exactly what had happened. Meanwhile, the Fusiliers had gathered themselves together in the highest traditions of their Regiment and gone on with 4th Brigade to attack and overrun their next objective, Tungsten.

By the afternoon of the twenty-sixth the Iraqis had begun to retreat northwards. The Tawakkulna Division of the Republican Guard was rapidly being destroyed by air attacks and the Medina Division was under attack from the American 1st and 3rd Armoured Divisions. The British forces prepared to go into the pursuit phase of their advance. First, though, they had to evict the enemy from Tungsten. The way to this was paved by a devastating artillery bombardment, which kept the enemy's heads down while 4th Armoured Brigade prepared to cross the pipeline, which was above ground and in places presented an obstacle three metres high. Chris

Hammerbeck gave a vivid eye-witness account of the MRLS bombardment:

> The rounds seemed to be falling just in front of us ... We heard a great tearing sound as thousands of bomblets began to fall on the enemy artillery group to our east. This was followed by one of the most awe-inspiring sets of explosions that I have ever seen as the enemy artillery ammunition blew up on the battery positions.

Chris later learnt from his interrogation team that at the start of the attack the enemy had seventy-six guns still effective; by the end of the bombardment only seventeen were left and ninety per cent of the crews were dead or wounded. The British battle groups crossed the pipeline safely soon after midnight and the battle for Tungsten raged on through the rest of the night in a series of confused company actions.

At first light on 27 February (G+3) only one Iraqi position remained and this was cleared by the Royal Scots, who interspersed their fire with loudspeaker calls from the psyops team, inviting the enemy to surrender.

By then the US Marines had reached the perimeter of Kuwait City and had sealed all exits, but left the triumph of entering the city to the Coalition's Arab troops. At 0630 that morning, I wrote:

> Dare I say it, but victory looks like ours. And what a victory, with the Iraqis suffering the most humiliating defeat of any army since 1945. Patrick's 7th Brigade have been quite outstanding, and Arthur has been the cutting edge of it so far. It is so sad about the blue-on-blue. I had hoped to bring the Division, indeed the whole force, home with almost no casualties. Even so, I may go down in history as the general who had the fewest casualties ever recorded, for the size of the command and the magnitude of the tri-service operations. It would be a great reputation to have.

Thereafter the Iraqis were in rout towards the north-east. The British had reached Phaseline Smash after less than two days – against Patrick Cordingley's estimate of four, and Rupert Smith's of ten. By 0930 they were poised on the edge of Wadi al Batin, the long, shallow, dry valley running north-east/

south-west, which marked the border between Iraq and Kuwait. The main difficulty now was exhaustion. Men were grey-faced after three nights and three days with almost no sleep and, although they still appeared to be making sense, their faculties were much reduced. In particular, the key need for commanders at every level to keep an eye on what other people were doing had begun to fail, as individuals concentrated their dwindling energy on the business of keeping themselves going. Recognizing this with his usual perspicacity, Rupert Smith started to issue all his orders in written form.

Phaseline Smash had been set as a 'limit of exploitation', a point at which Rupert had to obtain clearance from Fred Franks before he pressed on any further. It was also the point at which Franks estimated that his heavy divisions would come through from behind to smash the Republican Guard up ahead. Once on it, the British Division had to pause, because they had advanced so quickly that there was a danger of the Corps' right wheel turning into a left wheel and of the British putting themselves in a dangerous position, on the line of advance of the American 1st and 3rd Armoured Divisions on their left.

Franks now warned Rupert to be ready for two possible tasks. One was to clear Wadi al Batin southwards and link with the metalled road which branched off the Tapline road and came up a certain distance from the south, the aim being to shorten the logistic route from Log Base Echo at Qaysumah by some two hundred kilometres and make this the Corps' main supply route. The other task discussed was to head eastwards at high speed and cut the main road to Basra north of Kuwait City, to prevent the Iraqi army escaping.

At 1930 Rupert received a definite order to clear the wadi and 4th Brigade began preparing for the task, but only an hour later the order was countermanded. Now the dash to the east was the preferred option. Soon Corps issued further details and at 1030 that night Rupert issued his own orders, detailing 7th Brigade to lead the charge at first light. Soon after midnight news came of a possible suspension of offen-

sive operations and Patrick Cordingley went so far as to
unstow his camp bed and set it up beside his tank, hoping for
an hour or two's sleep.

In Riyadh that night, at Evening Prayers, I made an
interjection to attract everybody's attention just as the meeting was about to break up. I announced that I had something to say and did not expect any reply. At this unusual
intervention the room fell silent and I offered a few words
of thanks to Norman on behalf of the British forces. 'I just
want you to know,' I said, 'how proud we are to have
served with the US troops and to have played a small part
in what is *your* great victory. And the proof that it *is* a
great victory lies in the fact that so much has been achieved
with so few casualties.'

Except to say 'Thank you', Norman did not reply, but he
was visibly moved and I knew him well enough to see how
much he appreciated my gesture.

At 0530 next morning, 28 February, 7th Brigade headquarters
sent out an order to its commanders, warning them to be
ready to move at 0630. At once Arthur Denaro went on the
air and told Patrick Cordingley that he was ready to go and
could start at 0600, at the latest. After a brief delay, Patrick
himself came on the radio and said, 'OK, if you're ready to
go, go.' So away they went, at more than 40kph, with 7th
Brigade leading and the rest of the Division in column behind,
over difficult country still dotted with Iraqi positions, pitted
with deep berms and sown with mines. In spite of all the
hazards, they reached Objective Cobalt, astride the Basra
road, half an hour before the suspension of offensive operations was announced at 0800. Psychologically, it was an
all-important arrival, as it put Coalition forces firmly in control of the road. The Division had advanced over three hundred kilometres, destroyed most of three Iraqi armoured
divisions and taken more than seven thousand prisoners,
including several senior commanders. The prisoner-of-war
guard force – the Royal Highland Fusiliers and the King's
Own Scottish Borderers forward, with the 1st battalion of the
Coldstream Guards manning the compound at the FFMA –

were stretched to their limits in dealing with such huge numbers.

Although 7th Brigade had led for most of the way, 4th Brigade had also acquitted itself with no mean distinction. In ninety-seven hours – for fifty-four of which it was in contact with the enemy – it had travelled three hundred and fifty kilometres, knocked out over sixty main battle tanks, ninety armoured personnel carriers and thirty-seven artillery pieces, besides capturing some five thousand prisoners. Far from losing a hundred dead, as Chris Hammerbeck had feared it might, the Brigade had had nobody killed by enemy fire – the nine men who died in the blue-on-blue were the only fatalities during the battle. At the end, the officers and men justly felt that they had done everything expected of them and, in their Commander's words, 'were overcome by the sense of relief at having survived'.

For the moment, nobody was sure that the war had ended. Not knowing whether a ceasefire could be agreed, Rupert Smith spent the day preparing to head north for Basra, if he was ordered to do so. Physically, he could have gone on to Basra or beyond, for although seventy-four Challenger power packs had had to be changed during the battle, the REME support had been so excellent that only one tank was out of action at the end.

For the British, the battle never became a turkey shoot. Clearly they killed a good many enemy on the night of 25 February, in the artillery barrage and the ensuing actions when the tanks were firing at any heat source they could detect. But when, in the morning, they found they had created mayhem, they felt justified in this, for the Iraqis had been firing back at them. By the twenty-sixth, when our troops put in the attacks on Platinum One, it was clear that most of the enemy wanted nothing more than to surrender and the message quickly went round that it was much easier to take prisoners than to deal with wounded soldiers or bury dead ones. At no stage of the advance did our servicemen feel vindictive: seeking to destroy equipment, but to round up humans, they soon began looking for ways of encouraging the enemy to surrender. At no stage of the campaign did they shoot people unnecessarily.

Some soldiers, inevitably, had a feeling of anticlimax. For men who never fired their weapons, or had a real go at the enemy, it all seemed a bit of a waste of time. But Patrick Cordingley was glad that his brigade ended the battle astride the main road on the Matla Ridge, for there the worst horrors of war were displayed for all to see. American planes had detected and attacked a mass exodus of Iraqis desperately trying to escape in any vehicle which they had been able to commandeer, from tanks to fire engines, ambulances and ordinary cars, and the ground was strewn with dead bodies and burnt-out vehicles, the sky black with smoke, evidence of madness and destruction everywhere. As Patrick remarked afterwards, 'If you'd had to paint a picture of the horrors of war, that's what you would have painted and it was no bad thing for my soldiers to see it.'

For the Allied forces the war had been short and relatively simple, but for the Iraqis it had been precisely the opposite. The prisoners we took were in a wretched state, half starved, exhausted, louse ridden. Many were suffering from wounds which had remained untreated for days, and all had been terrified by their own propaganda into believing that if they entered any Allied field hospital they would be tortured by being operated on without any anaesthetics. So thoroughly were the Iraqis brainwashed that one dying man refused to call on Allah for his salvation and invoked Saddam Hussein as his saviour.

Brief though it was, the ground war included numerous outbreaks of hand-to-hand fighting, not least by the Royal Scots who fought their way from bunker to bunker to clear Copper South on the night of 25 February. The war also produced many outstanding acts of bravery. In the blue-on-blue incident, for instance, Fusilier Simon Bakkor was the gunner in Warrior Callsign 23, the second vehicle to be hit. The moment he saw the first explosion, he left his own turret and ran across in an attempt to extricate the gunner from the blazing vehicle. As he struggled to open the hatches, he was blown off the Warrior by a secondary explosion which left him with shrapnel wounds in the thigh. His selfless attempt at rescue failed, but his display of personal bravery in the face of acute danger was so exceptional that after the war he was awarded the Queen's Gallantry Medal.

The same award went to Corporal Michael Driscoll of the Royal Corps of Transport, whose medical convoy was caught by enemy fire and at the same moment began to detonate mines. An American medical officer was killed by the first explosion, and a young American woman medical assistant severely wounded by the second, which blew off one leg and left her with a large abdominal wound, besides causing four other casualties. The situation was extremely confused: Corporal Driscoll, himself wounded by shrapnel in the thigh, was surrounded by casualties and apparently in the middle of a minefield. He nevertheless behaved with exemplary coolness, doing what he could for the wounded, calling in an ambulance helicopter and directing the evacuation. In the words of his citation, he 'showed great presence of mind and devotion to duty', and it was tragic that after he had made such a tremendous effort, the woman died of her wounds.

The Navy, too, produced many heroes and none had a more striking record than one of its divers, Acting Petty Officer Andrew Seabrook, who was awarded the Distinguished Service Medal. Operating from the Royal Fleet Auxiliary *Sir Galahad*, he was part of a team tasked with the destruction of mines: on no fewer than five occasions he deployed from a helicopter and swam to place charges on buoyant tethered mines, knowing every time that a single accidental knock on one of the contact horns would kill him instantly. He also had the unpleasant task of recovering the bodies of two dead Iraqis and strapping their corpses together in the water for hoisting into a helicopter. Onshore in Kuwait, after the ceasefire, his unit began clearing mines, booby traps, unstable live ordnance and, again, dead bodies. Often he had to cross areas still sown with anti-personnel mines before work could start and dive in water with visibility reduced to zero by oil pollution, but his boldness, enthusiasm and vigour proved an inspiration to his team.

*   *   *

In Riyadh, the sudden end of the war produced a sense of anticlimax. As Tim Sulivan remarked, it felt a bit like the end of an exercise and it seemed uncanny that war should be the same. At a televised Press conference that evening, it was extraordinary to be able to relax and not to have to be on one's guard. I saluted the Allied victory, emphasized that the British had played a considerable role in it and declared how proud I was to have commanded our force of forty-five thousand people. But then I went straight on and asked, 'Who is the Man of the Match?' I immediately answered my own question:

> There is no doubt in my mind as to who that is: General Norman Schwarzkopf. It is his brilliance, his leadership, his drive, his determination and − I have to say it occasionally, although I work alongside him and am a great friend of his − his *rudeness** at times, that has got things done, and got them done so damn efficiently, and helped and enabled us to win this war.

I went on to describe the liaison and cooperation between British and American forces as 'smooth beyond the point of criticism', and to say that this in itself had made a major contribution to success in the land war. I also put in a particular word of praise for the Saudi Arabians and their commander-in-chief, Prince Khalid, singling them out from all thirty nations of the Coalition for the way they had adapted themselves to receive the immense influx of foreigners into the heartland of Islam.

In conclusion, after a brief review of our casualties and prisoners of war, I said:

> If I've got one message for the people at home today, it is this: get out there and ring the church bells, because the British servicemen and women in the Gulf have won a great victory, and they're coming home just as soon as we can tidy things up in the theatre and clear the battlefield.

---

* I meant to say 'abruptness', but somehow the wrong word slipped out.

Evidently the message about bell-ringing struck the right
note. I did not immediately know that my remarks made such
an impact in Britain, but evidence of the response to them
soon came pouring back in letters from parishes all over the
country. From Benhilton in Surrey, from Kinton in Shrop-
shire, from Kingstone in Herefordshire and many other villages and towns came assurances that quarter peals of 1260
changes of Plain Bob Doubles or Grandsire Triples had been
rung, and that the shutters of belfries had been flung open so
that the sounds of victory should travel as far as possible over
the British countryside. At St Paul's Cathedral in London,
where my former Chief-of-Staff Brigadier Bob Ackworth had
become the Registrar, all twelve bells were rung in a quarter
peal.

Since the war I have found that two questions, above all
others, dominate people's curiosity about the conflict. Did we
stop fighting too soon? And why did we not go on to capture
Baghdad?

The position of the Coalition forces on 28 February has
been widely misunderstood. Our United Nations mandate,
flowing from Resolution 678, authorized us to use all necessary means to eject the Iraqis from Kuwait. We did *not*
have a mandate to invade Iraq or take the country over,
and if we had tried to do that, our Arab allies would
certainly not have taken a favourable view. Even our limited
incursion into Iraqi territory had made some of them
uneasy. The Arabs themselves had no intention of invading
another Arab country. The Islamic forces were happy to
enter Kuwait for the purpose of restoring the legal government, but that was the limit of their ambition. No Arab
troops entered Iraqi territory.

In purely practical terms, there is no doubt that British,
American and French forces could have reached Baghdad. We
would have been there in another day and a half and we would
probably have met little resistance on the way. But in
pressing on to the Iraqi capital we would have moved outside
the remit of the United Nations authority, within which we
had worked so far. We would have split the Coalition physi-

cally, since the Islamic forces would not have come with us, and risked splitting it morally and psychologically as well, thus undoing all the goodwill which we had taken such trouble to achieve. The Americans, British and French would have been presented as the foreign invaders of Iraq and we would have undermined the prestige which we had earned around the world for helping the Arabs resolve a major threat to the Middle East. The whole of Desert Storm would have been seen purely as an operation to further Western interests in the Middle East.

Besides, if we *had* gone to Baghdad, what would that have achieved? Saddam Hussein would certainly not have sat there, with the enemy closing in to capture him. He would have slipped away into the desert and organized a guerrilla movement, or flown to some friendly state such as Libya and set up a government-in-exile there. We would then have found ourselves landed with the task of trying to run a country shattered by war, which at the best of times is deeply split into factions, with the Shi'ites in the south, the Kurds in the north, the Baathists in government, and the Sunnis on the periphery. Either we would have had to set up a puppet government or withdraw ignominiously without a proper regime in power, leaving the way open for Saddam to return. In other words, to have gone on to Baghdad would have achieved nothing except to create even wider problems.

On the other question, of whether we stopped the war too early, I believe that the answer is 'No'. Already there was mounting criticism in the Press that the battle had turned into a turkey shoot: certainly the Iraqi servicemen were totally beaten and in a state of rout. We could undoubtedly have mown down thousands as they queued to cross bridges which had already been knocked down, but what would that have achieved? Already the power of Saddam's army had been broken: a high proportion of his armour and artillery had been destroyed. It had always been our intention to leave Iraq with some ground forces, so that whoever was in power could defend the country and not be left with a vacuum. We certainly wanted to catch the torturers and murderers who had been wreaking havoc on the Kuwaitis, but once we had sealed the roads out of the city and blocked the escape of vehicles, there was simply no point in slaughtering soldiers by the thousand. Equally, could we have justified the deaths of further Coalition personnel which would undoubtedly have resulted? In an extremely complex situation, I believe we were right to stop when we did.

CHAPTER 13

CLEARING UP

Messages of congratulation poured in, from the Queen, the Prince of Wales, the Prime Minister, Tom King, the Chief of the Defence Staff, Paddy Hine and, not least, from Peter Inge, the Commander-in-Chief of BAOR. This last was particularly generous, I thought, considering that I had taken almost all his equipment and most of his soldiers for the conflict. All the messages, though directed in the first instance to me, were really for our forces and I duly passed them on. Some went immediately by signal and in due course all were published in the *Sandy Times*, together with the text of messages sent directly by John Major and Paddy Hine to Norman Schwarzkopf. I myself sent out a signal of congratulation and personal gratitude to all ranks under my command. In a letter to the Prime Minister, thanking him for his tribute, I wrote:

I believe that this has been a conflict in which, perhaps more than in most, the moral issues were clear cut. By their stand against Saddam's aggression, the Governments of the Coalition partners have conspicuously reasserted decent norms of international behaviour against the law of the jungle, which would let small nations fall prey to larger neighbours without penalty or recourse.

I can confidently say on behalf of all those under my command that we feel proud and privileged to have played our part in this achievement. We have all been greatly inspired and sustained throughout our deployment by the steady support of the British people, whose instincts in these matters are true and dependable.

A particular cause of thankfulness, as you mention, is the

remarkably small scale of our casualties. At the same time, our hearts go out to all those who have lost loved ones, or who wait anxiously for news of relatives or friends still missing or captured. I know of your concern for our prisoners of war in Iraqi hands and share your determination that no effort must now be spared to secure their safe return.

Although the fighting had stopped, several matters were far from resolved. The SAS were still deployed in the Western Desert and keen to flex their muscles by imposing road blocks on the highway to Amman. As one of their senior officers remarked, 'It would have caused great dudgeon if we'd started turning lorries round and sending them back to Baghdad with Union Jacks on them.' In the event I instructed the SAS to remain where they were for the time being, but not to engage in offensive operations. We were fairly certain that the Iraqis were holding several SAS prisoners, but because we had never declared that Special Forces had entered the war, or that any of them were missing, we were afraid that if we now made it clear that they had been involved, prisoners might just disappear and the Iraqis might deny all knowledge of them. As far as we could gather, the Iraqis never understood who the SAS were: certainly they thought some of the men they captured were Israelis and one, to prove that he was not, demonstrated that he was uncircumcised. In the end all were accounted for.

In the immediate aftermath of the battle, rumours swept the theatre. There was said to be growing unrest in southern Iraq. Basra was alleged to be in a state of anarchy. It was claimed that many of Saddam's closest henchmen had been killed in the last big bombing raid on Baghdad and that the dictator was about to be overthrown.

Reality was more prosaic. 'There is still the odd incident as the two armies glower at each other,' I told Bridget on 28 February, 'and we have every intention of shooting if there's any opposition.' With the fighting officially at a standstill, one of my main tasks was now to prevent our own people inadvertently killing themselves, either on the roads or on the battlefield. In the desert there were unexploded bomb-lets everywhere, mostly from MRLS rounds, for when the bomblets landed on something soft, like sand, they often failed to detonate and remained live. Now that the tension had been suddenly reduced, there was an inevitable tendency for everyone to relax and lose vigilance in the end-of-term atmosphere, and this was extremely dangerous. People who had survived the war could kill themselves needlessly by wandering into minefields, entering buildings which had not been cleared, falling asleep while driving or simply by collecting unstable souvenirs. Warned by my experience in other wars, I banned all mine-clearance operations unless specifically approved by me. I also put out detailed instructions across the whole theatre telling commanders to ensure that no deaths were incurred through negligence or stupidity and to make everyone aware, right down to the lowest level, that death might be lurking beneath every grain of sand.

One of my first concerns was to re-establish a British presence in Kuwait. During the battle only Arab forces had entered the city and I was anxious not only to repossess our Embassy as soon as possible, but also to set up a forward headquarters in the shattered city. The SBS were already in Kuwait, having flown in by helicopter on the afternoon of 27 February, and in the morning of the twenty-eighth I instructed them to launch Operation Trebor. They did so in characteristically decisive style, abseiling down from a helicopter on to the roof of the building. They had already acquired, from one of the last of the Embassy staff to leave the building, a precise account of how things inside were arranged and when they discovered discrepancies, they quickly withdrew, suspecting the place had been booby-trapped and blew in the front door. The British Ambassador, Michael Weston, who had flown in from Geneva the night before, was dismayed that the famous door, designed by Edwin Lutyens, had been destroyed, especially as the Embassy's Indian janitor was on hand and could have opened up for the SBS if they had asked him; but at the time it seemed better to take no chances. In fact it turned out that the Iraqis had never occupied the building and, although it was dirty and damp, it had suffered no looting or structural damage.

With the SBS, when they went into Kuwait on 27 February, was Lieutenant Colonel Ian Talbot, who had come out to Riyadh in the early stages of Operation Granby as adviser on armour to Sandy Wilson and later had gravitated to the planning staff in my headquarters. Recently he had been working on the preparations for Operation Trebor and on our general plans for going back into Kuwait. (It was Ian whom I sent back to the United Kingdom, for twenty-four hours, during the air war, with my first thoughts about post-war reconstruction.) Now he set up a small tri-service head-quarters in the departure lounge of the wrecked airport and he lived there for the next two days, not learning that the war had stopped until he heard an announcement of the ceasefire on the BBC World Service. His task was to pull together all the British interests in Kuwait: to protect the Ambassador, maintain contact with the Army (who came to rest about thirty kilometres north of the city), keep in touch with the Navy about the clearance of mines from the ports, coordinate British flights in and out, handle visitors such as myself, and liaise with other nations. With the war over, or at any rate suspended, international protocol had come back into play and it was important that we did not offend the Kuwaitis, the Saudis or any one else by behaving in an over-bearing fashion.

I myself flew in on the morning of 1 March and never in my life had I witnessed anything like the wanton devastation which the Iraqis had left behind. The journey itself was an astonishing experience. We travelled in one of the Hercules transports loaned to the United Kingdom by the Royal New Zealand Air Force and for most of the time we flew in clear air. But as we drew near Kuwait, we sighted an immense sea of oily black cloud beneath us and when we went down into it, the smoke was so thick that we could not even see the tips of the wings. All the airport's landing aids had been wrecked, so the pilot was talked down by a single American tactical air controller. Standing at the back of the flight deck, I could see our windshield rapidly becoming covered with smuts and oil until the pilot was flying blind. Eventually we broke through into a leaden twilight and found a huge civilian airport beneath us, much of it in ruins. Buildings were shot full of holes, and the place was littered with spent munitions and burnt-out aircraft, most conspicuously the wreck of a Boeing 747, British Airways' ill-fated Flight 149.

As we touched down, our crew streamed a Kiwi flag from the windows of the cockpit and I felt glad to have flown in with such spirited performers. On the ground, I could not for a few moments make out the source of the subdued roar which seemed to be coming from all round us, as if many other aircraft engines were running. Then I realized that it was the noise of the oil wells burning and there in the distance were hundreds of fires, flaming angrily beneath the black pall.

The passenger terminal, where Ian had set up his head-quarters, was utterly devastated, with all the windows smashed and the computer terminals ripped out, but when I discovered that he had commandeered various postal stamps, I at once sat down and scribbled a bluey home:

> Just arrived in Kuwait City. Devastation and oil fires every-where, forming black cloud – impenetrable. Came in Kiwi Hercules aircraft. Historic moment as British Commander arrives in liberated Kuwait.

Quickly sealing up the letter, I covered the outside with frank-ing marks and posted it, hoping that one day it might have some value as a unique first-day issue.

Later I discovered that the computer terminals had been removed not by the Iraqis, as I at first supposed, but by the head of the Kuwaiti air force, who had taken them away before the invasion to stop the Iraqis stealing them. Yet almost everything else in sight had been destroyed by the enemy before they fled. Kuwait was in chaos. Bursts of gunfire were constantly rattling out and even though we hoped they were in celebration, we knew that they might also signify the last-minute settling of scores. Most of the population had fled, but the people who remained, like their animals, were starving. Already we were hearing reports of torture chambers, in which Kuwaitis suspected of organizing the resistance had been brutally interrogated and then taken out to be shot in front of their families. Outside the city, it looked as though there had been a nuclear strike: tractors and cars stood about unattended, and no living thing moved.

After a visit to the Embassy, where, on my instructions, servicemen were making strenuous efforts to clear up and put the place in order, I flew up over the Matla Ridge and saw for myself the grim legacy of the Iraqis' doomed attempts to escape. More than five hundred burnt-out vehicles lay scattered about where they had tried to circumvent the road block ahead by taking to the desert. Then I went on to visit the Division, who were in good spirits, but very tired, suffering from reaction and already longing to go home. It was a measure of how exhausted they were that Arthur Denaro, a close friend, who had performed admirably during the battle, almost lost his temper with me in public when I said that I could not yet tell him anything definite about when his Regiment would be repatriated.

As we prepared to fly back from Kuwait to Riyadh, I got a striking first-hand illustration of the need for vigilance over live munitions. We were boarding the New Zealand Hercules when Bill Wratten noticed something lying under one of the canvas seats. When I asked what it was, one of the other passengers said, 'Oh, that's just a few bomblets we picked up.'

'If you think you're putting souvenirs on this bloody aeroplane, you can think again,' I told him. I immediately ordered everyone off, had the contraband carefully removed and the plane searched. The experience gave us all a nasty fright, for if the aircraft had taken off with the munitions on board, they would very likely have exploded with the change of pressure as we gained height, and down would have gone one Hercules together with about thirty men, including myself, Bill Wratten, Tim Sulivan and other senior officers.

In a longer letter, written that evening, I reported:

Kuwait City is a disgraceful example of the worst excesses of the Iraqis. The treatment of human beings is not for description in a letter – tenth-century behaviour or worse. Major buildings have been put to the torch, and all power and water destroyed.

The Coalition's priority was to stabilize the international situation by holding talks with senior Iraqi commanders. These were not to be peace talks, which would have to be handled through the United Nations, but discussions to settle vital questions about external boundaries, demarcation lines and above all Allied prisoners of war. The purpose was to agree a ceasefire until the complex arrangements for peace talks proper could be put in hand: the initial meeting would deal with military matters only and any agreements which it produced would be carried forward to the main meeting. We wanted to ensure that the Iraqis handed over all Allied prisoners and launched no further offensive operations. If they did, we reserved the right to go back on the offensive ourselves, without warning – and indeed we did just that on 2 March, on the main road to Nasiriyah, when elements of an Iraqi Guards Division tried to break through and escape, and were smashed to pieces by the US XVIII Corps.

Several alternative venues for the talks were considered. The Iraqis, who continued to prevaricate and create difficulties in spite of their total defeat, demanded that the meeting should be held in Basra. This was unacceptable to the Americans, because security would have been extremely difficult to enforce. Instead, Schwarzkopf suggested that the talks should take place on board a ship of the US Navy. This, too, was unsatisfactory, in that if the meeting was held on American territory, the rest of the Coalition would feel excluded. Kuwait City was also considered, but rejected. In the end we decided that the meeting should be held at Safwan, a small airstrip just inside Iraq, due north of Kuwait City, where we could bring home to the Iraqis the scale of their defeat by forcing them to meet us on their own territory and where we could arrange our own security.

The gall of the Iraqis was astonishing. On the morning of 2 March a senior officer somehow got straight through to Norman Schwarzkopf's Operations Room on the telephone and started making suggestions about the location of the talks, even though Safwan had already been settled. He also had the nerve to ask if the United States would extend the area

of its occupation to include Rumaylah and thus provide protection so that Iraqis could work there. Because of the threat
from his own people, he said, it was not safe to operate as
things stood. The answer was that the Americans might help
with some logistics, but that if the Iraqis wanted to negotiate
about the talks, they must do it through Moscow.

On the morning of 3 March I flew down from Riyadh to
Kuwait City with Norman Schwarzkopf in his private aircraft,
an executive jet like the HS125, but larger. The journey, lasting nearly an hour, gave us a final chance to discuss our
agenda for the talks, which had been thoroughly worked out
in advance both in theatre and between Washington and
London. It was an agreeable and civilized flight: sitting opposite each other at a table, we were served with coffee and
fruit, and had time to talk things over together. I think we
both felt the same mixture of elation and apprehension –
satisfaction that the job had been well done so far, tempered
by worries that we might be heading for a fiasco. The Iraqis
were so unpredictable that they might, even now, have no
serious intention of negotiating. They might not even come
to the rendezvous.

One of my deepest concerns was with prisoners of war. I
was determined to secure the release of all the Britons held
by Saddam Hussein, including the three civilians who had
been in prison before the war began, and I did not mean to
be satisfied by mere promises. All too often I had found that
it was not worth taking an Iraqi official's word, for he would
live up to it only if it happened to suit him. I wanted to see
all the prisoners back in our hands, and find out what condition they were in, before we agreed to peace proposals of
any kind. During the flight I once more stressed this to
Schwarzkopf and, on instructions from London, I added the
names of the three civilians to the list which he was to hand
to the Iraqis. He reiterated that he and Prince Khalid were to
be the Coalition's spokesmen in the talks, and that all the
other senior officers present would be observers, but that if
at any stage I felt that he had not covered some point
adequately, I should hand him a note.

At Kuwait we transferred into helicopters and proceeded

separately, each in a national aircraft, flanked by a swarm of about twenty armed escorts. Because the wind was from the west, the smoke from burning oil wells was being carried away to the east, and we were in clear air. Flying a thousand feet above the main road north, we could see countless armoured vehicles wrecked and abandoned in the sands, and our own armoured units tactically deployed, with their regimental and national flags fluttering in the wind.

In forty minutes we were descending towards an extraordinary scene. Because the talks were going to offer a perfect target — all the Coalition commanders sitting together in a tent at a predictable time — and because it seemed highly probable that an assassination attempt might be made, unparalleled precautions had been taken to defend the site against attack. An entire American armoured division had been deployed to guard the airstrip: a ring of tanks faced outwards round a small group of tents and the Americans had even staked out armour and artillery in the hills which rose from the flat desert fifteen kilometres in the distance. On the airfield dozens more helicopters were parked in rows: all the time one or two were taking off or landing and higher overhead, out of sight, fighter-bombers maintained a continuous combat air patrol.

We had agreed that we would come armed but surrender our weapons before we went into the conference tent, so that we could reasonably insist on the Iraqis doing the same and thus be certain that no bomb-carrying kamikaze specialist penetrated the security screen. So, having landed, we went through one cordon of troops after another, identifying ourselves. In the first tent, we handed in our guns to an American serviceman, who gave us tickets for them as if they had been coats in a theatre cloakroom, and proceeded to the conference tent, where a trestle table with bare wooden top had been set out, flanked by rows of chairs.

The Iraqis also came by helicopter, but were driven the last few hundred yards in an American armoured personnel carrier, and arrived half an hour late. The delegation was led by Lieutenant General Sultan Hashim Ahmad, Chief of Staff at the Ministry of Defence, and Lieutenant General Sala Abud

Mahmoud, Commander of III Corps, both of whom, to Western eyes, bore extraordinary resemblances to Saddam Hussein, with their black berets, dark olive uniforms and heavy black moustaches.

After the merest flicker of greeting and introduction, the two generals sat at one side of the table, together with an interpreter and junior staff officers. On our side, the front row was occupied by Schwarzkopf and Khalid, side by side, with the rest of the Coalition commanders immediately behind them. I was at Schwarzkopf's right shoulder. He led off in a frigid atmosphere. The proceedings were recorded on two tape recorders and by a stenographer, but no detailed text has been released.

Face to face with the enemy at last, I was not at all impressed. 'Instantly took a dislike to the Iraqis,' I reported to Bridget that evening. 'They were intelligent but shifty, and I decided there and then that I trusted them even less than before. My abiding impression is of dislike, distrust and a sense of all the evil that exists in Saddam Hussein and members of his regime.'

It soon became clear that Ahmad had the authority to do business and at first he acceded to all our demands. When Schwarzkopf asked that the International Red Cross should be allowed immediate access to all prisoners of war, Ahmad agreed, and said that releases would begin at once. When Schwarzkopf said he had a list of persons missing in action, but did not know whether some of them were alive or dead, the Iraqis volunteered to return dead bodies as well as live prisoners. Nor did the subject of mines produce any difficulty: when Schwarzkopf asked for information about minefields, both on land and at the head of the Gulf, Ahmad handed over maps which turned out to be surprisingly accurate. He also guaranteed without demur that no further Scud missiles would be launched and that no nuclear, biological or chemical weapons had been stored inside Kuwait.

Only when Khalid raised the question of the five thousand or more Kuwaitis who had disappeared after the seizure of their country did the Iraqis become evasive. Did they consider these people prisoners or not? Khalid demanded. Were

civilians rounded up and taken away by force not the same
as prisoners of war?

Ahmad deliberately sought to obscure the issue by claiming
that many Kuwaitis had chosen to go to Iraq when the war
started. Schwarzkopf retorted sharply that anyone taken
against his will should be considered a prisoner, and he offered
to fly a planeload of captured Iraqis to Baghdad to show the
world he was serious about a full exchange. An argument
developed, yet somehow, in the heat of the moment, the
Iraqis managed to fudge the issue of the Kuwaiti civilians
and the discussion moved on to the question of boundaries:
Ahmad was worried that the Coalition would try to re-draw
the map and move the international boundary northwards,
to the line on which the American and British forces were
established at that moment. Schwarzkopf said he had no
intention of doing any such thing, but he resolutely refused
repeated Iraqi requests that he should move his armoured
units one kilometre to the west so that they did not hold the
main road between Basra and Baghdad. Clearly the Iraqis
wanted all Coalition forces off their soil and, when they realized they could not achieve that, they pressed for a limited
withdrawal, only to find themselves obliged to accept the
status quo. They sought to escape from their immediate difficulty by saying that they would have to refer the matter back
to Baghdad.

Another argument flared briefly over who had been
responsible for starting the battle the day before, but Schwarzkopf cut it off by saying that the important thing was to make
sure no repetition occurred. Then Ahmad complained that
Allied aircraft were still flying over Baghdad. Schwarzkopf
dismissed the point by saying that it was 'purely a safety
measure' – although in fact the low-level sorties were being
flown to keep pressure on the Iraqis – and discussion moved
on to the vital question of whether or not the Iraqis themselves were allowed to fly. Schwarzkopf at once ruled out
flights by fixed-wing aircraft and reserved the right to shoot
down any that took off, but when the Iraqis pointed out that
because so many bridges had been destroyed, and so many
roads severed, they would not be able to administer their

country from the ground, he agreed that they might fly helicopters for civilian purposes.

As the talks drew to an end, the Iraqis handed over a list of
the prisoners they held: seventeen Americans, twelve Britons,
nine Saudis, two Italians and one Kuwaiti pilot. Ahmad also
admitted to having fourteen bodies, two of them already
buried, twelve not. Of the fourteen, eight were unidentified,
one British and five American. When he asked Schwarzkopf
how many Iraqi prisoners the Coalition forces had taken, the
answer was over sixty thousand.

All through the meeting the Iraqis tried to give the impression that they really wanted to settle everything: they sought
to exude goodwill and reassurance. At one stage they even
had the nerve to speak of a gentlemen's agreement, but as
nobody present had ever discovered a gentleman in Saddam's
regime, that ploy did not get them very far. All the same,
when the two generals got up to return to Baghdad, Schwarzkopf shook their hands and, once he had verified that both
recording machines had functioned, gave them one of the
tapes.

In retrospect, it is easy to say that we should have taken a
tougher line and been more demanding, perhaps even that
we should have made the talks run on into another day and
ground the Iraqi delegates into the sand. After all, we were
in complete control and had nothing to lose. We had defeated
Iraq utterly and if ordered could have smashed Baghdad. I
now think that we should have insisted on the release of all
civilians as a preliminary move and refused to countenance
any Iraqi request until everyone had been repatriated. I later
came to realize that the Arabs saw the question of prisoners
rather differently from us. Each Western country wanted its
own nationals back, of course, but to the Saudis it was intoler-
able that *any* Arabs should be held against their will by Saddam Hussein. Khalid did his best to press this point, but the
Iraqis managed to cloak it in a fog of ambiguity, clearly regard-
ing the Kuwaitis they held as hostages to fortune. I was
particularly disappointed not to secure the release of Ian
Richter, the British businessman who had been gaoled for life
on trumped-up charges of bribery and had already spent more

than five years in Iraqi prisons. (In the end it took much further negotiation and − according to Press reports − the release of £70 million of frozen Iraqi assets to secure his freedom.)

Later, Norman repeatedly said in public that he had been 'suckered', especially over allowing helicopters to fly. Yet the Iraqis did need helicopters for humanitarian reasons: with all the bridges down, they had no other means of moving people about, casualties particularly. Probably we should have laid a definite constraint on their use and positively banned the operation of armed helicopters, with the clear understanding that if any did take off, we would shoot them down. But at the time we seemed to have gone as far as we could. We were all tired, rather overwhelmed by the pace of events, and still off balance from the speed of our victory. Our immediate purpose was to make sure that the war did not start again and that there were no more casualties. With Saddam's army routed, his air force smashed or dispersed, and his country in ruins, it seemed hardly conceivable that he would almost immediately begin attacking his own people. We knew that he had carefully conserved his helicopters during the war, parking them out of harm's way and not letting them fly at all; even so, we could not imagine that within a matter of weeks he would start to use them for armed raids on his own subjects.

On the day after the Safwan talks, Rupert Smith took me for a helicopter tour of the battlefield. Mark Chapman came with us, a small reward for all the admirable work he had done, and we had a picnic out in the desert. For someone like myself, who had been obliged to follow events by radio from the depths of the War Room, this was a riveting experience. We went round like tourists, stop by stop, with a lecture from the Divisional Commander at each, and by the end of the day I had learnt an enormous amount.

It seemed extraordinary that the Coalition forces had broken through the minefields with so few casualties, but nothing struck me more than the absolute flatness of the terrain. I already knew, from many forays into it, that the desert was as level and featureless as a calm sea, but when I

looked at it in terms of having to fight across it, I was amazed
all over again at the sheer lack of cover, dead ground or
landmarks. I realized as never before how lucky we were to
have had our satellite-driven global position systems. Without
them, and without the TOGS night-sights, the battle would
have been entirely different and certainly would have gone
on much longer, for our armour would not have been able
to move and fight at night. Accurate navigation would have
been extremely difficult even by day and the probability of
blue-on-blue incidents would have been enormously
increased. Equally fortunate for us was the fact that the Iraqis
had relied on their dug-in positions and not started to move
about when they came under pressure. Had they done that,
our task would have been much harder.

Even with my knowledge of Saddam Hussein's military
incompetence, it seemed incredible that all the Iraqi guns and
tanks had been dug in to face a frontal assault from the south
and had not been able to turn round when they found enemy
coming at them from behind. The sight of all the burnt-out
vehicles on the Matla Ridge confirmed me in my belief that
we were right to stop the war when we did. One faction, I
know, believed that we should have gone on to capture Basra,
so that we could use the city as a bargaining counter to secure
the handover of Saddam Hussein himself, but how many
thousands more fleeing Iraqi soldiers would have been mass-
acred before that end had been achieved?

Altogether, our battlefield tour made explicit one major
lesson of the war. Although the Iraqis had one of the largest
armies in the world, they lacked the ability to use the considerable technology which went with it. Just as their pilots
were poorly trained, and could barely fly the sophisticated
aircraft which Saddam had bought from the Soviet Union, so
the ground forces had no idea how to exploit the mobility of
what was essentially a mobile force. Their use of the army as
a static defence, on the fortress concept, was entirely wrong.
It is people who win wars, not technology. If servicemen are
not properly trained and motivated to use the equipment they
have, they will achieve very little.

Withdrawal was the subject on everybody's minds. The one

question people wanted answered was, 'How soon can we go home?' For the time being, the only answer was, 'As soon as we can arrange it', and I used the *Sandy Times* to explain why immediate repatriation for all was not possible. In a front-page article I congratulated all ranks on the way they had conducted themselves, saying that they had 'earned the admiration of the whole nation', but went on to emphasize that officially we were still at war and had 'only halted offensive operations temporarily'. Some Arabs supposed that the British might take advantage of the occasion to hang on in the Middle East and to try to re-negotiate some of our former colonial privileges. This, of course, was very far from our intention, but the only practical way to demonstrate our goodwill was to pull out as soon as everyone was agreed that we should go.

For the time being we had an influx of visitors to deal with. 'The problem out here has switched from Iraqis to visitors,' I told Bridget. 'They are planning to come out in droves.' One of the first was Tom King, whose tour went extremely well – so much so, I reported, 'He was on a big high by the time he left, and told me how well I'd done. I have to say in private that I don't feel I've done very much. It is Norman's battle, and in some ways I feel a bit bogus taking the glory on his behalf.'

By now, at the end of the war, Tom King was greatly respected all round the Gulf. He had proved brilliant at dealing with the rulers and putting over the British point of view with firmness, but also with tact and fine political judgment. By giving me his full support in theatre, he had built up my standing as the senior British commander, to my own substantial benefit. His determination to work in hands-on fashion undoubtedly caused problems at all command levels, because he became too much involved in the detail of operations, especially in the matter of rate capping, and his obsession with the Press was another diversionary factor. Nevertheless, he was an immensely loyal supporter of the armed forces and did his able best to fight our corner in the War Cabinet. In my one-to-one dealings with him, I could appreciate his need for detailed information, to answer questions in the House of Commons and keep abreast or ahead of the media at their own game. Besides, I believe that the personal knowledge gained from our frequent talks gave him an understanding which he could never have acquired if he had not visited and kept in touch so keenly. As a result, he spoke about the war with exceptional authority at home and that in itself was a great help to us. It was a measure of how well he grasped in-theatre problems that he backed me wholeheartedly at one of the cardinal moments of the deployment, when I asked for our ground forces to be increased to divisional strength. Without this generosity of support, my own task would have been much harder.*

After TK, our next very important visitor was John Major, who flew into Dhahran from Moscow at 0500 on 6 March, the first Western leader to arrive in theatre since the war. I had gone down from Riyadh overnight to meet him and at 0630 we set off in a Hercules for Kuwait. Yet a combination of rain and east wind, which was driving the smoke from oil fires westwards, combined to defeat us: the plane was unable to land at Kuwait City and we had to fly back to the small coastal town of Al Mish'ab, some thirty kilometres south of Khafji. Against this very event, I had laid on two helicopters, but the change of plan meant that the Prime Minister had to leave behind most of his high-powered Press entourage, all of whom were longing to reach Kuwait. As we continued on our way, some distinctly overheated signals began winging their way back to the Ministry of Defence, but we had neither the time nor the facilities to manage the Press as well as the Prime Minister in this emergency.

In spite of this setback, the visit was a tremendous success and once again Major showed an unerringly sure touch with everyone he met, not least the servicemen. In Kuwait at last, we called on the Ambassador, who had collected together all the expatriates still in the city. The Prime Minister addressed them briefly and did much to restore their morale. Then

---

* Touring the Gulf with Tom King in June 1991 as his Middle East Adviser, I remarked on how useful it was for me to have been reintroduced into the area by the Secretary of State, and he came back with the generous quip, 'Everyone kept asking who the other man was travelling with General de la Billière.'

we went on to the Division in the desert, where he was presented with a captured AK-47 rifle. Hundreds of men had assembled in a huge semi-circle and when he spoke to them, standing on the roof of a jeep, he established an immediate rapport, evoking an extraordinarily warm response from the soldiers. A quick visit to the RAF was made memorable by the huge banner which the airmen had erected behind them, as they lined up on the wings of a Tornado to receive him. 'THE MAJOR ISSUE TODAY IS, WHEN ARE WE GOING HOME?'

In the evening I flew back to Riyadh with him in his VC10 for an audience with King Fahd. After the usual wait, we were ushered in to the Royal presence and everything went well and quickly, with the Saudis finally agreeing to pay all our in-theatre costs.

Major had certainly taken in the RAF's message, for he asked me to see if it would be possible to send a token batch of troops home by the following weekend. I set studies in hand and, as I reported to Bridget,

> That has of course set the lines alight, not least on the political front. Gossip from the UK has it that TK feels that the PM has taken his glory. If this is true, there will be blood on the carpet in Whitehall tomorrow.

Next morning Paddy Hine and Mike Wilkes arrived and we had a satisfactory conference to sort out our policy on decorations. As after any war, highly charged arguments had broken out about who should receive what medal. Who would qualify as having served in the Gulf? Where should we draw the geographical boundaries? Should medals be restricted to people who had served in Saudi Arabia, Bahrein and Oman? What about people who had been in theatre before the war, but through no fault of their own had left before hostilities began and had nevertheless done a valuable job? What about people in Cyprus, who had given a great deal of help on the fringe? What about those at the Joint Headquarters in England, who had done so much to set up the whole operation, and indeed those in Whitehall who had burnt the midnight oil for many a long week?

That same day, 7 March, I saw the coffins of our dead off

from Jubail in a simple but moving and beautiful ceremony, with a band and pipes, and no Press present. After a short service in a hangar, each coffin, draped with a Union Jack, was marched to a C130 by a group of bare-headed pall-bearers from the dead man's regiment. Such an occasion is difficult to manage, but this one was handled perfectly. The departure of the dead brought the formal phase of the war to an end, although there were still five British bodies to come from Iraq and eight international bodies, so-far unidentified, which in the end proved to include the three Britons not yet accounted for.

In the matter of Gulf medals it was decided that, as in the Falklands, there should be two forms: one with a rosette, and one without. The lesser award would go to people who had served on the periphery, or for a short time, the full medal to those who had done seven days in theatre during the war or twenty-eight days during the run-up. Of course this was bad luck on people who had done twenty-seven days, or only six of war, but the line had to be drawn somewhere. Separate arrangements were made for aircrews not based in theatre, who had flown in and out on the regular Hercules run, off-loading at Riyadh, picking up more freight, off-loading again at Dhahran and Jubail, and returning via Riyadh to the United Kingdom. They had taken as much risk as anyone and received the full medal if they had flown a certain number of sorties. There were problems with people who had been on the fringes, for instance, in the merchant navy and the crew of the Cunard liner *Princess* leased to the Americans for rest and recreation.

While these debates continued about the basic Gulf medals, we had also to deal with the more important question of awards for gallantry. Again, I knew that this would produce a great deal of argument and dissatisfaction. I had already heard that old Army hands in England were afraid that, because the ground war had been so short and casualties so few, soldiers would win awards too cheaply. Whatever we did, there would be accusations that one service or ship or regiment had got more or less than it deserved, and that the general allocation had somehow been unfair. I therefore took every possible step to secure an equitable division.

Having ascertained that the total of awards sanctioned by the Ministry of Defence was about two hundred, we split them into so many Distinguished Service Orders, so many Military Crosses, so many Distinguished Conduct Medals, and so on. Next I instructed all commanding officers to put in citations, on which decisions could be made, and asked a senior officer in each Service to weed through them, only sending forward those which he felt met all the relevant criteria and were fully justified. I also set up a board consisting of the three heads of Service – Bill Wratten, Rupert Smith and Chris Craig – who sat in Riyadh to make their adjudications and I laid down strict parameters for them.

The first and fundamental principle was that no award was to be given to anyone who had not measured up to the gallantry requirements prescribed by Queen's Regulations. Because numbers were restricted, I determined that the block allocation of awards to each of the three services should be based on the numbers deployed in the theatre and the extent of operations in which they had been involved. It was then up to each Service to present its list of recommendations.

The main selection board kept a small number of awards in hand as a reserve for particularly deserving cases and took special care to make sure that anybody downgraded from one honour was not missed out altogether, but was considered for a lower level of award. The final allocation was decided on a tri-service vote, taken by the three commanders, on a points system. It happened, inevitably, that a given ship or regiment won no awards, simply because it had never been far enough forward in the fighting.

The procedure was a fairly complex one, but also, I believe, accurate and fair. When the board had made its recommendations, I re-read every word of their reports and the citations, to be sure that I agreed with what had been said and decided, and in the end I think that justice was done. Inevitably there were some grumbles, but no serious criticism, partly because the total of awards was proportionally much smaller than that at the end of the Falklands conflict.

On 11 March I reported 'an emotional day', on which I went to say goodbye to 7th Brigade. Having come out to the

Gulf at the same time and seen the whole conflict through with them, I felt a special affinity with Patrick Cordingley's officers and men. Since the ceasefire, they had been living out in the desert, in horrible conditions, beneath the permanent pall of smoke from the burning oil wells, but they had certainly not wasted their time when it came to collecting booty. The rules of the game are that the victor is allowed to keep captured military equipment from the area over which he has advanced and 7th Brigade had brought in anything worth while, so that it could be taken home for training or display in barracks and museums. The rest they had blown up and destroyed, to prevent the Iraqis getting it. Norman Schwarzkopf and I had issued strict orders to our forces that they were to retrace their routes of advance during that battle and make sure that nothing serviceable was left behind. The operation of identifying, recovering or destroying equipment went on for at least ten days after the end of the war.*

Now I paid the Brigade a last flying visit, spoke to as many of the men as I could, thanked them for doing such a marvellous job, took a few questions and was ceremonially seen off on board a tank. Soon afterwards, the armour began moving down to Jubail, on the start of its long journey home.

Genuine military booty was one thing, smuggled Iraqi weapons quite another. After the Falklands War so many weapons were secreted in the baggage of returning servicemen that the Customs were thrown into a frenzy and I was determined that this should not happen again. I therefore issued a directive headed 'Repatriation of War Souvenirs' which laid down various categories. Definitely prohibited were firearms (whether functioning or not), explosives, pyrotechnics, live ammunition and knives with blades more than six inches long. Souvenirs permitted included empty shell and cartridge cases, enemy documents and maps. Things like badges, buckles, flags, helmets, clothes and boots were unre-

---

* The recovery of spoils was coordinated centrally under firm rules. Regiments and museums in the United Kingdom bid for particular items; equipment was also needed for training and, once these requirements had been met, the rest was left behind.

stricted, with the rider that 'any items of enemy equipment must have been found abandoned'. I believe that vigorous application of this policy, backed up by threats of dire recrimination against offenders and their commanding officers, reduced the homeward flow of contraband items to a minimum.

On 12 March we held a grand display in Bahrein, putting on show all the Army and Air Force weapons and equipment used in the war, with the servicemen who had operated them standing by to explain how things worked. We had invited senior officers from all friendly Arab states and, even if little immediate business was done, the occasion was a memorable success, for Sheikh Isa, the Emir of Bahrein, threw a magnificent lunch and the presence of so many visitors created a powerful sense of Arab togetherness. During the day the Emir held an investiture, at which he was kind enough to create me a Member of the Order of Bahrein, First Class. Norman Schwarzkopf was for some reason unable to be present and in his absence Admiral Arthur represented the Americans. He, too, received a decoration, but I could not help noticing that the Emir gave me mine first, either because I was the senior national commander present, or perhaps to make the point that Britain was his first choice among Western nations. Another highlight of the day was a classic remark made by one of the soldiers on our display. The man had spent at least six months in the desert and must have been through some hair-raising experiences during the land battle, but when I asked him what he considered to be his most abiding memory of the war, he instantly replied, 'Two days in a hotel in Bahrein, sir!'

My one major disappointment of this postwar period was my failure to secure a firm footing in Kuwait for British industry. Ever since Christmas I had been considering how British companies might win a large number of the contracts which were bound to flow once peace returned. The Foreign Office were also looking at the idea and got the Department of Trade and Industry to set up a team of high-powered businessmen who were leaders in their various fields, banking, construction, military sales and so on. I obtained permission from the

Ministry of Defence for the team to fly in an RAF aircraft –
there was no other means of reaching Kuwait at the time –
and when the party arrived, very soon after the ceasefire, its
assessment quickly revealed that the opportunities were
rather different from what we had expected. It turned out
that few buildings had been damaged structurally, so that
extensive refurbishment, rather than construction, was the
main order of the day. Nevertheless, the visit proved useful
and afterwards the team ran a series of briefings round the
United Kingdom, telling people what the possibilities were.

I myself had been taking careful note of the status of the
American Corps of Engineers, who are basically an Army
unit, but keep in close touch with United States industry.
Whenever a construction or reconstruction project comes
along which is not appropriate for the Services to tackle, the
Corps passes it across to industry. I saw that when our own
soldiers went into Kuwait and began to clear up the left-overs
of war – the booby-traps, burnt-out vehicles and so on –
they would identify jobs and make connections which could
well be handed over to industrialists for further exploitation.
Above all, the military could help civilian contractors reach
the shattered city, which was inaccessible by sea, air or
land, and accommodate their workmen in camps. I therefore
set up the British Reconstruction Implementation Team
(BRIT) whose task was to smooth the interface between
military activities and British business. I also obtained permission from the Ministry of Defence to sell businessmen
surplus military equipment, such as Land Rovers and other
vehicles, at full commercial prices, as no civilian transport
was available.

BRIT worked quite well at first. Some businessmen came
out and a few deals were done, but after I had left the Middle
East, the whole scheme seemed to fade away. I felt, and still
feel, that our arrangements for linking the Services with
industry do not match up to those of the Americans and that,
when another situation of this kind arises, we should have
some better medium of communication between the two, so
that businessmen do not have to batter on the doors of Whitehall before they can obtain a hearing.

Even with the handicaps I have mentioned, British firms did not in the end do too badly. In an audience with the Crown Prince, John Major had secured agreement that the British contribution to the war would gain proper recognition in the number of contracts handed out: firms still had to quote on a competitive commercial basis and British companies won between eight and ten per cent of the business going, which more or less matched the military effort we had put in. Yet I still felt we had missed an opportunity.

I myself had many farewell visits to make, not least to the Navy, who presented me with an elaborate personal gift in the form of a chart of the Gulf, handsomely mounted, framed and marked with the positions of all Task Group's ships on 28 February. I also visited 4th Brigade and, in spite of the pall of smoke overhead which put a foul, sooty taste into the air, I had a happy time in the desert having their battles explained to me. I stayed that night with the Fusiliers, as I wanted to spend time with them and discuss the blue-on-blue. By then some of them were living in tents and they generously gave me a 180lb four-man tent to myself for the night. We dined in what passed for an officers' mess, at trestle tables set out on the sand, surrounded by armoured vehicles. Having had the whole battalion assembled in a hollow square, I spoke to them briefly and found everyone most creditably composed, in spite of the disaster to the Regiment. It should be emphasized that the Fusiliers themselves had taken the setback in their stride: they knew they had been exceptionally unfortunate, but they did not allow the tragedy to blight their determination to press on with their operational job, nor did they let it weigh on their minds or obsess them. Next morning I had an excellent field breakfast with the Royal Scots and again spoke to the whole battalion.

Between these trips I entertained the Defence Committee from the House of Commons, led by Michael Mates, who had come out on a brief, fact-finding tour. I expected some awkward questions from John McFall who I knew had put down private questions about the Matla Ridge. 'I think he's trying to create a *Belgrano*,' I told Bridget, 'but he won't make progress, as the Brits weren't involved and in any case the situation can be fully justified.' My forecast proved correct. Mates's little squad was only nine strong – a very modest party, compared with the eighty US Congressmen who descended on the Americans – and their leader kept them under admirable control. After a briefing from me, we took them to Rupert's headquarters and showed them the Matla Ridge, an on-the-spot visit which changed McFall's preconceived ideas and demonstrated at a stroke the value of politicians travelling to see for themselves, rather than pontificating at a distance.

On 17 March the *Sandy Times* published its final issue. The front page carried the news that Her Majesty the Queen had approved my special promotion to General, with effect from April, when I would begin a one-year appointment as Middle East Adviser to the Minister of Defence. The same item announced that Ian Macfadyen would take over from me as British Forces Commander, Middle East, with the rank of Air Vice Marshal, for the remainder of the deployment. On later pages the paper found room for articles about its excellent printers, Maramer, and about its own small staff, which consisted more or less exclusively of Squadron Leader Pat McKinlay, the Editor, with supervision from Lieutenant Colonel Glyn Jones and practical support from Lieutenant Commander Nigel Huxtable, who described himself as 'photographer and theatre wanderer extraordinary'. These stalwarts were too modest to state the truth, that their publication had been an enormous success and that it had admirably fulfilled its role of binding all the far-flung elements of the British forces together by giving them a focal point. But now that the battle was over, there was no place for it any more: the only subject which interested people was home. And so, after a short but glorious career of twenty-five issues, the *Sandy Times* folded its tents and vanished into the desert.

Several of my own last days in theatre were devoted to visiting our embassies down the Gulf and giving brief presentations, so that our people had a first-hand account of how things had gone. In Abu Dhabi, after our briefing, the Ambassador, Graham Burton, threw a cocktail party for a hundred and fifty expatriates who had helped collect money during the war. Later in the evening I went to call on Sheikh Zayed, who gave me a very warm welcome and the honour of attending a Ramadan'breakfast'– a colossal meal, for which the Arabs who had fasted since dawn were ravenous. Zayed urged me to visit him again in my new appointment and told me that I would be welcome to come back every week, if I so wished. Next day we went on to Dubai, and after that to Muscat, giving our forty-minute presentation of the war in both embassies. In Muscat the generous loan of a helicopter for the day enabled me to revisit the Jebel Akhdar to see again the ground over which I had fought as a young SAS troop leader thirty-two years earlier: some things had changed, but much had not, and the trip brought back vivid memories.

Describing this on 19 March, in my final letter home, I reported that the war machine was fast running down and that there would be no point in my writing any more, as I should probably overtake any future missive. With a touch of pride I recalled that I had written home on every single day of the campaign, and concluded with a little paean of thanks to Bridget for her answering support:

> I can't tell you how I've valued your letters. It's them, and the close touch with you, that have kept my spirits up when I was under most pressure.

My final days in Riyadh were packed with administrative chores – writing reports, sealing off loose ends. I said goodbye to Prince Khalid with real sadness. I had grown to like him immensely and hoped that our friendship would continue after my departure. My farewell call took him aback, because he had not been expecting me to leave so soon and he learnt the purpose of my visit only a minute or two before I saw him. For his part, he expressed great satisfaction at what the Coalition had done, thanked me most handsomely for the British contribution and expressed his satisfaction at the way in which the conflict had enhanced the relationship between our two countries.

One of my most memorable farewell occasions was the

dinner party which Alan Munro laid on for me and senior
members of my staff at the British Embassy. Over thirty
people took their places at a U-shaped table, with Alan flank-
ing me on one side and Norman Schwarzkopf on the other;
Chas Freeman, the American Ambassador, was also present,
as was Chuck Horner, whose Air Force had done so much to
support us in the field. The fact that the ceiling had been
blown down by a Scud, making our surroundings more like
a barn than the dining room of an embassy, in no way
detracted from the warmth of the occasion. Both Alan and
Norman made generous speeches extolling the British contribution to the campaign, and I personally rated it as a high
compliment that the CinC had donned a civilian suit for the
evening – only the second time in seven months that I had
seen him wear anything but combat overalls.

   Somehow I never bade Norman a formal goodbye, but we
parted on the best of terms, confident that we would see each
other again. At a small ceremony in his headquarters, in the
presence of all his senior commanders, he was kind enough
to present me with a Legion of Merit, Officer Class. He made
a fine, short speech about the value of the British contribution, both to the Americans and to the cause as a whole,
and said how glad he was to have had our wholehearted
political and military support. He also made some embarrassingly flattering remarks about me personally. But he had
taken the precaution of preceding his serious statements with
the observation that never in his life before had he handed
out a medal to someone who had said in public that he was
rude – and this ensured that the occasion did not become
sentimental or maudlin. I responded with a fairly formal
appraisal of relations between ourselves and the Americans.
I said how much we had enjoyed working with them,
emphasized my belief that their leadership and commitment
had been a war-winning factor, and declared how much I
had enjoyed working alongside them on this, my last posting
and my last war. Norman then pinned the medal on my tunic,
we shook hands for the benefit of the photographers and that
was the last I saw of him for the time being.

   Some weeks earlier it had occurred to me that if all four

senior commanders returned to the United Kingdom together, it would round off the operational phase of the
deployment and emphasize the leadership given by the heads
of each Service, as well as making a good little news item for
the Press. My plan did not quite work out, as Bill Wratten
had to travel a day earlier than scheduled, but the rest of us
set off on 26 March and made an overnight stop in Rome,
where we were welcomed by the most senior officers of the
Italian forces and entertained most lavishly. We stayed in
their extremely luxurious officers' club, with jacuzzis in the
bathrooms, and were treated to a slap-up dinner – in the
middle of which, true to form, I fell asleep in the upright
position. I only wished that I could have responded more
enthusiastically to such overwhelming hospitality.

Next morning we flew on to London. As always when
returning from the Middle East, it was thrilling to see the
bright green of English fields beneath us and, when we
touched down, to smell the soft, moist air of home. At RAF
Northolt the pilot taxied straight to a special pan near the
officers' mess and we were delighted to find that Bill had
come to join us, together with Paddy Hine, his team from
Joint Headquarters at High Wycombe and all our wives and
families. After a grand reunion on the tarmac, we proceeded
indoors to a champagne reception. As familiar, smiling faces
gathered round, it finally came home to me that my latest
Arabian assignment was at an end.

INDEX